THE POLITICS OF EXILE

Written in both autoethnographical and narrative form, *The Politics of Exile* offers unique insight into the complex encounter of researcher with research subject in the context of the Bosnian War and its aftermath. Exploring themes of personal and civilizational guilt, of displaced and fractured identity, of secrets and subterfuge, of love and alienation, of moral choice and the impossibility of ethics, this work challenges us to recognize pure narrative as an accepted form of writing in international relations.

The author brings theory to life and gives corporeal reality to a wide range of concepts in international relations, including an exploration of the ways in which young academics are initiated into a culture where the volume of research production is more valuable than its content, and where success is marked not by intellectual innovation, but by conformity to theoretical expectations in research and teaching.

This engaging work will be essential reading for all students and scholars of international relations and global politics.

Elizabeth Dauphinee is Associate Professor in the Department of Political Science at York University in Toronto, Canada. Her research interests involve autoethnographic and narrative approaches to international relations, Levinasian ethics and international relations theory, and the philosophy of religion.

Interventions

Edited by Jenny Edkins, Aberystwyth University and Nick Vaughan-Williams, University of Warwick

As Michel Foucault has famously stated, "knowledge is not made for understanding; it is made for cutting." In this spirit the Edkins–Vaughan-Williams Interventions series solicits cutting edge, critical works that challenge mainstream understandings in international relations. It is the best place to contribute post disciplinary works that think rather than merely recognize and affirm the world recycled in IR's traditional geopolitical imaginary.

Michael J. Shapiro, University of Hawai'i at Mānoa, USA

The series aims to advance understanding of the key areas in which scholars working within broad critical post-structural and post-colonial traditions have chosen to make their interventions, and to present innovative analyses of important topics.

Titles in the series engage with critical thinkers in philosophy, sociology, politics and other disciplines and provide situated historical, empirical and textual studies in international politics.

Critical Theorists and International Relations
Edited by Jenny Edkins and Nick Vaughan-Williams

Ethics as Foreign Policy
Britain, the EU and the other
Dan Bulley

Universality, Ethics and International Relations
A grammatical reading
Véronique Pin-Fat

The Time of the City
Politics, philosophy, and genre
Michael J. Shapiro

Governing Sustainable Development
Partnership, protest and power at the world summit
Carl Death

Insuring Security
Biopolitics, security and risk
Luis Lobo-Guerrero

THE POLITICS OF EXILE

Elizabeth Dauphinee

Routledge
Taylor & Francis Group

LONDON AND NEW YORK

First published 2013
by Routledge
2 Park Square, Milton Park, Abingdon, Oxon OX14 4RN

Simultaneously published in the USA and Canada
by Routledge
711 Third Avenue, New York, NY 10017

Routledge is an imprint of the Taylor & Francis Group,
an informa business

British Library Cataloguing in Publication Data
A catalogue record for this book is available from the British
Library

Library of Congress Cataloging in Publication Data
Cleaver, Tony, 1947-
Understanding the world economy / by Tony Cleaver. -- 4th ed.
p. cm.
Includes index.
1. International trade. 2. Economic development. 3. Debts,
External. 4. Environmental economics. 5. Foreign exchange.
I. Title.
HF1379.C55 2012
337--dc23
2012016036

ISBN: 978-0-415-64085-5 (hbk)
ISBN: 978-0-415-64084-8 (pbk)
ISBN: 978-0-203-07798-6 (ebk)

Typeset in Bembo
by Taylor & Francis Books

For Kathe, whenever I may find her.

Foreword

Naeem Inayatullah

The Politics of Exile is not a standard theoretical treatise; nor would I call it an autoethnography, a memoir, or a novel. By utilizing a radically different form, Elizabeth Dauphinee produces a quantum jump in her path breaking work on the ethics of researching war.

Initially, I received it as a publisher's request for a review. The task went to the bottom of my list but I couldn't resist a glance at the first few pages. Within minutes it became my only priority as I surrendered to the narrative. Riveted, I laughed, held back tears, and read passages to Sorayya Khan – my spouse who is a novelist. Some hours later she picked it up and couldn't put it down. For the first time in ages we had a strong disagreement. She loves the book's ethical daring, its narrative drive, its sensibility for place, voice, tone, texture, and its rhythm. It reads like a novel, she said. But is it? She wondered why it was slated for publication in an academic series. More important, she believes that Elizabeth owes the reader answers to following questions: Is it a novel? A memoir? Autobiography? Is it a theoretical intervention? Why is the work silent on these questions? I replied that the text provokes these very issues. My answer did not satisfy. What purpose does the provocation serve, she wanted to know. Why not publish it as a novel?

★★★

Naming it a novel contains and limits the intervention by formalizing the dangerous intimacy Elizabeth generates. Elizabeth fuses the mandates of novelists and scholars. The novelist must not tell; she must show by painting with the subtle resins. The scholar must not merely evoke; she must explain with methodical precision. Elizabeth produces both: a world that combines affect with science, aesthetics with ethics. We can also read her book methodologically because it answers the "how" question: How does one present fieldwork so that it highlights rather than hides the process of obtaining information? How does one fathom the other's point of view? How does one tell the other's stories when they conflict with one's own?

Her intervention consists of weaving together at least three elements: a differentiated unity; an intimacy with otherness; and a pedagogy of complicity. Instead of a partial analysis that highlights international law, logic, and judgment, Elizabeth offers a holistic systematicity that incorporates emotions, feelings, and the thread of connectivity that binds us all; instead of foregrounding the distance between us and abhorred others, the book works within the overlap of "good" and "evil;" and, instead of subscribing to the authority of the lecture, it submits to a process whereby the teacher learns.

The unnamed professor of International Relations – Elizabeth's avatar – encounters a putative war criminal. The professor judges. She teaches. But with great difficulty she begins to realize she has everything to learn from those who her paradigm would frame as war criminals. Then, rather than rebuking, rejecting, or assimilating him, she opens up to his voice and vision. Even as doing so devastates her scholarly ambitions.

I love that when that putative war criminal is finally ready to confess, the scholar, cannot bear to hear what she has suspected all along. If we are not ready to internalize "evil" others, neither are we ready to hear their confessions. Anything to erase our overlap with their humanity.

★★★

For over two and a half decades I have read student papers and colleagues' manuscripts. Four hypotheses emerge from this experience: (1) Each of us writes about one substantive theme for the duration of our lives; (2) to get at this theme, we don't limit ourselves to one form. We can use poetry, fiction, autobiography, and academic analysis; (3) the theme emerges from a "trauma," or a "space/time wound." In Lacanian terms, this trauma is the "real" around which we orbit and around which we write; (4) the most important aspect of writing is allowing it to write back. We direct our conscious energy in formulating and executing plans for research. But surprises emerge when we strike the balance between control and letting go. Then the writing writes back. Producing this surprise is the unconscious purpose of writing.

Given these claims, I might say this book revives the theme of Elizabeth's first volume, *The Ethics of Researching War*. I find that book insightful and persuasive. Why then is she compelled to compose a second book on the same topic? Is it not because she understood, if only subconsciously, that the argumentative approach automatically activates our standard protective measures? She hoped to circumvent our defenses by changing the form. She aimed to transcend the usual academic venture but in ways that we cannot easily dismiss as an ideographic portrait or as "mere" fiction. She broke the shackles of the argumentative form in order to allow something to write back. And what emerged was this book. With it she means to redeem her words and our profession in the eyes of the other.

***

I find an undeniable love in this book. But this love assails standard approaches to scholarly activity and slices through notions of an objective, rational, even-tempered modern person.

Elizabeth's characters evoke our compassion. As they encircle impossible conundrums they also attempt to transmute their pain into forgiveness and redemption. Not by means of an instant alchemy but by honoring the durability of their trauma. As they work out the flaws in their humanity, they permit us to be merciful. Merciful to them and then to ourselves.

This book makes the impossible sing. Life, it seems to say, is not merely a matter of ascertaining right and wrong, the good and bad, the ethical and the profane. Rather, violence is set into motion by the very act of attempting the good. Elizabeth makes impossible ignoring scholars' complicity in structures of oppression and war.

She aims at a shift in the reader's consciousness, a shift that links to the larger pain of the world. I am tempted to say that Elizabeth gently places our hand in hers and leads us from this quasi-fictional microcosm to the world at large. But this misses something about how writing travels. Better to say: reading this book is a journey to a richer world, a journey that recovers the humanity already present in larger life.

I

I built my career on the life of a man called Stojan Sokolović. And I would like to explain myself to him. I would like to ask him to forgive me before I leave this life, but I don't know how to begin. We spent the better part of a single summer sitting on the balcony of his tiny apartment, drinking thick Turkish coffee from a copper džezva while the setting sun glowed against the sharp angles of a city that was home to neither of us. Ten stories below, the street was a teeming mass of exiles and expatriates perpetually on their way to somewhere else. The city was thick with high summer and shrouded in a fine film of dust, humidity, and exhaust from the idling traffic. We sat regarding each other with our differently colored eyes, each on our own side of the scarred milk crate that served as a makeshift table. The distance between us was immeasurable.

We talked about many things, struggling to accommodate and understand one another, but sometimes we just sat together in silence through the long, still summer nights. In the beginning, I stayed with him because I wanted to understand him. He had strange, colorless eyes that sometimes grew dark with grief and I wanted to know how that could be possible. I was still young and arrogant enough to believe that I could make sense of that from within the narrow contours of my own life. I wanted to understand how it was so that some people wear their souls on the surface of their skins, and why. I believed in my ability to order and classify my world. But later, as the weeks and months slipped by, I grew to be plagued more and more by impassable silences, and I found myself sinking deeper into a mire of terminal uncertainty. Later, I stayed with him for other reasons that I could not understand. He began to intersect me in some way that I could not grasp, and even though I could see it was destroying me, I stayed anyway. I stayed because of his coffee, and because of the lines on his hands, and because of the sonority of his voice. I stayed because he peeled oranges while sitting cross-legged on the floor of my office as he told me stories that ruined my research agenda and destroyed the life that I had spent so many years carefully building. He made me see the high ancestral hills of his home with other eyes—with eyes that were not mine—in a fleeting moment of madness whose shadow stayed with me afterward always.

II

I make my living writing books on war and teaching international politics to university students. Every spring, those students go heaving off as with one corporeal body, and they melt away into the cities and suburbs of this country until September draws them all back again. Students are like migratory birds. They mark the seasons like geese. They move in formation, and when some of them disappear, nobody wonders what happened to them. Universities are like that. You can walk around in a current of thousands of people and feel as alone as you have ever felt. In my case, I fended off this loneliness by writing books. But this was a cyclical, vicious thing, because the more I read and wrote, the lonelier I became. I was submerged so deeply in my work that I could not be distinguished from it. I lived in the dust of the mortar, ingesting the pollution of the city and the permanent silence that had come to envelop my life. I lived between the words of my carefully crafted sentences; in the chapters of my edited volumes and journal articles. Sometimes I slept on the floor under my desk. I had come to a point where I could no longer accept or reciprocate or initiate love, because I was incapable of recognizing its forms. I sat awake all night in my apartment, reading Emmanuel Levinas' *On Escape* and wondering if it was possible—as he suggested it was—to break the chains that bound me to myself. From time to time I would look up at the three pieces of furniture and the bare windows and the blank walls, and I would listen to the silence with straining ears.

When I met Stojan Sokolović, it was early spring, and I was bankrupt of love. I was looking for someone to proofread the small amount of Serbo-Croatian that appeared in my manuscript before it went to press. I was a shameful speaker of Serbo-Croatian. I could function, but I would never be able to express the sublime. I imagined there were some sublime thoughts in my manuscript that needed their translations checked. In an effort to demonstrate my expertise, I felt an uncontrollable urge to translate certain phrases, so I hastily typed up a brief advertisement that read: "Native Serbo-Croatian speaker required to proof manuscript. Standard research rate of pay," followed by my office location.

I walked down the street to the building that housed the support office. It was a mild day, still and rare with sunshine. The sidewalks were unusually dusty from the lack of rain. Undergraduate students were hanging around the pavement, smoking cigarettes and flirting with each other and complaining about the amount of work we had assigned them. They were such an easily identifiable species, with books in their arms or in bags on their backs or stacked on the cement retaining walls beside them. They were old enough to worry about the future, and young enough that they still dropped everything to build snowmen on the university commons in the winter. I navigated around them on the side-walks and climbed the stone staircase of the building where I would post my advertisement on the cork bulletin board. The windowless office seemed dim as I passed through the doorway, but the sun was not yet bright enough to cause that temporary blindness between outside and inside that serves as the true mark of summer. The bulletin board was a snowfall of requests and advertisements: "Spanish speaker wanted for conversation practice. Will exchange in kind with English lessons." "English as Second Language texts available. Cheap prices!" "Baby sitter required: Friday afternoons." And a strange one: "Aicha, if you find this, please call. I'm sorry. Love, Nizar." I paused at that one, wondering what Nizar had done to warrant Aicha's silence. How had he lost her? Where? I pondered it for a moment. Would Aicha call? Was she alright? Or was she *On Escape*?

I carefully posted my note with a yellow thumbtack and then I went back to hide in my office. For help or hindrance, research universities exist to both provide and profit from this luxury. In fact, they nurture and sustain people who want to hide, and I am one of those people. When I applied for my first job, I actually used those words in my application letter: "It is my goal to be a member of a collegium that can nurture and sustain my intellectual interests." This is just a way of saying that I want to be somewhere I can hide. University hiring committees understand this—after all, they are mostly composed of people who are also *On Escape*. I unlocked my office door and stepped across the threshold. I looked around, taking in my shelves of books, my file folders full of scholarly articles, a pile of unmarked essays, a manuscript that I was reviewing for an American publisher, and a couple of steadily slow-growing succulent plants on the window ledge that sometimes flowered just to keep me feeling like I had a purpose in life beyond all that solitary writing.

I stayed working for several hours on a funding proposal that I knew would never be successful, but the "leadership team" of the international politics working group had requested that all of us apply for research grants and this was beginning to be a culture in which one could not easily say no. Requests and suggestions have a way of becoming requirements in this world of commodity accumulation and exchange, and before you know it, even the things you thought were yours eventually belong to someone else: your copyrights, your royalties, your loyalties, your soul.

There was a tentative tap at my office door.

"Come in!" I called, and the door slowly opened. On the other side of the threshold stood a tall, broad-shouldered man with eyes that were so light it was unsettling. He was not one of my students—at least not one I remembered having seen before. I looked at him expectantly, inquiringly, waiting for him to say something. But he did not speak. I raised my eyebrows at him with the questioning, impatient countenance of a busy professor interrupted by a stray goose. He in turn raised his hand, and I saw that he was holding the note I had posted in the International Student office. I felt a brief flash of annoyance with him for taking the note down, as though he were the only candidate for the job.

"Native speaker?" I asked briskly.

He nodded.

"Alright," I said. "Come in." He balanced his long body on the edge of the chair opposite my desk as though he had no intention of staying for any more time than it would take to learn what was required of him. I retrieved the nearly completed draft of my manuscript from a smooth-sliding drawer in my desk.

"I need someone to proof my Serbo-Croatian," I told him carefully.

"Yes," he answered pleasantly, and smoothed out my note, which had crumpled in his hand. I dropped the heavy manuscript before him and it hit the desk with an impressive thud. He looked at it curiously. He crossed one long thigh over the other and cocked his head a bit to peer at the title page. I noticed that the sole of his shoe had torn away from the leather. I also saw that his dark jeans were too short for his long legs. I felt my hardness give way a little, because in some measure this made me feel sad. I could see the pulse at the side of his throat, the promise of life with its false assurances that things measured out in slow, steady meter were faithful and permanent—that illusion of illusions. For a second, I was confused. For a second, I forgot why he had come. I felt otherwise than myself that year. I regarded him pensively. Did he know me? It seemed that he might. I suddenly wondered what the grounds in the bottoms of his overturned Turkish coffee cups had told him about his future. I wondered if he knew when that pulse at the side of his throat would cease.

"Are you one of the ethics students?" I asked, referring to a course I was teaching.

"No," he answered simply.

We looked at one another in the silence of my office for a moment that felt very, very long. There were many possibilities for beginning a conversation, but it seemed that neither of us knew where to begin. In my case, I only knew how to begin discussions with colleagues and students, and even then it was an awkward task, because prolonged solitude makes it difficult to touch others, or to recognize their touch.

When I couldn't stand it anymore, I said to him in my brusque, business-like voice: "There is some phraseology that needs to be checked before the manuscript goes to press. The page numbers where the Serbo-Croatian text appears are listed on the back of the title page." I leaned over and lifted the first page so he could see what I was talking about.

He nodded again, and flipped through the manuscript. I expected him to leave. He didn't. He just kept turning the pages, reading. I stared closely at him, but this did not seem to affect him.

He looked up at me, and in a deep, casual, lightly accented voice, he asked: "Would you join me for dinner? I was planning to go to the Gurkha Grill."

I was stupefied. I must have looked at him incredulously, because he smiled at me and explained carefully: "Gurkha Grill? You know? The restaurant?"

I knew the place. It was a fluorescent nightmare, packed at all hours with unruly undergraduate students. I stared at him in silence for a few seconds, trying to decide what to say, and just when I was about to tell him how very busy I was, my stomach rolled over with an audible growl. I realized that I hadn't eaten a single thing that day, although I had swallowed down more cups of coffee than I had fingers on my hands. So when I opened my mouth to say no, what I heard was a surprising, "Yeah, OK."

He nodded and looked steadily at my lack of enthusiasm with a pleasant expression in his pale eyes. He gathered up my manuscript and carefully tucked it into his bag. We walked out into the corridor together. It was a strange walk. We passed through the fragrant gardens, which were cool with evening and silent in the long glow of violet shadows that leeched the color out of the flowers. The students were mostly gone, with only a few stragglers walking rapidly here and there along the pathways that intersected the grass. They appeared as strange, washed-out apparitions in the dying light. The silence was interrupted at irregular intervals by the low-throated call of a crow that lived in the tree outside my office window.

"Corvids are the only animals apart from primates who have demonstrated the capacity to use tools," I informed my proofreader.

He glanced at me out of the corner of his eye and suppressed a smile with marginal success. Then he said, "My name, by the way, is Stojan Sokolović." He said this carefully, as if the sounds that made up his own name were foreign to him.

I nodded. I felt ashamed that I had not asked him myself. After a few minutes, the obscene fluorescent lights of the curry house pierced the soft darkness. It would be a flawed memory to say that I felt alright with my new proofreader. I did not feel alright. I felt very uncomfortable. I didn't know what had caused me to agree to go with him. I tried to explain it to myself in different ways over the subsequent days, but I think now that it might have been the way the sole of his shoe had come unglued. There was something about that which caused the thickness of my skin to thin a bit. Or maybe it was something else, which I still can't identify. Maybe it was just loneliness. We walked softly through the gardens, and I didn't know what to say, so I said nothing.

The Gurkha Grill was eerily empty, and the servers were standing in a bored battalion waiting, it seemed, only for our arrival. They all moved at once when we came through the doorway and into the piercing orbit of those unforgiving lights. One picked up menus, one picked up a list of alcoholic beverages, one picked up silverware, and they all led us to a quiet corner table by the window. They were so sober and serious, I felt like we were being led to a firing squad. There was nothing to see outside the window, because the bright lights in the curry house transformed all the glass windows into reflective mirrors. We watched ourselves sitting down in watery superimposition on the tempered glass. That felt strange, as though we were watching ourselves from some point outside our own bodies. Mirrors always make me feel strange, both for this reason, and because I am always startled by my appearance when I come upon myself unexpectedly in this way. I do not look the way that I expect to: I am much thinner than I feel, and my hair is starting to be prematurely overgrown with white.

The servers, who were all students, tended us faithfully for a while. They tired of it quickly, though, as they tire of everything, and amused themselves instead by tickling each other behind the counter. One was studying, her lips moving in a whisper as she memorized the contents of some formula or other. From time to time she glanced over at the others in annoyance. They were laughing while trying not to laugh, a feat they could never accomplish, and which seemed most often to fail in my lecture halls. I watched them for a few moments, trying to think of something to say to Stojan Sokolović. Then I took refuge in looking over the plastic menu with its slightly sticky pages. When I had decided, I closed it and placed it gingerly on the edge of the table. Stojan did the same. We looked at one another. Where do I start? I wondered anxiously. My hands were sweating. I read somewhere once that sharing a meal is a moment of nearly unparalleled intimacy. But we hadn't even spoken to one another, except for my comment about corvids and his announcement of his name, which had shamed me because I had not asked it myself. I knew instinctively that we had nothing to say to one another. We had no mutual starting point. It was very difficult for me to think of what to say. I scoured myself completely, and came up with nothing. Stojan did not seem concerned. He propped up his chin with the upturned heel of his hand and regarded me with quiet curiosity. Mercifully, a server arrived with a basket of soft bread that revealed a lazy curl of white steam when it was torn open. It had just come from the oven, and it was piping hot.

Stojan Sokolović broke the silence with a single word spoken in his own tongue, "Lepinje." He smiled as he peered into the basket.

Lepinje: soft, low-leavened bread—the kind of bread that is made to accompany savory grilled meats served with peppery chopped onions and dished out with yogurt dumped over it all. I thought suddenly of the Muslim district of Baščaršija in Sarajevo, where war tourists walked around gawking at the splash-marks in the sidewalks that had been made by mortar fire, and where the international police still saunter around, staring at everything and everyone with a sort of bemused contempt. I watched Stojan Sokolović tear off a bit of the steaming soft bread, which he then reached over and handed to me. I accepted it with a murmur of thanks. From which of those dead republics had he come? I didn't want to ask. In that moment, I didn't want to know. The server came back with a silver thimble full of pickles. I was suddenly no longer hungry. I thought about what I should say. Somehow I was always plagued by this incapacity to start a conversation.

Stojan asked, "What is your book about?"

I felt myself bristle immediately. I hated this question. How could I describe the contents of a book over dinner, and to a stranger, and to a person who would not understand? It would be too hard to follow my own threads. I would leave too many things out and forget so many important elements that it would fail to make any sense at all. And it was nearly impossible to explain philosophies of ethics to people who are not trained in it, I thought doubtfully. I only realized later what a strange and telling thought that was for a university professor. I taught these things to hundreds of students every year, and I couldn't explain them to a man over dinner. Stojan was looking at me, waiting quietly for an answer. I thought for a moment, and replied in the most economical way possible: "It's an ethical meditation on the aftermath of the war in Bosnia." But that was not how I had wanted to describe it.

Stojan immediately laughed a lovely, genuine laugh, and then looked as though he instantly regretted having done so. "I'm sorry," he said, and cleared his throat. He looked at himself in the glass of the window, and frowned slightly at his own reflection. He stopped smiling, but the laughter was still evident in his eyes.

I shrugged, annoyed. How could I expect him to understand the philosophers I read? I expected his derision. And that was why I tried to avoid conversations about my research, I thought with triumphant self-pity. That was why I was less and less able to have conversations with people outside of my profession. I felt miserable, but also satisfied at having my rightness proven. I looked around the restaurant for a distraction.

"I'm sorry," he said again, perceiving my annoyance. "I didn't mean to hurt your feelings. It just seems impossible to me, for anyone to write about ethics in Bosnia."

I shrugged again. "It actually has nothing to do with feelings," I said coldly. "There are a lot of good ethicists and theorists who write on the war in Bosnia." I could hear the contempt in my voice.

"I can imagine," he answered seriously, but the laughter was still in his eyes. They were very pale and mirthful, with that liquidity still in them.

"Well, you'll read through parts of the manuscript anyway, so you'll see what it's about," I said, although I did not think he would probably understand it.

"How many books do you suppose there are on Bosnia?" he asked. He knew he had hit a nerve. I had many nerves at that time.

I thought for a moment. "I don't really know," I answered. "Probably dozens. Maybe more. If you add journal articles across the social sciences, probably hundreds."

Stojan Sokolović shook his head ruefully. "Stunning," he offered dryly.

"Not really," I answered, and I could hear the professor in my voice—the pedantic lecturer. "The war in Bosnia offered up one of the biggest political and ethical problematics of our time."

"Really?" he asked, and his voice was carefully neutral.

Was he joking? I couldn't tell. His expression looked to me to be one of disbelief. Or disgust. I couldn't tell. And because I took myself so very seriously, I couldn't let it go.

"Yes, really," I answered firmly. "The reappearance of concentration camps in Europe, ethnic cleansing and genocide, the dissolution of multiethnic states. That's worth at least a few hundred books to me." I heard the register in my voice rising.

Stojan looked down at his hands for a moment; his fingers were laced casually together on the tabletop. He didn't answer. I tore off another piece of the warm bread and tried to look out the window. I saw only myself in the reflection of the glass. He should just take the manuscript and go, I thought suddenly. I felt a heaving dissatisfaction at the pointlessness of the conversation.

"Are any of those books written by Bosnians or Serbs?" Stojan asked.

I considered this for a moment as I scooped up a fiery little pickle with a pinch of bread. I ate it and its hard sourness was unpleasantly overwhelming. "Not many." My tone was dismissive. "That shouldn't matter, though," I added.

He nodded, as though he had expected this answer. And then it seemed that he didn't know what to say, so he sank into silence, but instead of looking at himself in the reflection of the window, as I was doing, he was looking at me.

I could feel my arrogance embracing me like a cloak. It was heavy, familiar. I had been trained to wear it like armor in order to defend myself in conferences and seminars, in order to successfully challenge the views of others, and to propound my own. I wore it like it was my own skin, only tighter. I sighed, and Stojan gazed at me quizzically. Then the curries began to arrive, one after the other in rapid succession, and cold Indian beer; there was lamb and chicken, lentils and spinach, more pickles and bread and a bowl of minted yogurt. The arrival of the food prevented another awkward exchange, and the conversation died easily and completely. To my surprise, Stojan waved the server with the empty plates away and then there was no way to apportion the food between us. So we ate from the same copper pots. At the end of the meal, there was a last, small spoonful of each curry remaining because neither of us would take the final bit of anything. We left it for the devil.

And that was how I spent the first hour of my life with Stojan Sokolović: awkward and annoyed and self-righteous.

We finished the beer, which was still cold and refreshing, and wandered out into the spring evening. I paid with my credit card, and he allowed me to do so without protest, but with a nod of thanks. At the time, it annoyed me that he was not more grateful, but later I came to appreciate

Stojan's ability to accept good gifts without worrying about whether or not he deserved them.

Outside, the cool depth of the spring night embraced us like water. The streetlamps cast long, soft shadows across the grasses and the paths, and we walked off in the general direction of the now-empty social sciences departments. Stojan's left shoe made a slight slapping sound as we moved down the path. It was the one with the sole pulling away.

I said to him, "Your shoe is torn."

Stojan laughed another rich laugh. "Yes," he answered matter-of-factly.

"You need a new shoe," I went on.

"Yes," he agreed solemnly. And we kept walking until we arrived at the key-coded entrance to the block of offices where my life was beginning to fade away before it had even begun.

"I'll read the manuscript tonight," he said with his colorless eyes and his long-voweled accent.

I nodded. "Goodnight," I offered, and swiped the card through the reader. The door buzzed and I pushed into the building. When I turned back to make sure it had locked behind me, he was already gone into the night.

I walked down the hall and stepped across the threshold into my office, which looked very different in the dark than it had in the daylight. At night, it was a strange place of long shadows and deep corners, and the silence was palpable. The difference between day and night in the office was the difference between loneliness and absolute solitude. Solitude, I thought, was a prerequisite for true success in this profession. I was a lonely shadow, writing philosophy out of necessity and compulsion. I walked up to my shelves full of books in the semi-darkness, some of which were now ornamental, it had been so long since I opened them— the sad result, I thought, of having accumulated too many. I ran my fingertips along the avenue of spines—hardback, paperback, thick and thin, some of them dog-eared and bent with angular lines of commentary penciled in their margins. They seemed to speak to me in some secret, silent language that I had not yet mastered. I touched each book like this, murmuring to each of them. There you are! I haven't seen you in so long, Kierkegaard. Here is *Fear and Trembling*, which I removed from my mother's shelf when I was thirteen. I opened the cover and saw her unmarried name written in her earnest hand. There was a ring from a coffee cup burned across its old cloth cover—the difference between my mother and me.

I worked deep into the heart of the night, and slept under my desk. I kept a toothbrush in the top drawer of my office, for those increasingly frequent occasions when going home to an empty apartment was unbearable. I stayed there so rarely anyway, I sometimes wondered why I bothered renting the place at all. I guess I wanted to convince myself that I could go home if I wanted to. Had I given up the apartment, I would have been technically homeless, and while that was often the interior status of those of us who have bound ourselves to these institutions of knowledge, it didn't work as well in a world where one had to file an income tax return. In the middle of the night at some point, I was awakened by a sudden howl of wind that carried a curtain of heavy rain on its leading edge. A tree branch tapped wildly against the double-glazed window, which in turn rattled some unintelligible protest in its old wood frame. For a moment, I had no idea where I was. Then I went back to sleep.

III

I woke from a difficult sleep early the next morning. It was still heavy with rain. I brushed my teeth in the faculty bathroom with the toothbrush that I also use to remove the dust from the waxy leaves of my succulent plants, and sat down at my desk. It was early, and no one else had arrived yet. For an hour, I worked on the funding proposal that would never succeed. Then I went for coffee.

The café on the corner outside my office was just waking up, although its dirty brick exterior suggested that it was terminally exhausted. I struggled with my umbrella in the narrow doorway, trying to close it as I shoved against the heavy wooden door with my shoulder. I stood for a moment on the plank floor as the rainwater dripped from my umbrella, and saw to my dismay that my head of school was sitting at a table alone. He was the only customer in the café at this hour, and I could not pretend I hadn't seen him.

"Good morning, Bill!" I smiled as I passed by his table. A cup of tea stood steaming before him, and a newspaper was carefully folded beside the saucer.

"Hello!" he smiled.

"How are you?" I asked brightly, and I could feel the exhaustion threatening to break through in my voice.

"Oh, very well!" he answered. I looked closely at him. His graying, balding head gleamed under the spotlights in the ceiling. Under his apparently placid demeanor, it was possible to detect a furious hum of anxiety.

"Why don't you join me?" he asked hastily.

"Certainly!" I answered in a cheerful voice that belied the sinking feeling in my stomach. I leaned my umbrella against the wall beside the table, and it produced a small puddle of water on the floor that the badly worn, thirsty planks of wood began to absorb immediately. "Let me get a cup of coffee," I said, and turned toward the long marble bar where students-turned-baristas were absently wiping glasses with dirty dishcloths. I stopped in my tracks and turned again to look at Bill. "Bill, can I get you anything else?" I asked with what I hoped was a genuine tone.

"What?" he looked up at me. "Oh, no, I'm fine." He shook his head. "I don't need anything."

I nodded, and headed for the bar. Among the students pulling espresso shots all day behind the counter was a young Basque with eyes that alternated between green and a pale, milky brown. He was the most pleasant of all the staff in the café, and he pulled the best espressos, but his smile, which was ready enough, never touched his eyes. Because I appeared at his coffee counter like a Swiss timepiece every day (or perhaps there were other reasons that I had not thought about), he began to make me free lattes. This made me uncomfortable at first, but then after a while I got used to it, and at some point after that, I came to expect it. When he saw me, he sauntered up and smiled his tired smile.

"Latte?" he asked.

"Please," I answered.

He nodded. "I'll bring it over to you." He was accustomed to me. Every morning, I would come and sit at a corner table in the empty café, which smelled of stale food and freshly brewed espresso. I would smoke three hand-rolled cigarettes successively, one after the other. In those moments, I would not read or write or think of work at all. I would stare blankly through the window and into the street, listening to the music that piped out of speakers hidden somewhere in the corners where the ceiling met the walls. I always sat and tried to decipher the lyrics. The lyrics were all I cared about. But this would not happen today. Today, I would have coffee with Bill.

"Thanks," I answered the Basque student. "I'm sitting over there, with Bill," I gestured.

The Basque raised his eyebrows. "Bill?" he asked inquisitively.

"Head of School," I said by way of explanation, as though it mattered. He nodded, pretending it did.

The floorboards creaked under my feet as I walked back across the café to Bill's table. I sat down across from him.

"So!" exclaimed Bill as he adjusted the newspaper to line up with the edge of the table. "How's your research going?"

"Very well," I answered. "My book manuscript is nearly complete. I'm just having the translations checked now."

"Excellent! Who's publishing it?" he inquired.

I named the press and he smiled indulgently at me. "Wonderful," he murmured. "Congratulations."

"Thank you," I said firmly. "I'm very excited about it."

"What's the research about?" he asked. There were so many professors in his faculty, he had no idea who I was, I realized.

I thought about what I had said to my proofreader the night before, and said, "It's an ethical meditation on the aftermath of the war in Bosnia."

Bill nodded gravely. "Excellent," he murmured.

"It raises questions on the nature of war crimes," I went on. "And how we should think about them in the context of holding people responsible."

"Do you make recommendations on accountability?" Bill inquired.

"Of course," I answered. "The ad hoc tribunals are partially successful, of course, but the main question for me is how to deal, not with individuals, but with the trend toward collective expressions of exclusion."

"Genocide?" he asked.

"Yes, of course, as one manifestation," I nodded. "But what happens before genocide?" I pressed. "How are these exclusive identities formed in the first place, such that genocide seems to be a natural extension of the political process? That's the question I'm interested in," I said.

"Fantastic!" Bill responded. "And do you see a pattern there?"

"Yes, almost certainly," I answered. I was warming up now. "In Bosnia, the respective ethnic governments had a vested interest in turning populations against each other. And you can trace how the government and media primed their populations for war. It's just such a terrible loss that people on the ground couldn't see that they were being manipulated," I shook my head. "They really just went along—as they did in Rwanda and Cambodia—though of course it was not, strictly speaking, an ethnic conflict in Cambodia."

"Of course," Bill agreed. "Well, what's next?" he asked pleasantly. "You must be feeling ambitious."

Actually, Bill, I'm feeling exhausted and sometimes suicidal. "I'm not sure what I'll pursue next," I said slowly. Bill looked at me with confusion. This was clearly not the answer he was expecting to hear. So, I tried to save myself. "Well, there are a lot of spin-off projects that are possible from the book. There are many things I didn't get a chance to expand on, which I still want to pursue."

"Have you thought of external funding?" he inquired.

"Yes, I'm working on a proposal now," I answered and we fell into silence. Bill was almost certainly waiting for me to explain my proposal—to help me work out in his helpful way whether it was viable or not. I didn't think it was viable. But I couldn't say that. Slowly, I said, "I am interested in further exploring the effectiveness of war crimes tribunals. I think I can build nicely on the case studies in the book."

Bill nodded, and seemed reasonably impressed. "Will you undertake interviews?" he asked.

I nodded, and tried to move into more vague intellectual territory. "Yes, I want to identify the people who are affected by the tribunals."

"Have you identified people yet?" he asked.

Yes. I had identified Slobodan Milošević. And then Slobodan Milošević died. So I deleted that section. "Not exactly," I confessed finally. "It's still in the planning stages."

Bill seemed satisfied with my answer nonetheless. "You should speak to me when you have some more concrete sense of the project," he said. "I can proofread your funding proposal for you. I spent several years serving on the adjudicating committees for the research council."

"I would appreciate that, Bill," I nodded.

"My pleasure," he smiled.

We sat awkwardly for another moment or so, while I tried to think of excuses to leave. There were many plausible excuses, but executing them had the potential to seem rude. I had to let some more time pass first before I could reasonably employ an exit strategy.

Bill cleared his throat and toyed with the edge of his neatly folded newspaper.

"What's happening for you these days?" I asked, and heard the unintended flatness of my own voice. I covered it over with a smile.

"Oh, well," Bill sighed. "We are trying to pilot an international exchange program, and it's taking up a lot of time."

"Any countries in particular that we're targeting for recruitment?" I asked.

"Well, actually, yes," Bill answered. "Uzbekistan, Tajikistan, Kazakhstan, Romania, Moldova, and Bosnia. It's called the 'Young Leaders of Tomorrow' program, and we're trying to recruit students from democracies in transition."

Democracies in transition, I mused.

"We're trying to work out the curriculum requirements at the moment," Bill went on. "There will need to be mandatory courses in governance and economics."

"Great!" I answered. But something in me felt uneasy. I remembered a conversation I had had with a professor of literatures from the University of Banja Luka that last time I had been in Bosnia.

It was early March, not quite warm. The leaves were starting on the trees. I was drinking coffee with the professor—a slight woman called Mia with dyed hair that was more red than the brown she intended it to be. We sat together in a small, stylish outdoor café situated in an old Austrian fortress on the Vrbas River. Mia was telling me about the funding crisis in the university. She said it had reached critical proportions. The union was considering strike action. We both knew it would make no difference, but we didn't say it. The international "donors" had a vested interest in seeing the old socialist guard disappear from the universities in that part of the world, paving the way for neoliberal-minded faculty who would teach their students about the inevitable triumph of progressive capitalism and the virtues of structural adjustment. We both knew it. But this was a tide that was bigger than any who might want to oppose it, and the recognition that this was so made any conversation pointless. Mia knew this, but I think she was telling me because she believed that I could help her. She never said it directly, but at one point she sighed and said almost wistfully, "If only some Western university could be convinced to help us—to fund us … " She trailed off like that, careful not to look at me, hopeful that I would take the hint. I watched the Vrbas slide past, swollen with spring. Mia did not understand that the vast proportion of our own funding was generated by the exorbitant fees that international students paid—perhaps some of her own among them—for the privilege of a diploma from a Western university. Mia did not understand that our students were swallowing down neoliberal economics like mothers' milk and that any of her students who were "lucky" enough to study at my institution would come back to be exactly those neoliberal-minded professors whose job it was to bury once and for all that old, annoying socialist order.

So we pretended together that the strike action might be successful. It was the only option for saving a nice spring day from total ruin. I drank my espresso while the sharp breeze murmured in the willows on the banks of the river that had been named for them. When we parted, I walked along the Vrbas for a while, and then back to the city center through the old marketplace. The villagers were selling eggs and cheese and smoked meat. There were strings of peppers and garlic, early hazelnuts and walnuts and waxy-leaved leftover cabbages from winter storage cellars piled up in pale green pyramids. I paused to admire a pair of raw woolen slippers. The women were laughing together over some private joke. I resolved to buy the slippers and rummaged around in my pockets looking for banknotes. And then a young girl came running between the stalls, her hair flying behind her, and she was shouting something about assassination and Djindjić and Belgrade. At first I thought I had misunderstood, but the stall keepers around me went quiet with pensive shock.

The news spread like an electrical current through the marketplace. Zoran Djindjić, the prime minister of Serbia, had been assassinated in Belgrade. He was shot from a concealed window above a Belgrade café that had absurd pink umbrellas on its patio. A friend of mine in Belgrade later reminded me that we had once had espresso together in that café, after the seventy-eight days of NATO bombing that had (maybe) ended the war in Kosovo. Later, I would convey this to my undergraduate lecture hall: "I had an espresso in the café where the assassin was waiting," followed by a rueful shaking of the head. It was my mark of authenticity as an academic and a researcher. It was supposed to have secured my place at the front of the room, where one hundred fifty pairs of eyes were supposed to be trained faithfully on me. "Sometimes, we experience politics without even knowing it," I said authoritatively, and a few students bent over their notebooks to write this down.

But really, it was all just stomach turning. Zoran Djindjić's aides stuffed him, mortally wounded with a single shot to the chest, into the back of a black Audi, which tore out into the heavy traffic on Knez Miloš Street. The window flew down and the man in the passenger seat bellowed from the car at another motorist as he waved his arm violently in a desperate attempt to halt the traffic: "Stani, bre!" Stop, man! I watched this on BBC satellite over and over again. Over and over, the Audi dove into the street with tires screeching. Over and over, the window came down and the passenger howled at the traffic. Over and over, Zoran Djindjić, who had a mother, a wife, a son, a daughter, and a Ph.D. supervised by Jürgen Habermas, the great communications theorist, was dying in the back of the car. Over and over and over again, he died. Three days later, I watched the funeral on television with an even more dejected Mia and a few of her colleagues.

"Takav je život ovde," they clucked at the screen. "That's the way life is here." Some of them wept. I didn't weep. I felt hollow. And after all, Zoran Djindjić wasn't mine to mourn. But later, in Vienna on my way home, I stood under the shower and wept my guts out without ever really knowing why.

The café began to wake up while Bill and I looked at one another across the table. He was looking at me with a small, puzzled smile on his face. I wasn't sure how much time had passed since one of us had last spoken. I smiled back, and risked saying, "I wonder what good our exchange programs actually do."

"They generate fees," he responded evenly.

I forced a lighthearted laugh and nodded at him. "On that note," I announced, perceiving that the moment for a pleasant departure had arrived, "I should go and prepare my lecture notes."

Bill nodded. "I should get back, too. I have a meeting with the program directors."

"Good luck!" I offered brightly as I gathered up my umbrella.

At noon, I went off to deliver a lecture on inter-ethnic war to a theater full of students who didn't really care about anything I had to say. I shouldered past them with my folder full of lecture notes clutched in my sweating hands as they congregated in a loose throng outside the lecture hall. When they saw me, they began to slowly—resentfully—trickle through the doorway and disperse into the folding seats like ducks lined up at a rifle range. They hated that monotonous seating. I didn't blame them. I walked down the shallow, carpeted steps to the front of the room and took a moment to organize my notes at the lectern, glancing up from time to time at the bursts of laughter that rang out from the general chaos that echoed through the theater. I took a deep breath.

"We have a lot to cover today, so let's begin," I announced briskly.

The students began to quiet down, but slowly. Little pockets of whispers popped up here and there, scattered across the lecture hall like broken clouds after a deluge. Most, however, were bending down over their notebooks and laptops, waiting for me to drop the precious hints indicating what might be on the exam. The study of the post-Cold War world for its own sake was a pointless endeavor for more than only a very few of them. These days, they mostly just worried about law or business school applications and came slinking around the office, pressing for grades to be raised.

"OK, last week we looked at how the Cold War gave way to a less clear geopolitical situation. We looked at how different theories attempted to cope with the "brave new world" in which we found ourselves after the fall of the Berlin Wall. We focused on the rise of inter-ethnic conflict and civil war as one defining feature of the contemporary scene in global politics."

I paused and looked up to scan the lecture hall. A number of students were still scrambling to find paper and pens. One was struggling with a cassette recorder. And still, there were little whispers emanating here and there from the ones who would undoubtedly go on to fail the exam. That, of course, was the revenge that students seemed almost terminally incapable of anticipating. There was a giggle from up top somewhere, and I trained my gaze on the last row for a long, considering moment.

"Today, we're going to look at one conflict in depth—and that is the war in the former Yugoslavia. Now, the recurrent themes here are going to be human rights, genocide, and justice. And we're going to look at the impact of the Bosnian War on ideas of democracy and multiculturalism. We'll face some recurring questions about how to think about the relationship between ethnic groups and the nation-state—specifically, why the multicultural model has so often failed in transitioning democracies."

For an hour, I talked. For an hour, most of my students were busy scratching down what I said with their faces bent over their notebooks, or tapping away at their laptops. And for an hour, I waged a battle of long looks with the ones whose whispers bubbled up in the back rows of the lecture hall. When the time was up, I watched two hundred students bolt all at once for the doors. And then, up in the very top row, I saw Stojan Sokolović making his way toward the aisles and the door. I felt my skin crawl with unease as I watched him. I tried to imagine what he would think of my lecture. I also realized that I should feel annoyed that he had come in the first place. Lectures were not for public broadcast. But I didn't feel annoyed with him for coming. I felt annoyed with myself for not delivering a better lecture.

On my way back to the office, I was acutely anxious. I wanted to get back and close my office door. Navigating through battalions of students in the corridor leading down to my office, I could hear the tide of blood pulsing in my eardrums. I fumbled the key against the lock for a moment, balancing my briefcase and my file folder full of lecture notes. Then I was in. I closed the door behind me and regarded my mercifully silent office.

The rain outside suddenly turned to sleet, and then to hail, and there was a clap of thunder that shook the building and sent the car alarms in the parking lot wailing. I walked over to my computer and checked the airport website, to see if there were flight delays. This, for me, was the gauge of whether or not the world was alright. If the airports were working, things were alright. I saw that the hail and winds had canceled a number of flights. Then, somehow, all the words on the monitor seemed to shrink and fade away. The hail clicked against the window more insistently. I struggled out of my wet raincoat.

I was interrupted by the sound of knocking on the hollow wood of my office door.

My heart sank.

"Come in!" I called. And I realized right away, as soon as the door began to open, that all our preparations actually anticipate nothing. We cannot know what is in store for us.

Stojan Sokolović stood at the threshold of my doorway for the second time in less than twenty-four hours, dripping rainwater on the carpet. The leather of his shoes had gone dark with the rain. I sat regarding him. I had expected him, certainly. But I was not ready for him. He stood there, filling up the doorway with the form of his body, soaked through to the skin with rain. There was something in his eyes that I could not read. There was something in the set of his mouth. I waited. He seemed surprised to have found himself at my door. We looked at one another. He stepped into the office and brushed the rain out of his dark hair with the palm of his hand. It cast a fine spray of water across the room. I motioned silently to one of the chairs that sat opposite my desk. He came in and sat down. I waited. He waited. We were gauging each other, as we had the night before, each trying to form a picture of who the other might be. I thought that we must both seem strange figures there, facing one another across the piles of books on my desk.

The hail turned back to rain, which pattered against the window. The tree scratched against the glass. Stojan Sokolović sat facing me. Droplets of rainwater were collected on the lapels and the shoulders of his jacket. What do I want to know about you? I wondered suddenly. What do I ask? Your place of birth? The name of the country on the cover of your passport? Who are you? Why do I want to know? Why did you come to my lecture? These thoughts, piling up like cars on a freeway in the fog, caused my anxiety to increase further. I waited for him to deposit my manuscript on the desk, so I could pay him from my research account, and have him go away. I might have already had the sense that he was disrupting me in some way. But I proceeded anyway, because he was here, and there was nothing I could do about that now. I had invited him. Was he a Serb? A Muslim? Both? Neither? He could have been either, with that name, I thought. He could have been a Croat, too, but I didn't think of that. I remembered a conference on Bosnia at which I had once presented a paper, where one of the audience participants finally dragged out of me what I had been subtly trying to say all along: that, way back in 1997, I had supported the partition of Bosnia. That was a shameful position, I knew, but it was my own. When the conference broke for coffee, a man with a long body and a shaved head and dark eyes walked purposefully up to the panel of presenters. He asked me: "Do you have a chainsaw in your briefcase?" This was amusing and strange. I wanted to laugh. "Why?" I was both suspicious and amused (but not quite amused, because I took myself so very seriously). He regarded me with a steady, even gaze. "Because you will have to cut me in half if you partition my country. I am half a Serb and half a Muslim. To which entity do you suppose I belong?"

I couldn't answer him, so, true to my arrogance as I always was, I promptly forgot about him. He compromised my position. He compromised my politics. He had to be forgotten in order for me to remain who I was.

And here, now, I was faced with Stojan Sokolović, who may or may not have needed cutting in half. And I couldn't help myself: "Are you a Serb or a Muslim?"

Stojan laughed as though he had not expected to. "Does it matter?" he asked, raising his eyebrows.

"No," I answered honestly.

"Then why ask?" he inquired gently.

"Curiosity," I answered defensively. I wanted to place him. I wanted to make sense of him for myself. I wanted to judge him, to feel out his contours, despite the fact that I knew better.

He looked at me for a few seconds, as if trying to guess something. Then he conceded. "Serb."

I nodded.

He reached into his bag—it was crafted of worn brown leather with a long strap that crossed his chest—and pulled out my manuscript. "I have read it through," he announced.

"And?"

"Everything seems alright," he said coolly.

I waited for him to say something about the argument of the book, but he didn't.

"I hope it didn't bore you to death," I offered, fishing for his views so I could correct them if necessary.

"No. I was not bored. I just didn't agree with it," he answered slowly, carefully.

"Well, I guess it's a good thing that you're not writing the reviews of it," I smiled and felt the tightness of my lips.

"Yes," he smiled back, but his was genuine.

"We didn't talk about payment," I said crisply.

"That's right," said Stojan Sokolović.

"How long did it take?" I inquired.

"I don't know," he answered.

"What do you mean?" I asked, confused.

He shrugged. "I really don't know how long it took."

I thought for a moment. I could pay him for a day's work. It hadn't yet been twenty-four hours since he first appeared in my doorway with the crumpled advertisement in his hand. I calculated the standard rate for research assistants and stopped to consider for a moment. Then, feeling magnanimous, I tripled it. He needed new shoes. I named the price and asked him if it seemed alright to him.

"Don't worry about it," he said evenly.

"Worry about what?" I was really confused.

"I don't want to have the money," he said slowly. His voice was deep and sonorous.

"Well, the department will pay it back to me, so I might as well give it to you," I answered.

He didn't respond. He was looking at me with a certain sort of hardness in his expression.

"Look," I insisted, "you did the work, I'm going to pay you, and the department will reimburse me, so no one loses anything." I was feeling generous, because it was easy to be generous with other people's money. I paused and asked him pointedly: "Why don't you want to be paid for your work?" And while this was a genuine query on my part, it sounded patronizing and I regretted it.

Stojan laced his fingers together and rested his hands on the edge of the desk as he had done at the table the night before. He looked closely at me. "I don't want the money," he said.

"Why not?" I asked.

"I just wanted to see what is being written on Bosnia," he said evenly.

"Well, you could have gone to the library for that," I said reasonably. "And anyway, you didn't agree with what I wrote, so you should at least get paid for having to read it."

"That's true, I did not agree with it," he conceded.

"Forget about it," I told him briskly. "Let me pay you. It's only fair." I struggled with the temptation to ask him what his objections to my book were. I reminded myself that it was not up to him to make that determination. It would be decided by academics.

He finally nodded. "Alright."

He signed the claims form, and then he rose to leave. I watched him walk toward the door.

At the doorway, he turned back to face me. His strange light eyes rested on me, and he seemed to be trying to decide something. His gaze was unwavering. And then he asked, "How long were you in Bosnia?"

"Probably around five months or so, altogether," I answered slowly. "Why do you ask?"

But he answered with another question. "And when were you there?"

I looked at him. I saw that he wanted to discredit me. "I was there several times from 1999 onward."

"After the NATO intervention in Kosovo," he confirmed.

"Yes, about two weeks after the war ended," I said.

"And were you in Bosnia during the war?" he asked.

"Of course not," I answered smartly. "I'm not a journalist. I'm an academic."

Stojan was silent for a moment, considering. "Will your students read this book?" he asked.

"They'll pretend to," I smiled.

But he didn't smile at that. Instead, he was looking closely at me. "You are writing about war crimes," he said.

"Yes."

"Do you think that what you wrote is really possible?" he asked.

"I do," I answered firmly.

He looked at me sadly, and I felt like a child. It made me feel angry. "Stojan, my research follows on from a well-established body of literature on ethics and post-conflict institutions."

"Did you ever talk to anyone who committed those crimes?" he asked.

"Well, you and I probably both know that there's no need to look for people to talk to in this case. War criminals are not likely to admit to an academic researcher that they are war criminals … "

"How would a person know if he was a war criminal or not?" Stojan asked pointedly, interrupting me.

I looked at him sharply, unsure of how he could ask such a question. "What do you mean?" I asked slowly, and I could hear the incredulity in my voice.

Stojan looked closely at me. "How would you know if you were a war criminal? It's a simple question. How would you know?"

"What do you mean, how would you know?" I retorted.

"Well, is everyone who is responsible for another man's death a war criminal?" he pressed.

"Of course not. There are international agreements determining what constitutes a war crime," I answered.

"But not everyone agrees on the criteria," he reminded me quietly. "And not everyone knows them."

"That's a different argument," I said abruptly. "Ignorance of the law … "

"No," he said steadily. "It's not a different argument. You said that war criminals would not admit to you that they were war criminals. I am asking you how you would determine that they are war criminals in the first place."

"Stojan, the courts determine those things, based on evidence," I sighed. "I'm just trying to say that people who kill people don't usually want to admit it to foreign researchers."

Stojan seemed to consider this for a moment. "There are some situations where no matter what you choose, you will be responsible for something that you couldn't anticipate," he offered quietly.

He was right, of course, but I ignored him. Something about the tone of his voice made me uncomfortable. I shrugged in an effort to lighten the unease that I felt. "Well, whether we can determine who is a war criminal, or what a war crime is, doesn't matter. The point is that I didn't need to talk to people who killed people in order to write my book. The ones who have been convicted and imprisoned have already signed statements that say everything I would want to know," I finished. But my speech had been deflated.

"Everything?" Stojan asked.

I paused and sighed. "Well, of course, not everything," I said. "Researchers have to make choices. In this case, I think I've covered everything I need to for the purposes of my book. There is always going to be the dilemma of what to include in any analysis."

"But you did not include the fact that there are some situations in which there is no good decision to be made. Your book is written as though each one could decide for himself what he should do, and what he should not do. But something is wrong there. The context is not right." He trailed off, struggling to try and put his finger on what he thought the problem was. I stared at him in cold silence, waiting for him to get to his point. He shook his head, obviously frustrated. Then he shrugged, and seemed to let it go. He could not figure out the problem. He knew there was a problem, but he didn't know exactly what it was or how to say it.

I stared—maybe even glared—at him, waiting for him to leave. And amazingly, as though it had never crossed his mind that he might have insulted me deeply, he said, "Let's go for coffee."

"What?" I asked. But my disbelieving tone did not seem to register with him.

"Coffee," he repeated, as though he thought I just hadn't heard him properly.

I glanced at the piles of unfinished things on my desk that needed attention. Stojan was supposed to have proofread my manuscript and gone away. I stared at him, considering. I didn't want to wrestle with him over this. I didn't want to hear him say what so many Serbs say: *We were not guilty. We did not do it. We were defending ourselves. We were unfairly prosecuted.* I didn't have the energy to try and convince him otherwise. I examined myself very closely in that moment, and encountered an opacity that was surprising. The seconds ticked by while Stojan Sokolović stared patiently at me. And I saw that I wanted to go with him, but I didn't know why. Against my rational judgment, I gathered up my coat and my wallet in silence.

We waded through the teeming rain back to the café under my battered umbrella. Stojan held the umbrella over us, and I struggled to avoid the frozen puddles that were spreading across the sidewalk. The Basque student greeted us with his customary smile and steamed us two free lattes. We found a quiet table near the window. The rain kept most people in their offices, so the café was relatively empty. There was no sign of Bill. Stojan and I walked together across the creaking planked floor and sat down facing one another across a scratched tabletop. The café was fronted with long, Victorian windows framed by cracked molding and they allowed a generous amount of light into the room. This light, which today was muted and grey, illuminated the eyes of my proofreader. His eyes were really very strange, I thought—really nearly colorless so that the contrast between the pupil and the iris was actually rather jarring at first. They were very different in the light of day. He seemed nervous now. His lips were pressed together, and this changed his face, making him seem more severe. I thought that he might have picked up some nervousness from me. I was quietly berating myself for having agreed to come with him, and still wondering why he had been in my lecture hall. Stojan didn't say anything. He didn't seem to have a problem with the silence. He drank his coffee and rolled a cigarette and gazed out the window into the rain for a while. I was squirming in my own skin, and the more uncomfortable I felt, the more I wanted to go back to the office. I regretted how far I had already allowed this to go. I simply did not have time for him.

Finally, I asked him gently: "So, can you try and explain what you mean about the book? I really can't stay here very long."

He turned his strange eyes back to me and smiled quietly. I thought his smiling must be over something other than my question. It seemed out of place with the expression on the rest of his face.

"Patience," he admonished me quietly. "I have to find the right words, and this is not my language."

"Alright," I answered. I reached over for a cigarette. "What do you do for a living, Stojan Sokolović?" I asked.

He shrugged. "Different things, here and there," he answered vaguely. "Translating for the courts, sometimes. Painting houses. Simple carpentry. Things like that."

"What did you study?" I asked.

"I wanted to study African languages. But it turned out to be engineering instead." He sipped his coffee. And though I didn't ask, he said, "I didn't like it."

"I wouldn't like it, either," I offered by way of sympathy.

"Do you like it?" he inquired pointedly.

"Like what?" I asked.

"Your living," he said.

"Of course," I answered.

He nodded thoughtfully.

"Of course," I repeated.

He nodded again.

"You're an American," he announced in an unequivocal voice.

"Yes," I answered slowly.

He nodded.

"Why does that matter?" I couldn't help asking.

"It explains your discomfort with silence," he said.

"What do you mean?" I asked, genuinely confused.

"Americans are uncomfortable with silence, in my experience," he said.

"And your experience consists of … ?" I prompted.

"Humanitarian aid workers, soldiers, international police," he answered. "They would come and drink in the bars at night, and they always talked the most out of everyone. I got the sense that they were scared to be quiet."

I shrugged noncommittally.

"I got the feeling that they were afraid of themselves," he went on in a musing tone.

"Afraid of themselves?" I echoed.

He shook his head. He could not—or would not—explain it further.

I looked at him for a long moment. "Stojan, what do you want to say?" I asked slowly. "Do you want to tell me that Serbs were not responsible for the Bosnian War?" I heard a quiet sadness creeping into my voice.

"No," he answered quietly, distinctly. "I do not want to say that." There was something strange about his eyes in that moment. They seemed to get darker. It gave me the odd sensation that something had changed with the lighting around us. I looked around the café and then to the window to see what had happened. It did not occur to me to consider then that a man's eyes could change color—could deepen like that—with the tenor of his mood. I felt that I should leave. But I didn't.

The hail began again outside, bouncing off the long windows of the cafe. I thought about the airport. Would it close? I stared out the window. The few students on the pavement below the café were put in the difficult position of having to run to get out of the hail, but not really being able to because the sidewalks were too slippery. So they skidded along the pavement, barely bending their knees because they were worried about falling down. They looked both sad and silly, and I suddenly felt an urge to laugh.

But I didn't get the chance to laugh, because then Stojan said, distinctly and without hesitation, "Why I didn't agree with your book is because you write that everyone can choose freely and then be personally responsible for all the consequences."

"Yes," I said simply. "We *are* responsible for the choices we make."

"What if we can't see the consequences beforehand?" Stojan asked.

"Well, we should be able to at least predict major consequences," I answered.

"How?" he asked.

"Stojan, you should be able to predict that pulling a trigger will kill someone," I said firmly.

He didn't answer.

I toyed with the little package of thin cigarette papers and looked at him.

"Do you know where Bijeljina is?" he asked suddenly.

I nodded. Yes.

"Have you ever been there?"

I shook my head. No.

"I know a man from Bijeljina. His name is Petar Petrović. He moved to Pale in 1990, and that is where I met him." Stojan spoke slowly, carefully, as though weighing his words before he spoke them.

I waited.

"Petar was thinking of studying to be a priest when the war overtook him in the spring of 1992 and destroyed all his plans," Stojan said. "The war destroyed many people's plans," he added thoughtfully. "In fact, the war made it so that a person could not plan anything at all."

I looked at him in silence as he paused, considering what to say next. He looked out at the hail for a moment, and then back at me. Then he went on.

"Petar traveled around all the monasteries of eastern Bosnia and also in Serbia, talking to priests and asking them for direction for his studies. He would drive around in his car, looking for churches in the hills. There are several monasteries that do not appear on the road maps," Stojan added, rubbing his cheek absently with his fingertip.

"Anyway, one day, Petar found the one he had been looking for, and he decided as soon as he saw it that he would one day be a priest there. He found it by accident, up in the hills around Višegrad." Here, Stojan paused again. "Have you ever been to Višegrad?"

I nodded. Yes.

"Have you read the famous novel about Višegrad?"

I shook my head. No.

"It doesn't matter," Stojan said. "Petar walked through the iron gate in the wall of the monastery, and he knew he wanted to stay there. He said he knew because he saw that painted into the plaster above the gate was a fresco of the Old Testament Trinity—the archangels that are supposed to be the prophesy of the three forms of God-to-come."

"Rublyev painted an icon like that," I announced, trying to indicate that I did, in fact, know something. Stojan nodded in acknowledgment, but did not pause in his story.

"Like in all our monasteries, the air there was very serious." Stojan laced and unlaced his fingers on the tabletop. "It was very devoted. Our monasteries might be sometimes simple, but there is something in their architecture that they all share. And they always smell the same. I don't know if it's because of the incense they burn—the *tamjan*—or if it's something else—something in their age. You know," Stojan said, changing his tone from one of musing to one of declaration, "it seems that time never touches those monasteries. Priests and monks come and go, but the character of the monastery doesn't change." He sighed, and toyed with the spoon on his saucer. "Petar told me so much detail about everything there. I can't imagine how he remembered it all so well. He said that sheets were out on a clothesline between the living areas and the kitchens. Copper pots were sitting in the sun. Things like that. He saw orange kittens sleeping under a bench against a wall. For a while, Petar stood at the gates, and no one noticed him. But he noticed them. He watched them for a long time, and said that he knew it was the right place for him to study."

"So, did he study there?" I asked.

"No, he didn't," Stojan answered evenly.

I sipped my coffee and waited for him to continue.

"He stood there for a while, and then a priest emerged from a doorway with a bowl of milk for the orange kittens, and he saw Petar, who was standing just inside the gate. The priest stood slowly, and came across the grass to greet him … "

IV

Stojan closed his eyes against the shadows of the little café for a moment, thinking of Petar Petrović. When he opened them again, he saw the young professor looking at him intently with her dark eyes. She was waiting for him to continue, and it seemed to him that his frequent pauses were beginning to annoy her. There was something very anxious about her—something economical in her speech and in her movements and in her purposeful questions that sought out clear answers and could not settle for ambiguity. She looked like she wanted to know what the point of all this was. So Stojan went on, narrating the conversation between Petar and the priest as Petar had told it to him when he came back to Pale.

"The blessings of Christ be upon you," said the priest.

"And upon you," nodded Petar.

"What brings you to Holy Trinity?" the priest asked affably.

"I want to devote my life to God," answered Petar without hesitation, and he could feel the ecstasy of that statement breaking his voice.

The priest frowned slightly.

They walked slowly toward the kitchens together, and the coarse cotton of the priest's black cassock rustled a whisper in the warm gust of a spring breeze.

"Will you share coffee with me?" asked the priest.

"I will," answered Petar solemnly.

The priest called the novices to make the coffee, and then reached down to lift one of the kittens to his shoulder. He invited Petar to sit at a solid pine table under the trees. Petar did, and the kitten bounded across the tabletop and into Petar's lap.

"The sacrifice of one's life to God is a sacrifice for country as well," the priest offered by way of beginning.

Petar was confused. The novices came with the coffee on a metal tray and set it before them on the table. Petar scratched the cat in his lap behind its ears, and it licked his fingers appreciatively.

"There is now going to be war," the priest said slowly. "It is the duty of the Serbs to defend their country."

Petar considered this. "Defending countries requires men to die, Father," he answered quietly.

The priest looked at him closely. "Only a Serbia pure of heart can be devoted to God," he answered.

"This is not Serbia," Petar wanted to say, but didn't. He wondered for a moment if he had indeed crossed into Serbia on his drive, but he was sure he hadn't. Petar looked at the priest, now unsure of which republic he was really in, and the priest went on, "God asks us to defend the land where his Word is held sacred, and to protect it from those who want us to worship a false deity."

Petar was confused. What false deity was this that the priest talked about? Was he talking about the Muslims in Bosnia? "They worship the same God as we do," he wanted to say, but something told him that the priest would not hear him. Petar did not touch the coffee that had been placed before him. He felt shocked, and hurt. "Countries are not much more than stone and wood," Petar finally managed to say. "It is people—not countries—that matter, and I want to comfort them with the love of God."

"Sheep need their pastures," answered the priest. "How shall you comfort men in exile?"

"Only those who are in exile *need* comfort," Petar whispered in reply.

The priest drank his coffee. In a definitive tone, he said to Petar, "This is our land, and if you want to serve God, go and defend it for Him."

"Am I in Serbia?" Petar pointedly asked the priest.

He nodded solemnly. "You are."

Petar arose and left without touching his coffee. He placed the little kitten carefully on the grass and walked away without looking back. It followed him for a moment, wobbling across the churchyard. Then it gave up. At the bottom of the hill that led up to the monastery, Petar saw a farmer walking down the dirt road. He slowed and rolled down his window.

"Brother!" he hailed. "Which republic is this?"

The farmer laughed. "Do the priests say Serbia?" he asked.

"Yes," Petar nodded.

"This is Bosnia," declared the farmer. "And the priests knew it, too, before all this craziness started."

Petar thanked him and drove on. When he arrived home that night, he knocked on Stojan's father's door. In his hand was a letter asking him to report to be mobilized.

"Come in, Petar," murmured the older Sokolović. "My sons are inside." He opened the door to his home wider so that the man could pass through into the warm little rooms where his friends were finishing their evening meal.

"What is it?" Stojan inquired when he saw Petar's frozen face.

"The war has really come now," Petar answered flatly, as though he still did not believe it.

"No." Luka Sokolović, Stojan's older brother, was adamant. "There will not be war. This is Europe!"

Luka's dark-haired lover, Jelena, reached over and took his hand.

"I've been mobilized," answered Petar.

"It's precautionary, maybe," Stojan offered.

The older Sokolović was silent. Stojan took note of it. He wondered what his father was thinking, but did not want to ask. He knew the old man would say what he wanted to say when he felt the time was right.

"I want to be a priest," Petar murmured uselessly.

"And you will," said old Sokolović with conviction beneath his frazzled gray brows.

"The priests have gone crazy," Petar replied.

Luka's lover stood up from the table to make coffee. Her long, slender hands organized the china cups quietly.

Stojan spoke, and the young professor listened. "So, Petar returned to his unit. He had two weeks of re-training, to reacquaint him with tactics and weapons, and to convince him that the Muslims wanted to wipe out every trace that Serbs had ever been in these hills." The warning of the priest of the Trinity haunted him—and he worried that all the churches and monasteries might be destroyed if the Serbs were defeated. But then he began to hear stories, reported over crackling radio transmissions at night, about how certain villages and districts had been "cleaned" by the Serbs. They used the word "*čist*." And he began to feel a deep dread welling up in his heart. Petar would not have taken even one Muslim life for the resurrection of the whole of the lost federation, and he had loved the federation that was now disintegrating without purpose all around him. He would not kill a man to save a monastery. It was absurd.

"Why didn't he run away?" asked the professor innocently.

"Where would he go?" answered Stojan with surprise.

She didn't answer. She turned her face away and looked for a moment out the window and into the street. She looked like she wanted to say something more, but she didn't. Stojan suddenly felt regretful that he had said Americans are uncomfortable with silence. She now seemed to struggle with her desire to speak, and he thought it was because she had interpreted his comment as a criticism.

"There was nowhere he could go," Stojan reformulated. "And this is the point of what happened to Petar. He had nowhere to go, and he could not change anything, even though he desperately wanted to. Night after night, he lay awake, knowing that he could not avoid the front, and knowing that he could not get out of it."

Stojan stopped here, and raised his finger to stress his next point. "Petar resolved that he would not participate in killing anyone, no matter what happened. He tried to make that ethical decision that you talked about in your book."

The professor looked at him quietly, and there was a baleful, helpless sort of anger in her face, he thought. Stojan ignored it.

"But Petar did not know what to do under the circumstances. And then, he made a decision. On his first night at the front he walked away from the others, and he traded the full clip in his rifle for an empty one. Then he came quietly back to listen to the radio from Belgrade, and to laugh a bit with the others. Just as morning began to break, the Bosnian unit on the other side began firing—they had managed to get close enough that they could be heard taunting the Serbs across the trenches.

Petar was in a particularly exposed position, but was determined to keep his commitment to kill no one."

"So, I guess he got killed," the professor interjected sadly.

"No," Stojan felt himself smile a small, terse smile. "No, it was worse than that. With Petar was a kid from Vlasenica. He was very young. His hair was wet with sweat," Stojan breathed, closing his eyes to visualize the boy as though he himself had been there. "Petar said that the boy was just whispering over and over again, 'God, God, God.' He was trying to replace the clip in his rifle, but his hands were trembling too much, and he couldn't do it. Then, someone yelled for him to take some cover. And because Petar was an experienced reservist, an officer called to him to clear some of those bastards out so this kid could get out from under their fire."

"Please shoot them," the kid from Vlasenica spoke with Stojan's voice. "Please help me."

"Petar raised his rifle and betrayed the boy from Vlasenica. Petar could not cover his escape with an empty rifle, but the boy took the raised rifle as indication that he should run. He died ten seconds into his sprint."

Stojan stopped then, and began to roll another cigarette. The professor was staring at him with big, liquid eyes that had not anticipated this terrible twist to the story.

"Thus, the man who had decided he would not be responsible for death was, in the end, responsible for it anyway," Stojan added. "What do you think he could have done?" he asked her quietly.

"I don't know," she whispered in a deflated voice. "I don't know." She looked down at her hands, which were wrapped tightly around her chipped coffee cup. And Stojan realized that he felt sorry for her. Her fingernails were bitten painfully short. They sat together in silence while the hail ticked against the window. Stojan lit his cigarette and rubbed his forehead.

The Basque student came with fresh lattes and half a smile.

"Do you need anything else?" he inquired unobtrusively.

"No," Stojan answered kindly. "We're alright."

When the student had gone, the professor cleared her throat and said quietly, "Stojan, I don't know what to say."

He smiled without meaning to. Her pride was a huge thing, he realized, and it had cost her something to admit that she did not know what to say or how to respond. He liked her for her honesty, for the ease with which those layers of arrogance could be peeled back. And she could pronounce his name properly, a precious rarity in this city.

"I like how you say my name," he said suddenly, hoping to make things a little easier now.

"What do you mean?" she seemed surprised. "How do I say your name?"

"You say it perfectly, and it seems so unusual for me here, to hear it perfectly like that," he explained.

She smiled a small smile, but it was a sad, confused sort of smile, and it was not convincing.

Stojan smoked his cigarette with a measure of uncertainty that he tried not to show. He could see that what had happened to Petar had now injured her. He sighed and said, in an effort to make it easier, "It's probably not worth wondering about this."

"Why not?" she asked, surprised.

"Because it's over now," he answered.

Stojan heaved a heavy sigh and rested his chin in his hand. It seemed to him that they had reached a place where there was nothing more to say.

"What happened to Petar?" she asked thoughtfully.

"He became a priest, and he emigrated, along with everyone else."

She nodded. She was still looking down at the coffee cup in her hands.

"I'm sorry," said Stojan unexpectedly.

"When did you leave Bosnia?" she asked, ignoring his apology.

"1988," he answered quietly. "In the summer."

"When did you serve in the army?" she asked.

He looked closely at her, unsure of whether to tell her the truth. She was looking at him with a totally open expression on her face, as though she already knew the answer and was only awaiting confirmation. So he sighed again and said, "I served over the course of four years,"

"When?" she pressed, and he was surprised at her tenacity.

He stared closely at her. "When do you think?" he asked openly, challengingly.

"I don't know," she answered, but her uncertainty was clearly feigned. She wanted to know who she was dealing with, Stojan realized suddenly. And he wondered himself what the answer to that question was.

He looked steadily at her out of narrowed eyes. "I was mobilized three times between 1992 and 1995," he said quietly.

She didn't ask anything else. They rolled cigarettes and drank coffee, each struggling in their own way with the intertwined fates of Petar Petrović and the boy from Vlasenica who died as a result of Petar's ethics. Finally, the professor roused herself and announced that she had to go back to her office. Stojan did not object. He was grateful for it to end, even though he had initiated everything. The sky was just appearing in little blue patches here and there between the clouds when they emerged out onto the street and went in opposite directions.

Stojan thought that he would probably never have occasion to see or talk to her again, so as they looked at each other for what he expected would be the last time, he cleared his throat and said sincerely, "Thank you for the translating work."

She smiled sadly, and murmured, "You're welcome."

They nodded at each other, and then she turned toward her office. Stojan stood for a fraction of a second longer, looking at her back as she began to walk away. Then he turned in the opposite direction for home.

"Stojane!"

He circled back immediately at the sound of his name being called in the vocative case. This was the form of his name that demanded a response. Spoken in the imperative, a person responded without even thinking about it.

"Evo me," he answered automatically in Serbian as he turned to face her—"Here I am."

She was standing on the pavement with her hands on her hips and a puzzled look on her face. Her raincoat billowed out behind her in the wind. She opened her mouth, and then closed it again.

He stood still, waiting for her to say what she had called him back to say.

She cocked her head to one side and asked him, "Why were you in my lecture today?" There was a demanding, accusative tone to her question that perfectly matched her use of the vocative case of his name.

He smiled easily, and the corners of his eyes creased gently. "I wanted to learn about the war in Bosnia," he answered without hesitating.

She half-laughed, hearing the good humor in his voice.

"What did you think of it?" she demanded.

He considered her for a moment, still smiling. Then he waved her away jokingly. "I'll tell you another time!"

"Right!" she called out in mock sarcasm.

He laughed. "I will, I will," he promised.

She shook her head, still trying to smile, and turned away from him again.

Stojan continued home. The hail had stopped for good now, though little clusters of the strange, misshapen stuff were still collected here and there around the bases of trees and along buildings. The young leaves on the spring trees rustled in the wind. Stojan saw this, but could not hear it over the sound of cars and busses grinding through the slushy streets. He buttoned his wool coat up to his neck and was grateful that his shoe had dried somewhat. He tried to avoid the puddles here and there that would certainly leak through the split in the shoe and soak his foot again. People were moving fast along the sidewalks, overtaking him on all sides with purpose and direction.

He never got used to how quickly people moved in this city, and how seldom they stopped to look at or appreciate anything; like leaves on trees rustling in the wind, or the way the sun occasionally burst through a break in the clouds. Stojan wondered if he was the only one who noticed the transition from winter to spring, or if it meant anything to anyone else. It reminded him of home in some way—when the spring thaw over-swelled the little creeks that suddenly poured down the mountainside in great torrents of fresh, frigid water. Those freshets were so pure that you could drink from them with your cupped hands, if your mouth could stand the cold. They came from deep springs in the earth that the villagers had expertly tapped into. One could wander all over the place in the hills above Sarajevo and along the way find hand-hewn troughs into which endless streams of good water poured all year long without fail.

Stojan walked across the city and thought about Pale, his small town in the high hills of Romanija that swelled exponentially in population during and after the war. By the time the peace agreement was signed at Dayton, Pale was almost a city. This was perhaps a predictable outcome for Pale, which had been the seat of the nationalist Serb government throughout the war. Stojan had liked it better when it was a village that no one paid much attention to. He liked its quiet, clean snowfalls and its gigantic coniferous pines. He liked the way the sun set on the white-washed brick and the terracotta tiles of his father's rooftops. He liked to walk in the surrounding forests, listening to the snow crunch beneath his feet. He couldn't be bothered with Sarajevo, sprawling out dirty and in disrepair in the valley at the foot of the hills. He had never liked cities, and now he lived in one that was larger than any he had been to.

He remembered the first time he had left the hills and gone down with his mother and brothers into Sarajevo. It was the year before she died, and she had taken them to buy a copper coffee pot from one of the tiny shops in the narrow little alleys near the Bey's mosque with its marble, laughing fountain. She bought them each a brick of pure white Turkish halva, made with honey and pistachios. They were piled up like walls of snow-bricks in the sweet shop windows. Stojan ate his halva as he walked, peering into the dim, scented shops that sold hand-hammered copper pots for brewing coffee.

They stopped in front of a shop that had windows piled up with all manner of copper things. "Help me pick a džezva," his mother offered.

It was the only task he had ever undertaken in Sarajevo that had distracted him from his dislike of its ceaseless hum. He and his brothers poured over every džezva in the place while their mother watched them affectionately and the shopkeeper smiled indulgently.

"How many are you?" he asked Stojan's mother.

"We are five, with my husband," she announced. "These are my sons." She was proud of them. It showed in her voice, Stojan felt. It showed in the gentle curve of her spine, and in the way she held her shoulders.

"Three sons, eh?" the old shopkeeper exhaled sharply, showing his admiration.

"Three sons," she confirmed. "Three falcons." She touched Stojan's dark head with her pale hand as he moved down the line of shelves, inspecting the coffee pots.

"I found it!" announced Stojan.

They all turned to look. Stojan was crouched down on his knees pointing to the very back of the lowest shelf. Luka walked over and crouched down beside him to inspect the džezva that he had chosen.

"Stojan is right," he said after a moment of serious consideration. "It's the best one."

"Go on and pick it up," encouraged the shopkeeper.

Stojan reached back carefully and took the džezva. It was tall and deep and had a voluptuous arc that ended in a solid copper base. The seamless body of the pot was covered in hand-stamped desert animal figures interspersed with stars and crescent moons. Under the dust, it was possible to detect a muted, burnished glow.

"Perfect," said their mother crisply. "We'll take it." She paid the shopkeeper, and he dusted the džezva with a scrap of linen cloth before wrapping it up in a page of the Sarajevo daily *Oslobodjenje*.

"Happiness," called the shopkeeper after them in blessing as they filed out of the tiny shop and into the street again. With the džezva wrapped safely and stowed in their mother's cloth shopping bag, the four of them walked back the way they had come, toward Princip's Bridge, which spanned the Miljacka River. She told them the story of how Gavrilo Princip had bravely assassinated the Archduke of Austria in a classic act of Serbian defiance that would kick off the First World War.

And Luka asked a question that he had wanted to ask when they learned about Princip in school, but hadn't the guts to ask the teacher. "Is it right or wrong to assassinate people?"

Their young mother was speechless for a moment at this. She paused, and thought, and answered, "History judged Princip to be a hero." Then she qualified: "But those were different times."

Years later, when the Serbs were shelling Sarajevo to death, Stojan longed to ask his mother this question again, and he wondered if she would make the same answer. She had believed in the federal socialist republic. He didn't know where she would have turned her loyalties once that republic was gone. But when it came time for each of them to decide, his mother had already been in her grave for many years, and on this matter she would be forever silent.

After the war, the Bosnian government officially declared Gavrilo Princip a common terrorist and they removed the plaque on the bridge that had for nearly a century commemorated him as a hero. And Stojan's mother's pronouncement of his heroism—like she herself—was blotted out. But he remembered reading what Princip had scrawled on the wall of his prison cell before his death: "Our ghosts will wander through the streets of Vienna and roam through the palaces, frightening the lords."

Later, when they were teenagers, Stojan and Luka and their friends would sometimes go down to Sarajevo to look in record stores or visit nightclubs. But Stojan could not grow to like the chaos of Sarajevo, and he was always happy to head home. His ears would pop on the road around the turnoff to Mokro. He would watch the craggy hills rising up from the riverbed below, counting the numbers of houses precariously balanced on the edge of the canyon's precipices. And he would feel at home.

Stojan's family had been in those hills for hundreds of years, as the dates on the gravestones in the family cemetery attested. And they all had the same light eyes. The Sokolovići passed on their strange eyes generation after generation. No matter how many people were married in with their varying depths of dark eyes, that strange blue persisted. When the war started, there was not a born Sokolović on the mountainside without those eyes. Everyone knew which Sokolović was born of blood and which was married in, because the blood Sokolovići were light-eyed, and the acquired Sokolovići were dark-eyed. Not all of them were in Pale, but most of them were in the ancestral mountains of Romanija, tucked away in small villages and big towns alike with their light eyes. They were in Pale, Mokro, and Sokolac, from where it was said they had originated and obtained their surname (though Stojan did not believe this tale, because in his view Sokolac was not old enough to confer itself as a surname). Some had migrated down to Sarajevo and its drab suburbs of Vogošća, Ilidža, and Lukavica. There were dozens of them along the river in the Grbavica section of Sarajevo, and there they stayed until the Federation army decided that it was time for them to go. When they left Ilidža at the war's end after learning that their village would fall into Federation territory, they exhumed their ancestral dead and carried them up the hillside to be reburied in Serb territory. They burned their own houses when they left, so that there would not be a trace of anything useful to the Bosnian Muslim refugees who would be resettled there.

Stojan shook his head as he walked through the city, as though he might spill out these thoughts that were now rising like the slow, steady encroachment of an incoming tide. He thought it must have been reading through parts of that professor's book and his now pointless story about Petar Petrović that had caused these memories to well up in him. Stojan felt angry with himself for telling her that story. He never talked about the war, with anyone. He lived in the hope that it could be forgotten. But then he had been drawn to attend her lecture, and to invite her for coffee, and he did not know whether these things were the cause or the effect of this welling memory—or whether they were related at all.

When Stojan arrived at his small apartment, the clouds that had brought the bad weather were nearly blown out and the sky had become a muted deep blue. He closed the door behind him and looked around at the shabby, well-ordered room. He walked over and stood for a moment before the window, gazing out across the street with thoughtful, considering eyes. The tiny apartment was warm, but Stojan still felt the cold in his body, and a trace of the wet, frozen feeling in his toes from the tear in his shoe where the rain had leaked through. He crouched down, still in his coat, before the vent in the floor that forced heated air into the room. It seemed to him in that moment that he could have never anticipated finding himself here as he now was: in a country to which he did not belong, speaking a language that did not have words for the things he wanted to say, and with a soul that always seemed just slightly out of place. Even when he knew that the war had arrived—and even when he knew it would not end quickly—Stojan could not have anticipated this life. He could not have anticipated that he would one day be so intimately acquainted with loneliness—like a mountain laurel dug up and transplanted to a soil in which its roots could not find purchase. He held out his cold hands in front of the forced air for a moment, and then went to the kitchen, where he filled the copper pot with the desert animals stamped into it with water for coffee.

V

Stojan Sokolović, the youngest of three brothers—three falcons, as his mother had proudly told the shopkeeper those years before—stood on the threshold of the door to his father's house. The old pines whispered to one another in a gentle breeze, and Stojan could not decide if it was announcing the end of winter, or the beginning of spring. The television inside talked only of the war that was coming, and Stojan couldn't stand listening to it anymore. His father was perched in front of the screen like a watchful bird.

"Father, turn it off, please," Stojan begged him after a while.

"There's a war coming," his father answered without looking up.

"The Serbian people must defend themselves," opined the news anchor from Belgrade.

"Oh, for God's sake!" Stojan sighed. "I'm going out." But he felt uneasy. The air in the house seemed heavy and fetid. So Stojan stepped outside with a cigarette in one hand and a cup of coffee in the other. He was barefooted, and the black earth was cold beneath the sun-warmed grass. He walked toward the hand-hewn bench and table under the trees and sat down, looking for some peace.

As he finished his cigarette, he saw Luka and Jelena walking toward the house. The morning sun glinted on her hair. They smiled and waved at him, and he raised his arm in return.

"Stojane!" called Luka across the distance.

"What?" Stojan called back.

"Make coffee for us! Please!"

"Fuck you!" replied Stojan cheerfully. "Make it yourself!"

They walked up to the table under the trees and sat down across from him.

"I'm not going back in the house until our father turns the television off," Stojan announced as he sipped the last of his coffee and set the cup decisively back in the saucer.

"Why not?" asked Jelena.

"All they talk about is war," answered Stojan shaking his head.

Luka laughed. "They're insane, man. How will we go to war with ourselves?" he asked rhetorically.

"I'll make the coffee," offered Jelena quietly.

"No," replied Luka as he stood up. "I will." And he looked down at his younger brother with mock superiority. "I'll bet you I can get the old man to turn that shit off," Luka laughed.

Stojan waved his arm toward the house magnanimously. "Go for it," he answered as though he were making his brother a particularly generous offer. He wanted to laugh, but he found that he couldn't.

Luka walked across the grass, long and sinewy. His shadow followed behind him with exaggerated length. When he had disappeared into the house, Jelena looked up at Stojan and said, "I think Luka is wrong. I think there will be war."

Stojan looked back at her, and felt a little coal of disbelief blaze in his stomach. A gust of wind lifted Jelena's hair off her shoulders and it danced for a moment around her face like dark silk. He wanted to deny it. He wanted to tell her that she was wrong. But instead, he felt himself nodding in assent. "I think so, too," he murmured.

"Luka doesn't believe it," she said. Her hands were folded together tightly in front of her on the table. "What do you think is going to happen, Stojan?" Jelena asked, searching his face.

"I have no fucking idea," he answered helplessly.

She grew pensive, and a little furrow of worry appeared on her brow between her eyes. "What is going to happen to us?" she asked again.

Stojan looked at her pale countenance. He looked at the curve of her neck as it disappeared into the collar of her jacket. She was scared. And she said, "I think you and Luka should go to Belgrade."

Stojan considered this.

"Don't laugh at me," Jelena warned.

"I'm not laughing," he answered.

"What if you are mobilized?" she asked.

"Well, then I guess we're mobilized," Stojan shrugged. "I don't know anyone in Belgrade. How will I live there?"

"No one is going to fight a war!" Luka called from the doorway as he came out balancing the tray of coffee.

"Petar was mobilized," Stojan reminded him.

"You said yourself it was precautionary," Luka answered.

Old Sokolović came out of the house, moving slowly, and joined them all at the table under the trees.

"Stojane, son, why are you barefoot?" his father asked sadly. Over the years, he had slowly taken on his wife's role. She would have been shouting at him from the doorway of the small house.

"I'll go in a minute," Stojan promised.

"Listen to me," his father announced.

"I'm going!" Stojan replied exasperatedly.

"I'm not talking about that, idiot!" his father said sharply.

They all looked up at him in muted surprise. He looked back at them steadily, seriously, his hands sunk deep into the pockets of his wool sweater.

"My sons, I think the Turks mean to kill us," he announced.

Luka laughed. "What Turks? Don't be stupid! Why would Turkey invade Yugoslavia?"

"He's not talking about Turkey," said Stojan quietly. "All the Muslims in Bosnia are called Turks now. Why do you think I want the old man to turn the television off?"

"I know what he's talking about, Stojan," interrupted Luka. "I'm trying to make a point. Look, it's time to calm down. This is Europe." Luka looked at his father, who was staring gravely at him.

"No, it's not Europe," Jelena replied tersely. "Stojan?" she turned to look at him with her bloodless cheeks, and the expression in her eyes was one of insistence. "Back me up," this look begged.

Stojan looked at his brother.

"Luka," he began.

"What?" Luka looked back at him with a confused expression on his face.

"Luka, I think Jelena is right," Stojan offered. And then, ashamed of his fear, he looked away with a frown.

"About what?" he asked.

"There will be war."

"That's ridiculous," Luka answered emphatically.

"Luka, you're going to Belgrade tonight," his father announced.

Luka wanted to protest, Stojan knew, but there was something in their father's voice that prevented him. He looked at Jelena, who looked back with her quiet, urgent eyes. Stojan regarded her closely and saw that her eyelashes were trembling.

It never occurred to Stojan to wonder why his father wanted to send Luka to Belgrade, and not him. It was Jelena who asked, "What about Stojan?"

From the pocket of his lamb's wool sweater, old Sokolović withdrew a piece of paper that had been folded many times. It was worn from being held in his hands. He carefully unfolded it, and his old eyes scanned its print slowly, as though he had not already read it a dozen times over. They were all silent while Sokolović re-read the creased paper. Finally, he looked up and said, "Stojan has been mobilized."

Stojan felt his stomach roll over beneath his ribs. But still, his feelings came from what felt like a great distance. A wash of disbelief flooded through him and seemed to numb the marrow in his bones.

Jelena raised her hands to cover her face.

"God," Luka sighed.

"It's not Europe!" Jelena shouted. "It's not fucking Europe! Stojan, run away! Go to Germany. Vladimir is there," she said, referring to their older brother, who had left over a year ago on a temporary employment visa. "He will give you a place to live."

Old Sokolović shook his head. "It's too late for that," he said matter-of-factly. And Stojan knew that he was right. They wouldn't let him cross the border. And Germany wouldn't issue him a visa under any circumstances at this point. But Jelena did not agree. She saw the trap, just as they all did, but she couldn't accept it. She couldn't accept her powerlessness. She said again, in an imploring tone, "Brother, listen to what I'm saying. Go to Canada! Go to America, if you don't want to go to Germany! But don't report to them! Fuck them!"

He shook his head sharply at her, as if he meant to ask her to stop. So she did stop, but she looked at him with her deep, helpless, angry eyes.

Luka left for Belgrade that night. When he had placed his small bag in the back of the car, he went out to the fields where Stojan was sitting. He knew instinctively that he would find his brother stretched out with his back against the oldest pine at the edge of the smallest pasture. Stojan could always be found there, when he couldn't be found anywhere else. When Stojan saw Luka coming, he stood up and walked halfway to meet him. They looked at each other with their identical pale eyes.

"It won't last long, Stojan," Luka promised.

"Stop," Stojan whispered.

Luka stopped. They stood regarding each other quietly for a moment. A lamb bleated thinly from the pasture below.

"Come on," Stojan said to his brother, and slung his arm across Luka's shoulders. "I'll walk with you."

Luka nodded, and they walked back to the house together with their arms around each other. It was a perfect spring afternoon. The wind sang in the trees. The birds were building their nests in the safety of the tall, dense pines. The lambs had all been born or were about to be born. Stojan thought that the roofs might need to be retiled soon, or at least repaired. The carpets should be taken out of the house and washed, too, he realized. Maybe they should put a fresh coat of paint on the walls. He looked around at the cluster of little buildings that had belonged to his family for uncounted generations. Nothing about the place suggested that anything was wrong at all. It was a day just like any other day—just like all the days that had come and gone all of his life, he thought disjointedly. And suddenly everything started to feel absurd.

Jelena was standing against the whitewashed wall of the house. She was wearing one of Luka's sweaters against the chill that was creeping into the high-altitude air. Luka turned to embrace his brother. "I'll see you soon," he said as he kissed Stojan's cheeks. "Be safe."

Stojan nodded, because he didn't trust that his voice would work if he tried to answer. He held his brother tightly for a moment, and then went into the house so that Luka and Jelena could have their last moment alone, to say goodbye.

VI

The long light of late afternoon fell through my office window and stamped a thinly illuminated square on the opposite wall. I pushed my chair back from my desk and regarded the dust that hung in the air, pierced by that shaft of faded light. I felt tired and restless. I was sick of the funding proposal. I was pouring myself into it like milk, and it wasn't going anywhere fruitful. From somewhere out in the corridor, a door thumped closed quietly and I heard a key turning in a lock. I stood up on legs that were asleep from having been immobile for so many hours, and I limped over to my bookshelves. There were meters of books lined up, each waiting for its turn to be read, re-read, marked, dog-eared, commented upon, and then lent to graduate students. I ran my fingertips across their spines as I walked down the length of the shelving, looking closely at each one. I stopped at a thin, black-bound volume that was particularly tattered from having been over-read, and took it from its place. Emmanuel Levinas' *On Escape*. I opened it at random, and read a sentence that I had once underlined with a hand much surer than it would later become. "The necessity of fleeing oneself is put in check by the impossibility of ever doing so." I smiled at this, and passed my bloodless fingers over the type. They rasped against the heavy stock paper.

Suddenly, there was a tap at my window that made me jump nearly out of my skin. *On Escape* fell from my hand and landed on the floor with a loud rustling of pages and a thump of protest. Stojan Sokolović was standing outside with an uncomfortable smile on his face and an urgency in his expression that suggested something was wrong. I could still feel the surge of adrenaline from having been startled so badly. I walked over to the window purposefully. Couldn't he use the door? My annoyance must have shown, because his smile faded and then he grew sheepish as I struggled to unlatch the window. It wrenched open with a loud squeal. A crow was startled out of the tree behind Stojan, and it took off with a mad flap of its wings.

I looked at him through the open window and said nothing.

But Stojan didn't say anything, either, and we just stood staring stupidly at each other for a few seconds before I finally asked, "What's up?"

Stojan opened his mouth to say something, and then closed it again.

"Is everything alright?" I prompted.

He nodded. "I just thought you might have time for me to tell you what I thought of your lecture," he said.

"I'm really busy," I answered automatically. "Can you come back tomorrow?"

He looked away for a moment, and then changed tactics.

"Well, I wanted to make up to you for the dinner you paid for when we went out the other night," he said with a note of hope in his otherwise reserved tone.

"I'm writing a funding proposal," I said, gesturing weakly to the computer. He looked over at it. The galaxy was meandering its way across my screen saver.

"It will still be there tomorrow," he said quietly, insistently. I studied his face in the deepening light of the courtyard. There were many fine lines around his eyes. I hadn't noticed them before.

"Alright," I conceded, and began to turn away. "Let me lock up, and I'll meet you outside the doors."

He nodded and took a step back form the window. "OK."

"Why didn't you use the doors in the first place?" I asked in afterthought as I reached up to close the window.

Stojan looked surprised. "It's after seven o'clock," he said. "Everything is locked."

"Oh," I answered feebly.

I closed the window, locked my office door behind me, and went out. It was already evening. The sun was sinking fast. Stojan had walked around the building and was waiting for me. We started down the street together in a silence that was slowly becoming characteristic of us.

"Where are we going?" I asked after a while.

"I thought we would go to my home," he said in an apologetic tone.

"Oh," I answered awkwardly.

Stojan Soklović lived in a small apartment on the tenth floor of an old concrete building with balconies that looked like they were going to collapse in a heap of tangled, flaking rust at any moment. He had a few books on a few shelves, mostly in Cyrillic, and a dictionary that went from Serbo-Croatian to English and back again. He had some old, cheap furniture—a few chairs, a scratched table, a desk, and a worn-out couch. It was more than was in my apartment. Somewhere off in another room, I presumed there must be a bed and a bureau, and maybe a nightstand. The walls looked tired. The floors were interlocking hardwood. They were scuffed and worn in the high-traffic areas, where thousands of feet had crossed and re-crossed and crossed again back and forth over the years since it was laid. Things were clean and well cared for, but that was the most that could be said for the place. The pictures on the wall were generic poster prints of green fields and sunsets and sailboats in plastic frames. One would be tempted to forget them on moving day, I thought.

I stood looking around for a moment while Stojan hung up my coat, and then I followed him into the kitchen, where there was an ornate, long-handled copper pot for brewing coffee on the stovetop. The hand-hammered copper glowed in the light.

"God, that's beautiful!" I exclaimed. "Where did you get that?"

"It belonged to my mother," Stojan answered.

"I love it," I offered.

Stojan smiled appreciatively. He filled the pot with cold water from the kitchen tap, and returned it to the flame he had coaxed out of the burner. It crackled madly for a moment.

"What made you decide to write about Bosnia?" he asked me seriously as we waited for the water to boil.

"I don't know," I shrugged. Standing in this place, it suddenly seemed like it had all been some kind of accident.

He looked at me, disbelieving. "What do you mean, you don't know?"

I shrugged. "It bothered me," I said.

"What bothered you?"

"The war," I answered. "It bothered me. I wanted to understand how it could have happened."

He nodded slowly, considering this, and I shrugged a third time. I could see that sympathetic shine in his eyes again as he looked at me. I was the professor, and he the one who worked at odd jobs that probably barely covered his rent. I didn't know then that poverty was a relative term.

"It's just strange for me," he said.

"Why?" I asked earnestly.

"Well, why would you spend so much time thinking about something that isn't yours, and which you can't change?" he asked.

I considered this. "To prevent it happening again?" I asked.

Stojan laughed, not unkindly. He measured the fine-ground coffee and took the copper pot with the water in it off the flame. He stirred a heaped spoonful of coffee into the water, and returned it to the stove.

"Sweet or bitter?" he asked me.

"Bitter," I answered.

He left the sugar out, and removed the coffee from the stove just as the rich foam rose exponentially and threatened to overspill. His timing was perfect.

He saw me watching him and murmured, "This coffee is an art. It doesn't matter whether it's made in a good džezva or in some other kind of pot."

I nodded. "I hear that you can read the future in the grounds, too," I added.

Stojan smiled. "Maybe," he offered noncommittally.

He poured the thick coffee carefully through the bubbling foam into two small blue china cups. Each cup got a saucer. Each saucer got a spoon. Each spoon got a lump of yellow sugar. And then he carried it all on an old tray out onto the rusting balcony, where he set it on a scarred plastic milk crate between two wood folding chairs that were held precariously together with tarnished brass hardware. Each chair had a blue cushion, but it was a different hue than the blue of the coffee cups. And these were both a different hue than the blue in the eyes of Stojan Sokolović, which were so strangely pale.

We sat down, and I waited for the grounds to settle on the bottom of the cup before drinking it. I could only drink coffee when it was first taken from the flame. As soon as it started to cool, it would make me feel sick. So I had to find the right moment to begin drinking—while it was still as hot as it could be, but after the grounds had settled enough to make it drinkable. I counted out twenty seconds and looked down at the stained concrete floor of the balcony in the meantime.

"So you were going to tell me what was wrong with my lecture," I reminded him after a few minutes.

He shrugged. "I don't really have anything much to say about it, I guess," he began.

"I don't believe you," I said evenly.

He laughed.

"Seriously," I pressed. "You can tell me."

He looked closely at me with a mixture of perplexity and indecision on his face. He sighed. "I don't know," he said thoughtfully. "I don't think there was anything wrong with it. It's just strange for me, to hear about that war in a lecture hall. For me, it was something very different than what you described."

I was quiet, considering this.

"I mean to say, you tell it as though it is a clear story." He seemed to struggle with finding the right words. He spoke as though what he was saying was not what he wanted to say. "But while it was happening, it wasn't clear at all. I mean … " He paused and scratched his unshaven jaw absently. "I mean that, you know, just when the war began. Well, it was unclear when it began. Me, for example, I was just at home in Pale at the time you say it officially started. And I didn't know it had started. I didn't believe it. My brother promised me it would only last a few weeks. You know, on the day that I was mobilized, nothing looked wrong to me at all up in the mountains. It was just a nice spring day." He shrugged, and thought for a moment.

"For me, the war began when my brother left for Belgrade. It began when my father's friends came to see him to ask advice on what to do with their sons. They wanted to protect their sons from being mobilized, but they felt also that we had to kill the Muslims before they killed us. After they talked about their sons, they talked about their women. What would their women do if the Bosnian army managed to come up the hillside? How would they escape, and things like this. So my father's friends came to ask his advice because he knew all the paths in the mountains and they wanted to speculate on military strategies." Stojan smiled ruefully. "He knew all those narrow paths which just look like the grass is slightly pushed down between the trees. You would have to be a tracker to find those paths, and to follow them across the hills. But my father knew them all, because he spent his life up there in those hills, and his father before him. He argued that we had to protect our hills. So they sent their sons."

Stojan was not looking at me. He was staring out over the railing on the balcony, and I watched his profile as he talked. "There are three of us sons, and no sisters. Vladimir went to Germany the year before, to work. Luka went to Serbia. And I went to the army. When war came, people behaved strangely. The very old got nervous like herd animals, because they had seen it before, and they knew what it meant. But the young weren't worried. They either thought, like my brother, that it would be over in a few weeks, or they just couldn't believe that they might die. They grew up hearing their grandfathers' stories, and they knew that those old men exaggerate. They exaggerate endlessly. We never believed them. And we should have. There was evidence enough. In my family graveyard, there are whole generations of men just destroyed in 1945." Stojan trailed off for a moment, his gaze trained far away, seeing, perhaps, the stones in the cemetery that illustrated his point. He lifted his tiny cup and sipped his coffee.

"Soon, we believed it, though," he went on, "because it did come: artillery and exhaustion and donations of feta cheese from the humanitarian aid organizations. We all ate so much feta cheese that we wanted to die." Stojan laughed a short, rueful laugh at this, remembering.

"But at that point, it was still early. We didn't imagine what was coming. There was only the sense that we had to defend ourselves. Diplomats came from the United States. And they came from Germany. That didn't go over well, because Serbs don't trust Germans. Most people don't know about what happened to Serbs in the Second World War. Most people don't know about the mass executions of Serbs. Today we would call it genocide. And that was what we thought of when the Germans came to make promises to us. We thought of genocide." Stojan trailed off, thoughtful for a moment. "And when we thought of Turks, we thought of the towers they built, made of the skulls of Serbs who resisted them."

"You were afraid of genocide, so you committed it," I offered quietly.

Stojan smiled a dark, wry little smile at this, but did not indicate whether he agreed or not. He went on talking as though I had not intervened.

"So Vladimir was in Germany. I went to the army. And Luka, who went to Belgrade, decided after seven months or so that he couldn't live without Jelena. So against the wishes of our father, he returned to Republika Srpska, where he was immediately mobilized and killed outside of Sarajevo." Stojan's voice took on a flat quality. He spoke in a detached tone, clinically, using language that suggested he was not talking about his own brother, or himself.

I was silent.

"My brother was killed with one shot to the head. No one questioned the facts surrounding his death—the official story was that he was 'shamelessly murdered while serving his nation by Muslim terrorists who had performed a raid behind the Serb lines' or some shit like that." Stojan squinted his eyes and stared out beyond the balcony, as if the official text that narrated this death was written somewhere there for him to read.

"It was the feast of Saint Nikola, the month before Christmas," he went on. "At first, no one questioned his death, or who was responsible for it. We believed that each Serb died at the hands of a Muslim, and then all the Muslims had to be killed in compensation. And it went on and on like that." Stojan paused, almost musing, and then he smiled a tight, painful smile. "But then, much later, I heard another story," he went on. "I heard that Luka might not have died as they said. There was supposedly one witness, who told a different story. For a long time, the only thing I knew about him was a rumor that his heart beat in his mouth instead of his chest." Stojan paused to consider what he had just said. "Strange, isn't it?" he commented, turning to look at me.

I had no answer for any of this. I scoured everything I had read these long years, and thought of my research trips to Bosnia. I had never gone to Pale. I had never seen those pines. I had no idea what to say about Luka Sokolović's death. I was perfectly blank, looking back at him silently.

"I'll make you dinner," he said, suddenly changing course. He stood up and stretched his arms over his head. It was already growing late. The sun was long gone beyond the balcony, leaving an unremarkable purple ink stain on a horizon choked with pollution.

"No, don't worry," I answered doubtfully. "I should go." I had work to do, articles to write and books to read. I had essays to fail, exams to prepare, plants to water.

"I will bet that you have not eaten anything all day long," Stojan replied evenly.

I looked at my watch while Stojan looked at me intently. I sighed, and said, "Alright. But it's already late, and I still have to go back to the office."

And Stojan Sokolović said firmly but pleasantly, "Fuck your office."

I thought I should take some measure of offense to that, but I found that I couldn't. Somewhere inside of me, despite myself, I knew he was right to some extent. But I couldn't concede this, so instead I heard myself protest, "No, really. I have things to do. Deadlines to deal with."

Stojan looked closely at me with an unmistakable sympathy on his face. "When you come to the end of your life, you will be alone with all your books, and they will not talk back to you."

I looked back at him for a long moment, unsure of what to say.

I shrugged.

Stojan looked closely at me. "You're wasting your time, writing on Bosnia the way you do." He delivered his verdict quietly.

"Why?" I asked tentatively.

"What can you hope to know about Bosnia?" he asked pointedly.

I felt exasperated at this. "Are you saying that because I don't come from there that I can't say anything?"

He shook his head in surprise. "Of course not. You can say whatever you like. But some things can't be made sense of, and trying to do it will only ruin your life."

"What do you mean?" I asked. I thought of the professor of literatures in Banja Luka, and about the university strike that could never succeed. I thought of Zoran Djindjić dying in the back of the black Audi on Knez Miloš Street in Belgrade. I thought about how I had wept in the shower in Vienna.

"I mean that you can write about Bosnia or talk about Bosnia to students, but what does this actually change? Everyone who died there will stay dead. And the truth in Bosnia is so covered in lies that you can almost never know if you'll ever know the truth," Stojan answered thoughtfully.

"Well, dead people are true," I retorted. "Missing people are true."

Stojan considered this, and because he was silent for a few moments, I assumed that he had conceded the point.

Then he said, "How do you know who's doing the dying when each side is claiming the victims for their own?"

"What do you mean?" I heard myself snap at him.

"I mean, when Muslims were killed, film crews would come and say that they were Serbs. When Serbs died, Croats would come and say they were Croats. In the middle of that, how do you know what to do?" Stojan asked thoughtfully. "I mean, what do you do when the things you think you know might not be real at all?"

"War always generates problems like that," I offered.

Stojan looked over at me sharply. "That is not an abstract problem. The lies are also a part of what happened, and they had their own consequences."

"Listen," I responded slowly, "murdering people and bulldozing their bodies into mass graves seems pretty clear to me. I don't understand what's questionable about that."

"Nothing is questionable about that. That's the easy part," Stojan explained.

I stared at him in puzzlement, not quite sure what he was trying to say. "Easy part?" I echoed in disbelief.

"That's the easy part," Stojan repeated firmly. "They count bodies in order to decide who is guilty, and who is innocent. That's how Serb guilt was established. But we didn't know that we were guilty until it was all over."

I didn't know what to say to that. It seemed unbelievable to me.

"I loved my brother," said Stojan quietly as he sipped his coffee.

I didn't know what to say to that, either.

Stojan leaned back against his chair and sighed gently, almost imperceptibly. I reached over to roll a cigarette.

"I'm sorry," I said in a remorseful whisper as I drew the smoke from the first lighting down into my lungs.

Stojan lowered his cup and it clattered gently against the saucer. "It's not your fault," he answered.

"He was called Luka, your brother?" I asked.

"Luka," he confirmed emphatically.

I nodded.

Stojan Sokolović turned his face away again and gazed out over the balcony. There were lights glowing behind the curtains in the windows across the street. His eyes scanned them slowly.

"And you're the youngest brother?" I asked after a while.

"I am the youngest," Stojan replied, and he smiled. It was a sad, slow smile, but it was genuine. It touched his eyes, and the lines around them creased deeper.

"What about this other one?" I asked.

"What other one?"

"The one who has a different version of events—with the heart in his mouth," I elaborated.

"Yes," sighed Stojan. "He had a different version of events."

"Do you know where he is?" I asked.

Stojan nodded, and gestured with a nod of his head toward the edge of the balcony. "He lives two metro stops away from here." Stojan pointed northward from the balcony railing. "His name is Milan."

I was surprised at this. "Are you going to go and see him?"

Stojan thought for a moment. "I don't know."

I nodded. I drank my coffee. Stojan put out some cold cuts of ham and cheese, which he meant to pass for dinner. And later, I walked back to the office through a soft veil of rain, which mixed with the oil on the streets and made delicate stripes on the asphalt where the cars had passed. There was a fine mist on my cheeks. It clung to the pores of my skin. It was soft rain, and never enough collected in any one place to form a droplet. It hung in the arcing glow of the streetlamps like dust.

VII

Two days after the feast of Saint Nikola, Milan Milanović was given an unexpected week's leave from the lines in the hills above Sarajevo. He was surprised to have received it, because he had already been forced to give up the last two scheduled leaves that had come due. Maybe they were feeling generous because it was nearly Christmas. He didn't know, and he didn't care. He just wanted to go home. He was constantly freezing, constantly hungry, and he felt as though he had been there already for half his life.

"Cousin! Where the fuck are you off to?" Milan heard a cheerful voice boom out behind him.

Milan whirled around to face Ivan Vuković, his new best friend. Ivan was looking at him with an expression of sincere suspicion. Milan did not answer right away. He was not sure what to say.

"Are they sending you on a special mission?" Ivan changed his tone and narrowed his eyes. "Because if that's the case, I'm going to fucking complain. I haven't had any special missions at all, and I think I'm overdue."

They heard the puff of a mortar shell exploding somewhere in the distance, and Ivan's face lit up as he paused to listen. He was young and thick-browed with a broad chest and rough hands, and he was nearly beside himself with excitement at the prospect of war. He would walk around with the safety on his rifle flipped off, fingering the barrel from time to time and boasting about how many Muslims he would kill. He boasted that he could fill his father's whole granary with dead Muslims— no, all the granaries in the whole country. And the silos would be full of Muslims, and the quarries, and the mineshafts, and the rivers, and he would personally not stop killing until all the Muslims in Bosnia were either dead or in Saudi Arabia.

After a while, the other men in the unit began referring to him as "the Ivan," adding the English article, because Serbian does not have a designate word for "the." When Ivan heard about it, he was pleased, because many Serb men are called Ivan, and he imagined that the addition of the English article was intended to signify that he was "the"—the one and only— Ivan. But the quiet, thoughtful soldier who added the article had studied for a Master's degree in English literature in Manchester some years before. Now he was standing behind an artillery piece and, after he met the Ivan, he added the article with the intention of insulting him—"the" Ivan, no longer a man's name but a simple noun, as in "the dog," "the pig," "the Ivan." It was probably a good thing for the artillery man with the Master's degree that the Ivan did not get the joke which had been crafted at his expense, because Ivan announced one day shortly afterward that not only the Muslims, but also any unfaithful or disloyal Serbs should be killed immediately. After that announcement, the others either avoided him out of contempt or befriended him out of fear. Milan had chosen the second option. He stayed close to the Ivan as though he respected him tremendously. He listened to the Ivan soberly, and nodded appreciatively at the Ivan's desire to burn the whole of Bosnia. Milan was a pragmatist. He was also a man of little faith. What it came down to was this: the Ivan wanted to shoot things, and Milan didn't want to be one of the things that the Ivan shot.

He stood regarding the Ivan in the cold light of that early winter morning. Behind them, the snow-dusted hills of Romanija stretched up and out hundreds of meters high. The Ivan was waiting for Milan to answer his question about the "special mission."

"No," Milan finally replied weakly. "No, it's nothing."

"So what are you doing then?" Ivan asked.

"Nothing. I have a week's leave," Milan admitted.

The Ivan narrowed his eyes further.

"What did you do to deserve that?" the Ivan inquired suspiciously. His voice was hard, demanding an answer, and he absently rubbed the stock of his rifle with his fingertips.

"I didn't do anything," Milan assured him rapidly. "I was due two times before this, and each time I was overlooked. I don't know why they gave it to me now. I was due for it before, you know. And they didn't give it to me. I don't know why. Maybe it's because of Christmas coming," Milan tried to speculate in order to assure the Ivan that he hadn't done anything special to deserve the leave.

"Maybe because it's Saint Nikola Day," offered the Ivan easily.

"Maybe," Milan agreed.

"Although I don't think so," the Ivan went on, still staring intently at Milan.

Milan shrugged, trying to appear nonchalant—trying to appear at ease with the Ivan.

But men like the Ivan can smell fear on other men's skin. And their strength grows as a result.

"Are you a Serb, Milan Milanović?" the Ivan inquired seriously.

Milan tried to laugh. "Would I be here if I wasn't?"

"Maybe," the Ivan answered slowly. "Maybe the Turks sent you to infiltrate our defenses."

Milan looked at him, confused.

"Man, I'm from Sokolac!" he replied, treating Ivan's inquiry as a joke.

The Ivan ignored this. "Maybe you're a Turk, and maybe you're here in order to secretly kill us all, one by one."

"Come on, Ivan!" Milan offered weakly.

"Maybe your mother is a Muslim," the Ivan suggested darkly.

"She's not!" answered Milan defensively. "That's insulting."

"Maybe you fucked a Muslim once?" the Ivan continued.

Milan stared at the Ivan, and did not know which answer would be the right one.

"Ivan, please, man. I have to go," Milan responded feebly.

The Ivan stared at him out of bloodshot eyes and leaned in very close to Milan. He put his arm around his shoulders and Milan could smell the shadow of last night's brandy on his breath and in the sweat on his skin.

"Are you going to say things to other people that you shouldn't say?" inquired Ivan in an easy, affable tone that made the threat all the more explicit.

"Of course not!" Milan answered in the most sincere tone he could muster. "Do you think I want to go to jail?"

"You might want *me* to go to jail," the Ivan offered.

"Why would I want that?" Milan asked. "You're my friend."

The Ivan brought his face so close to Milan's that he lost focus. Only the Ivan's grayish eyes were clear. His stomach turned and a wash of vertigo came over him. He put his own hand on the Ivan's shoulder and gripped tightly to avoid collapsing, although he hoped his grip would be interpreted as sincerity of friendship.

"Ivan," Milan whispered seriously. "This army needs you. Men like you are going to win this war for us." His heart was pounding.

A slow smile spread across the Ivan's face as he withdrew his arm from around Milan's shoulder.

"That's right, Milan. Most of these men are complete cunts." The Ivan waved his arm expansively across the lines. A trail of laughter and a waft of marijuana smoke floated across on the wind from a loosely gathered group of men on the other side of the tree line, as though confirming the Ivan's assessment that they were indeed cunts.

Milan nodded. He wanted to go home very badly, to eat well and sleep in his childhood bed for twelve hours at a time. He wanted to wash the dirt and sweat that had collected in the pores of his skin. He wanted to clean the micro-traces of Luka Sokolović's blood out from under his fingernails. He wanted to forget that needless death in the woods in the hills above Sarajevo.

The Ivan slapped him between the shoulder blades with a massive blow that caused Milan to sway on his feet. "I'll see you next week, then!" he said gruffly.

So Milan started for home. But as he moved further and further up the hills toward Sokolac, the heart in his mouth began to beat more insistently, his guilt magnified exponentially, his belief that he had washed his hands had already started to fail, and he was plagued over and over again by the memory of the sound Luka's body had made when he collapsed on the frozen ground. It was a unique sound, unlike anything he had ever heard—a stomach-turning thud that he felt in his own ribs.

He thought that the further away from the lines he traveled on his way home, the lighter the burden of that death would be. But it happened in exactly the opposite way. His guilt staggered up to a steady, hammering pulse in the back of his throat. The further he went, the worse it got, so he started to think that maybe if he attended Luka's funeral, he would recover. He pressed his hands against the sides of his head. He wanted to forget what had happened, not go somewhere where it would never be forgotten. But he had determined that there was a penance to be paid, and he knew that this was so. Funerals bring closure for victims and perpetrators alike, he told himself. So he changed direction almost against his own will, and went toward Pale instead of Sokolac.

Halfway up the side of a hill called Gornji Pribanj, above Pale, Jelena Dragojević was standing at the front door of her mother's house with dish-cleaning wet hands and a defiant glare of disbelief on her face. Jelena stared at the neighbor who had come to bring her the news that Luka had been wounded. The neighbor was known to be filled with more gossip than blood—a dramatic, nervous woman prone to exaggeration, and already made old by fear of war long before the war arrived. The children that Jelena had grown up with, Luka among them, had always dismissed her as insane, though they all secretly loved her stories and went out of their way to see her in the markets or on the street. Still, those stories were mostly known to be untrue, so Jelena refused to believe it. She stared at the neighbor across the threshold with cold, hard eyes.

"Why would you say something like this?" she asked sternly, angrily, as though to a child.

The neighbor assured her gently that such a matter would never be an acceptable joke. "My soul," the neighbor addressed her sadly, "I am telling you the truth. I saw the man who delivered the news that Luka was wounded. He came from the army." Her hands were trembling. Jelena thought it must be because of the cold, and she reluctantly invited the woman inside.

"I'm sorry, my dove," the neighbor went on.

"Alright. Stop. It's not possible." Jelena was emphatic. But the panic was already beginning to gather between her ribs—that crushing feeling that announced a grief whose inescapable arrival had not yet been confirmed. The army always announced a dead soldier as "wounded," and it was always a lie, but it was a lie that allowed for that tiny particle of hope that this time it would be true. It was not yet death. It was the suspicion of death, and the suspicion of death allows that last pinpoint of hope to remain, no matter how small and cold. Jelena clung to her droplet of hope by virtue of the absurd. With numb hands, she made coffee for the neighbor who had come with the news that could not be swallowed. She saw Luka's lovely, light eyes, which sometimes went dark when he wept. And she held onto her hope. When the foam in the džezva rose up in its exponential volume, Jelena did not notice, and the coffee spilled over the edge and flashed violently on the flame. It sputtered and sizzled everywhere, and was ruined.

At nightfall, they came with the body. By that time, the roads in those mountains were nearly impassable with snow, and even the chains on the drab green army truck were not enough to prevent it skidding off the road on the last turn that led up to the house where the dead man they were bringing home had been born. The truck slid off the road and Luka's uncles had to go down in the dark and help the two young soldiers carry the pressboard coffin for the last fifty meters up to the house. Luka was still in his uniform. Only his boots were missing. No one would say what had happened to them. The huge trees—some of which had seen four generations of dead soldiers returned—stood implacably in the snow like sentinels. The driver from Trebinje looked down at his own feet sheepishly when the coffin was opened. He was glad to get the body out of his truck. He said he was worried that if they took too long to get him home, Luka's soul would get confused and remain in the truck. And the snow was really slowing them down.

"Don't be a fucking idiot!" warned the passenger, who was from Banja Luka, and proud to be less superstitious.

"I'm just saying it's possible, is all!" protested the driver. "Not that I believe it!"

"Peasant!" accused the passenger.

So the driver kept quiet, but silently worried as they inched along in the lowest gear through the drifting snow.

The old man with his creaking bones shuffled out of the house to receive the body of his son, supported under one elbow by the priest. He had called the priest in the afternoon after the telegram had arrived and before the snow started. He knew that word of a badly wounded soldier was really news of death, and he knew that word like this does not come unless it is true. He knew his son was dead. He had seen it only once in his life, that a man had been announced dead, and was not. The bizarre story had been spread by the friends of the man, who had hoped to die in name only, so he could leave his wife for another woman without having to face his children in shame. The old man stood at the threshold, watching his brothers and the two soldiers slipping through the snow with the coffin balanced precariously between them. They took the body into the house and Luka's aunts washed him and dressed him carefully again while they waited for the temporary cross to arrive, which would bear his name and stand watch over his grave until a proper stone could be crafted and raised in the summer. The old man had waited until he saw his son's body before asking Rade the carpenter to carve the name of Luka Sokolović into the soft wood. He had called the priest for support, but it was obscene to ask for a grave marker for a body that had not yet arrived. Rade wept through his old, milky eyes as he carved the ornate Cyrillic letters and retraced them with gold paint, remembering the days when the child Luka had tottered after the milk-laden goats in the high hills of summer.

Word spreads fast in small villages, among friends and enemies alike, and especially in wartime. Neighbors began to seep out of their houses and into the snow-filled street. Death notices were prepared. Luka Sokolović, born 27 July 1970, killed in the district of Vogošća, 19 December 1992, in his twenty-third year of life. Among the neighbors emerging from their houses was a young soldier on his way back to the front in the ancestral mountains of the east after two weeks of leave. The soldier's mother was wailing over him, clutching uselessly at his sleeves as she wept. He tried to extricate himself from her. Finally, he shoved her in anger—a thing he had never done before—because he was afraid that her low, inconsolable crying was a foretelling of his own death. As he was shouting at her to stop, an uncle of Luka Sokolović by marriage, who had dark eyes that could never be passed on, floundered up through the drifting snow and asked him to take the news of Luka's death back to his brother, Stojan. The soldier extricated himself with a violent jerk from his mother's tenacious embrace and nodded. "Stop it!" he nearly shouted at her. His sister emerged from the house and cajoled their mother to come inside out of the snow.

"What a fucking mess," he said to himself as he turned and walked away. On his way, he saw Jelena Dragojević flailing up through the snow toward the little cluster of gypsum-plastered houses that belonged to Sokolović and he was washed over with relief that he couldn't stay to witness all that was about to follow. It was easier to do the killing than the mourning.

Jelena had tricked herself into believing that she would find Luka smiling at the doorway of his father's house, waiting for her. And if human hope could make such a thing happen in this world, Jelena could have done it, so great was her certainty that he would be well when she found him. She saw the priest standing in the courtyard, and she heard the women wailing from somewhere deep in the house, and her legs faltered. The priest saw her coming and blocked the door with his body to prevent her going in. He was young, and it was instinct, not experience, that caused him to stop her. When he moved to block her at the threshold, Jelena knew it was true, and she threw the full weight of her body at the priest in an effort to dislodge him from the doorway. She tore at his cassock, trying to pull him out of her way. They struggled together over the threshold. Jelena wrenched herself out of his arms and sucked in her breath to scream in his face "Let me go!" But no sound came out. The priest held fast to her shoulders and did not move, but neither did he speak, because he did not know what to say to her. He had no experience with this. The old man appeared from somewhere behind the warm, dark shadows of the house, swaying toward the doorway on unsteady legs as though drunk. Jelena had never seen him move thus. The droplet of hope evaporated, and she stood in the snow with hard, silent eyes in the arms of the priest who would not let her pass.

"Luka is gone," Sokolović said to her.

Jelena stared at him wordlessly, her skin crawling with shock. And then, suddenly, everything seemed to slide smoothly into a sort of dream. Jelena understood that it was true, but she did not yet believe it. The years without Luka had not yet come and gone. The endless hours in which there was nothing but empty loss had not yet begun. This was the effect of the shock, before the experience of life without Luka really began. She looked dumbly around the house that was now missing all of its sons.

The vigil began at sunset, and kept on through the night until morning. According to Orthodox tradition, the body of Luka Sokolović could not be left alone under any circumstances. The living room was cleared of its tables, and the chairs were arranged with their backs against the walls so the coffin could fit, and the men kept watch in brooding silence. Eventually, Jelena was allowed to enter the house, but only after the coffin had been closed and laid out across the sawhorses that had been dragged up from a neighbor's stable through the snow. The aunts who had bathed and dressed Luka emerged from their task with clouded, grief-filled eyes and trembling, pale lips. The priest went in to anoint the body with a small flask of consecrated oil that would come over the next four years of war to sit permanently ready in the deep pocket of his cassock. The old man stared impassively at his son's coffin hour after hour as his family, friends, and neighbors poured in and out and the women silently made coffee. People moved around the house with devastated eyes on silent footsteps, and everyone spoke in whispers. The door between the kitchen and the living room was open, and the mourners moved in and out quietly, trading places between the vigil and the kitchen, which was warmer. They had shut down the radiators in the room where the coffin lay. The women drank coffee without sugar at the kitchen table while the men sat vigil, and then, from time to time, one or two of the women would slip through the doorway for a while, re-emerging with fresh tears and crumpled red faces. And then one or two of the men would break the vigil to fortify themselves with coffee and bread, secretly grateful to get out of the thick atmosphere that was beginning to permeate the living room, but which could not be talked about or acknowledged. They would bury him tomorrow, whether the snow stopped or not. They would have to.

Jelena sat silently beside her mother in a hard-backed chair situated in the corner of the whitewashed room. She stared at the six-foot polished wooden cross with the name of her lover carved into it; it rested against the wall at the head of the coffin, with the embroidered blanket into which he had been born wrapped around its crosspiece. The women were whispering about Jelena in the kitchen. Her silence unnerved them.

"She is in shock," said one sorrowfully.

"She will kill herself," whispered another, and the rest hissed at the one who had spoken to be quiet. As the night wore on, the warm little house began to slowly fill with death. It could be smelled in the plaster of the walls. The priest moved around quietly with his prayer rope wound around his hand in a silence that was punctuated from time to time by the muffled sobs of those who had come to watch over the coffin. He was also worried about Jelena. Her refusal to speak frightened him. He tried to approach her, to entice her out into the kitchen for coffee, but she just shook her head in silent, emphatic refusal. She would not look at him, even when he called her by name. Her eyes were hard and dead. She did not cry. The horror of this present had melted protectively into the comfort of the past, and memory after memory welled up in her, unbidden and unasked-for. She did not call upon them, she did not seek them. They simply came, and she scrutinized each one over and over again. She felt the flat palm of Luka's hand on the small of her back, his fingertips, feather-light, tracing the contours and curvature of her spine in his absent way. She felt his colorless eyes burning through her, the warmth and the weight of his body, the tenor of his quiet laughter against the darkened room, as though that darkness could be cleared out by laughter alone. It seemed to her even then—in the comfort of delusion— that he would always laugh into the sun, would encircle her waist with his arms, would kiss the insides of her hands and the places where her body bent. It seemed to her that she would always bear his weight in secret nights marked only by the sound of their breathing together. And her eyes were hard, looking out on a world in which she now could not live.

After some time, old Sokolović disappeared into one of the bedrooms, and returned with a bottle of brandy. In some villages, Serbs make brandy when a baby is born. And when the person for whom it has been made leaves this life, they drink that brandy at the funeral. The bottle was covered in dust, and old Sokolović spent the better part of the night carefully cleaning the dust and grime from the twenty-three-year-old bottle. The priest worried. The women wept and worried and whispered in sorrow and disbelief. But Jelena was elsewhere entirely, because Luka had been hers in a way he had not been anyone else's, and there was no one who could understand that, because there was no one else who knew the feel and the scent of his skin; there was no one else who knew exactly how it stretched over his bones; there was no one else who knew exactly how he breathed, or what he whispered into her hair when they were alone.

Jelena stayed through the night, keeping watch over the unadorned coffin of her lover and in the morning she went home to hang herself with an electrical cord. She waited until everyone had gone from the house—one to have the bread consecrated by the priest, one to call on an old neighbor who was unwell, one to help post the death notices for Luka on trees and lampposts and bus shelters. Jelena tied the line up carefully to a light fixture in the well-made ceiling, and climbed up on the kitchen table. She was perfectly calm. Her eyes were still hard, and she had still not wept.

Then Jelena hesitated, not because she was not determined to die, but because one particular wave of memory suddenly washed over her, and she wanted to be immersed in it for a moment before she stepped off the edge, because she did not have the perfect faith of the priests. She did not fully believe that she would in fact see Luka again when she stepped off the table's edge. So she stood for a moment and lingered on the rising crest of that last memory. He was lying beside her in the spring grass beyond the row of pines that delineated the space between two of his father's fallow fields. He was holding her hand, lying on his side looking at her closely, strangely. He promised that he would come back—he promised that the war would end in a few months at the most. "How can the world let us all kill each other?" he asked reasonably. "It can't happen. This is Europe. And if you're right—if it's not Europe, then when I come back, we'll go to Canada. Canada is cold, but there you can live well, and be a citizen in three years. Canada is cold, but there are no wars in Canada, and no military service, and there is a chance to be something else—something other than what we have become." Luka smiled. "Will you go with me?" he implored her. Jelena smiled despite her fear and wrapped her arms around his neck. She remembered. Her ribs felt too tight in her chest. The electrical cord was hanging slack, waiting with dumb patience to do its strangling work.

And then Milan Milanović was coming around the back of the house. Milan Milanović was coming to attend the funeral with his heart beating in his mouth instead of his chest. Milan wanted to absolve his soul. He wanted to get his heart back into his chest where it belonged. He wanted to forget what he had seen. Through the frost-laden window of the kitchen door, Milan saw Jelena standing on the table. He dropped his rifle, shoved the frozen door open and burst into the kitchen, leaving a trail of haphazard frozen mud behind him on the floor. And, for once, finally, it was not too late. He tore the cord from her neck and his fingers were trembling crazily. "No no no no no," he whispered over and over. He dragged her down off the table and then they were crouched on the floor together, Milan settled on his trembling haunches in fatigues with his hands on Jelena's back as she curled up with her head between her knees. Under the fingernails of his splayed hands were the micro-droplets of Luka's blood. And from somewhere inside Jelena, there began a low, long wail which grew steadily in strength and depth and volume. Milan could not see her face—she had covered it, buried it—and his stomach rolled horribly, hearing again the shot that sent the soul from the body, that stilled the heart, that ruined lives without any awareness of or regard for that ruining. Jelena's mother came through the door with the consecrated bread, and when she saw her only child huddled between the boots of this soldier with his deep skin and his dark eyes and hair, the bread slipped out of her hands and hit the floor, smashing against the tiles in a volley of brown crust.

Luka Sokolović was buried that afternoon beside his mother, and the thought that she might have greeted her son on the other side of this life provided a bit of thin comfort to the old man. Throughout the funeral, Jelena was crumpled with grief. She clung to her mother, swaying back and forth on her feet in the deep snow. Milan watched her weep, growing sicker and sicker. He was sick with guilt as the priest chanted over the coffin and the smoke from the frankincense danced away with the winter wind. And then the priest made some comments about the Muslims, who could not be permitted to kill the sons of the Serbian nation with impunity. God and the Serbs would seek revenge, the priest promised. Milan knew then that he could never tell what he had witnessed. He resolved that he would keep quiet. He would pretend that none of this had ever happened. He would to go to Canada, like everyone else.

The priest stopped chanting the psalter, and the time came for the mourners to close the grave. Luka's father picked up the spade with faltering hands. For a moment, he sagged, and it seemed that he would not be able to lift it at all. But then he recovered himself enough to take up a small shovelful of snow-covered soil. He let it slip into the grave of his son, and then his brothers and brothers-in-law took his arms and led him away. The spade was passed on to the son of old Sokolović's youngest brother, who looked at Jelena and nodded at her. Because she was not his wife, Jelena should not have been among the first to throw the soil on Luka's grave, but the cousin felt sympathy for her, so he motioned for her to come and be the second one. So Jelena came and picked up the spade, and dropped another small shovel of soil on a grave whose newness would inevitably begin to fade, which would several seasons later be indistinguishable from any other grave, save for the life span on the stone that was too short to be acceptable in any nation on earth.

One by one, the mourners lined up to throw soil into the grave of Luka Sokolović. Milan could not feel his hands when it was his turn to lift the shovel. He threw a load of dirt into the grave, and a heavy rock that happened to be mixed in with the soil in his spade bounced off the side of the coffin with a sharp, hollow crack that sounded like it had split the wood. He dropped the shovel into the snow. Luka's father was given a cigarette, and he smoked it quietly by the metal gate in the fence that meandered drunkenly around his family cemetery. He narrowed his eyes against the cold. His brothers thought he was not ready to leave his son's grave yet, and they stood beside him patiently, a flock of old men like tired birds in the winter wind. Old Sokolović, however, stayed by the gate not because of his grief, but because he was waiting for his youngest son to appear on the side of the snow-covered hill. He waited thus for a long time. But Stojan did not come.

VIII

Milan walked along the waterfront of a new, safer country with his hands thrust deeply in the pockets of his spring jacket. The newly risen sun dispersed the thin silver clouds like smoke as it climbed up the side of the sky. There was a chill in the air that lingered over from the night. It would not be long now before no trace remained. These were the moments that Milan recognized most easily; the quiet moments just at the border of where one thing ended and another began—the three-second space between songs on an album, but also less definitive borders: the constantly negotiated place where water met earth, where day met night, where lies met truths, where lives intersected. These spaces changed all the time—altered with seasons or tides or with the waxing and waning capacity to choose between things. This made him uneasy, but he recognized these moments just the same. They were not comfortable spaces, but he was familiar with them.

Milan liked to walk alone along the water in the mornings before going to his job as a clerk with the city's health department. He would quietly rise from the bed while his wife still slept, breathing softly, warm and sweet-scented, a lock of dark hair curled over her left ear. He watched her each morning like this, briefly, furtively. He did not linger. He always felt there was something betraying about watching her sleep. Maybe it was her defenselessness—the vulnerability of sleep. Or maybe it was the gentle slope of her shoulder against the bed sheet; or the shallow hollow at the base of her throat. Milan would watch her, balanced precariously at the border between sleep and wakefulness—the border where dreams are still believed to be reality and reality dreams. She would sometimes roll over suddenly, stretching her arms above her head, and Milan would retreat.

Every morning, Milan quietly kissed his sleeping wife's shoulder and slowly backed out of the bed. He dressed quietly, so as not to wake her. He crossed the boundary between the warm interior of the overheated apartment building and the crisp chill of early morning on the waterfront. On most days, he experienced an almost complete cerebral emptiness—a sort of comatose bliss. And this is why he walked. He was in search of emptiness. But sometimes, on other days, memories and fears seeped through his skin and filled him like rain. It was impossible to determine beforehand which sorts of days would be which. There was no pattern. There was no way to guess. It only became apparent once he had arrived at the waterfront, and by then it was too late to turn back. All along the water's edge he walked as the sun rose higher in the sky, glaring with staggering brightness, a solitary figure at a solitary time of day.

Milan was demobilized in the spring after Luka was killed. He continued to visit Jelena, and she encouraged him to study, saying she thought it might be a form of insurance against being mobilized again. She had heard that there would be a need for physicians as the war dragged on, and that studying for medicine would likely protect him from being mobilized a second time. He made it through the entrance exams, which were becoming more and more irregular. Everything seemed to have fallen apart or gone crazy. The best students were rejected, and the worst were accepted, and it all became a matter of who one knew or how much one could pay. Thus went the Yugoslav republics in the south, one after the other, until everything was in such a state that no one had any idea of what was going on. But classes went on despite the war. Students studied and teachers taught because they did not know what else to do, and Milan, who had passed the exams despite the stubborn presence of his heart in his mouth, finally got a space when the son of a local functionary was accidentally killed while he was in a bar showing off the antipersonnel mine he had found.

"Watch this," he commanded his admiring friends, but whatever it was he was trying to show them did not work out as he had planned it, and the thing exploded in his hands. The son of the functionary was killed instantly and his place in the medical school was suddenly free. So Milan Milanović went to study in his place, and his heart continued to beat steadily in his mouth.

After Luka's death, Jelena slowly recovered a tentative, precarious stability, and Milan stayed in Sokolac with his mother so he could visit her in Pale. For a while, he bought gasoline for his little silver Volkswagen from a neighbor-turned-entrepreneur on the street corner. Then the pumps at the stations opened again, and it was a little easier. He piloted his car between Sokolac and Pale along narrow roads flanked by steep canyons that dropped down to the rock-strewn riverbed below. He made this journey first out of guilt, and later out of a combination of guilt and love. After a while, it grew so that he could not distinguish between the two feelings. But he knew that it was guilt that kept him returning to her in the beginning, because she didn't smile even once for six months after Luka's funeral, and that was not easy to swallow down and live with. He came to see her whenever he could, and she always let him in, and always made him coffee, but she never smiled and he could never really tell if she was happy to see him or not. He sometimes wondered whether she secretly hated him for thwarting her plans for death on the day of the funeral. She didn't seem to feel the need to talk to him. Sometimes she talked. Sometimes she didn't. Sometimes her dark eyes were raw and red, sometimes they were hard and distant, and other times they were wet and deep and vulnerable. It started out very uncomfortably, very awkwardly, because Milan was constantly haunted by the memory of what had happened to Luka, and of what he himself more and more felt that he had unforgivably allowed: the dark-eyed woman who had lost her lover; the house on the side of the hill which was now without its middle son. At first, Milan tried to make her laugh with silly jokes and questions. But she did not respond. She would stare into some distance that he could not see and ignore him. So he stopped.

After a while, he discovered that she seemed content to just let him hang around. She made coffee and they would sit together throughout the afternoons and sometimes into the evenings. Sometimes, Jelena would read during his visits, as though he was not there at all. He felt angry at this—it was a long journey from Sokolac to Pale in winter to be ignored. From time to time, on his way home at night, he told himself that he would not return to Pale. But a few days would go by, and his heart would beat more insistently in his mouth, and his guilt would magnify, and before very long, he would find himself in Jelena's kitchen, drinking coffee and wondering what he should say and what he shouldn't. Eventually, he discovered that neutral, intellectual conversations were safest. He mapped out his family tree for her, and asked her to do the same. He discovered that she had a natural gift for math-related problems. She could solve in her head equations that took him several minutes with paper and pencil to work out. And she was good at identifying birds.

One afternoon while Milan was visiting her, Luka's father came to the door of Jelena's house to give her a pile of photographs, which she carefully placed in a drawer without looking at them. She would look at them later, Milan knew, when she was alone with her memories of Luka. And he was right. Jelena would lock herself in the bathroom and rifle through the photos with the water running so that no one would hear her weeping. On this occasion, Luka's father was pleased to see Milan, and invited him for coffee that evening.

"You must come, and tell me about the time you and Luka spent together," he pressed. Milan's blood went cold, trying to think of a way out of it, but he knew it would be impossible. So at sunset, Milan slowly climbed the side of the hill and, with his heart beating heavily in his mouth, he tapped feebly at the door. The old man opened it immediately, and the coffee was already waiting. Milan walked across the threshold.

The house had low ceilings, but high windows, and the long light of the fading sun flooded through the handmade lace curtains on the west-facing wall of the house, illuminating everything with intricate, warm patterns. Old Sokolović invited Milan to sit down at the table, which had a fresh cloth draped over it. His pale eyes had gone dark, but they were still friendly and welcoming. Milan sat as unobtrusively as possible, and the pit of his stomach was now throbbing in time with his heart. Sokolović brought the coffee to the table with old, unsteady hands, and the cups rattled against the saucers, and the saucers rattled against the tray.

"Milan, son," old Sokolović began.

"Yes," Milan responded automatically.

"I have been without my Luka now for six months," Sokolović said slowly.

"I know, father," answered Milan quietly.

"And Stojan does not return, either."

"Where is he?" Milan asked through numb lips. His voice sounded strange to him, as though it belonged to someone else. He wondered for a moment whether maybe his relocated heart was resting against his throat, and changing the pitch of his voice.

The old man rubbed his hand over his cheek as though he didn't know, or couldn't remember where his youngest son was. Then he said, "Višegrad."

"And Vladimir is gone to Germany," he went on, placing his three sons, who had all vanished in one manner or the other.

"Where in Germany?" Milan asked politely.

Sokolović looked up over Milan's head, as though the answer might be written in the air somewhere. It took him long seconds to answer.

"Konstanz," he finally answered with an authoritative nod of his head.

"Konstanz," Milan repeated.

"Konstanz," Sokolović confirmed.

Milan nodded. He had never been to Germany. "I would go to Canada," offered Milan honestly.

The old man nodded. "Yes. I would like my Stojan to go to Canada. Canada is a good state." He slurped his coffee. Will you take Jelena with you?" he asked pointedly.

Milan did not know what to say. He thought for a moment before answering, "I don't know if she wants to go ... ," he began awkwardly.

Sokolović interrupted him with a sharp burst of laughter. "Milan, don't be a fool." He looked at the young man intently. "There is nothing left here in these mountains. Take the woman with you when you go. Make a life for yourselves in a normal country. Give your sons the passport of a country that will not send them to die. Trust me. I know. I have lost my son. And I may yet lose another," he said, referring to Stojan, who was somewhere on the lines around Višegrad. "And Germany does not accept what is not its own," he added thoughtfully.

Milan was mute. "Jelena loves Luka," he whispered truthfully.

Sokolović became pensive. He thought for a moment. Then he said, "He returned from Belgrade because of her, even though I told him not to. Even Stojan asked him to stay in Serbia. But Luka wouldn't listen, because of his love."

"I know that she loves him still very much," whispered Milan, struggling to keep his voice neutral.

"And this will not change." Sokolović looked pointedly at Milan. "Don't try to take that away from her. Don't be jealous of a dead man."

"I wouldn't," protested Milan. "I wouldn't do that."

Sokolović nodded, satisfied.

"Luka was always quiet and shy," Sokolović mused. "Did you find him this way? Or did the war change him?"

Milan felt such a wave of sadness wash over him that he thought he would cry. He struggled with this for a moment. Milan did not know who Luka was, but he knew how Luka had died. Then there were these people, who knew him and loved him and missed him, but didn't know what had really happened to him.

"He trusted," Milan answered simply. That was why he died, he thought. He trusted us in those cursed woods. He trusted us like a child. And why wouldn't he have? We were all wearing the same colors.

"Yes!" the old man exclaimed, slapping his palm on the edge of the table. "That was very well put, Milan." He nodded. "He trusted. That's why I didn't want him to serve in the army. It is not a place of trust."

Milan did not answer.

"They brought him home without his boots," Sokolović said. And he shook his head.

But Luka had been wearing sneakers when he died, Milan remembered, because his army had run out of proper boots. They had mobilized so many.

Sokolović was quiet for a moment. Then he said, "When my wife died, Luka was the most devastated. He refused to leave her grave. We had to drag him out of the cemetery."

"I didn't know," Milan whispered through lips that had grown numb.

Sokolović went on as though Milan had not spoken. "Only Stojan could get him on his feet. Luka was ten. Stojan, seven. They were close as Siamese twins. They slept in the same bed."

"I didn't meet Stojan," Milan said, just to say something. And a shadow passed over the old man's face.

"No," he said. "Stojan did not come for the funeral. He sent a letter back with a neighbor's son, but it didn't arrive until long after Christmas." Sokolović considered for a moment. "Maybe he will be able to come for the raising of the stone," he said, referring to the gravestone that was being carefully prepared by Rade.

"That would be good," Milan answered uselessly.

"Yes." He trailed off. Then he said, "You served with Luka. How did you get to know him? He was always so quiet."

Milan looked at Sokolović. His eyes were creased with lines, more from grief than age, it seemed. Milan began to speak slowly, "We were assigned to the same brigade—the same task force."

"Luka never mentioned you," Sokolović mused. "I don't know why. You are a good friend, to come to his funeral and look after his Jelena."

Milan sank into silence. He was not used to lying. He did not like it. Then he said, with a smile that felt like it had been carved into a stone face, "Luka talked about Jelena a lot. So I wouldn't expect him to talk about me."

Sokolović nodded. "I hope you don't feel badly that I told you Luka didn't mention you. I hope you are not offended, I mean."

"Of course not," Milan shook his head.

"These are not easy times," Sokolović asserted.

"No," Milan answered, grateful that he could drop the smile he had manufactured.

"Do you love her?"

"I'm sorry?"

"Do you love Jelena?"

"I don't know," Milan answered hesitantly, and it seemed immediately to be the wrong answer. He didn't know how to answer this. It seemed to him that there was no answer that would make it alright for the man who had lost his son, and who knew he would now lose the woman who was meant to be his daughter-in-law. He didn't want to insult Luka's father by saying he loved her, but he also didn't want to insult Jelena by saying he didn't.

Old Sokolović looked closely at Milan and said, "Son, you should love her, and do well by her. She deserves to be well loved—as loved by you as she was by Luka—she deserves to be happy. Can you make her happy?" His eyes shone in the western sun.

"Yes," Milan whispered. "I mean, I'll try."

Sokolović nodded, satisfied. "She needs time. Don't be jealous. Be patient."

Milan nodded.

"She is young. She will recover."

"What about you?" Milan surprised himself by asking. But he needed to know—needed to believe that maybe this Luka had not been so well loved after all. He needed to believe that their lives would go on, because his guilt was a torment. "Will you recover?"

Sokolović smiled a small, sad smile. "The space between my oldest and youngest sons is empty now. It will always remain so."

Milan nodded miserably.

"But for Jelena, there is still a chance."

Milan swallowed around his altered heart.

Sokolović, misinterpreting the look on Milan's face, felt a rush of sympathy for him and said to him, unbearably, "You have my blessing for all the days that you live. If you need anything, you must simply come and tell me. You are not my son, but you were Luka's friend. I will not deny you."

Milan felt a rush of horror climb up his throat. "You don't know what I've done!" he wanted to scream. "You don't know! You would shoot me yourself if you knew, right on the doorstep, and there would be no blessings and no good wishes. You would never have allowed me across the threshold of your house. You would put a bullet through me, and rightly so."

But Milan said nothing. Sokolović stood up and kissed him three times on the cheeks and Milan ducked out of the warm little house wishing that he had died in place of Luka.

After that, Milan's heart kept him up for many nights. He dreamed that it was he who had killed Luka Sokolović, and he dreamed this over and over again, bathed in cold sweat and waking in a horror that could not be entirely shaken. He became extremely depressed, sometimes refusing to get out of bed no matter how long his mother stood in the doorway of the darkened bedroom and begged. He studied less and less and began to spend more time in the bars and cafés with the soldiers who would come back up the hills to Sokolac on leave from their positions above Sarajevo. He began to think that he should go down, too, and ask to be remobilized. But he didn't have the strength to go back down to those positions. He was afraid the Ivan would be there, stuffing the granaries with dead Muslims. In the summer, they raised the gravestone, and Milan feigned illness to avoid attending the six-month anniversary of Luka's death. His guilt bloomed like a vicious sunburst which burned over many days. And in this state, Milan went out one pleasant summer evening, and he got very drunk with a small group of soldiers, one of whom was still serving in Milan's first unit. They were exchanging stories—some true and some partially true and some complete fabrications.

Milan grew very, very drunk. His heart beat in his mouth. His guilt shone across the skin of his face like oil. He leaned over and, without thinking about what he was about to do, told the soldier the story of how Luka Sokolović died in that little hollow in the woods back behind the lines. The sunburst of guilt had eclipsed his judgment. And he was drunk enough to have lost his sense of consequence.

The young soldier exhaled sharply, shook his head and drank his brandy.

"I know his brother, Stojan," said the soldier.

Milan had not calculated this.

"Brother, you can't repeat this," Milan implored him.

"Of course not!" said the soldier.

After that, Milan silently vowed that he would never say anything about it again. But it was already too late. The soldier eventually told another, and that other one told a third, and the third a fourth. And Sokolac, of course, was full of Sokolovići, both light-eyed and dark.

For weeks, Milan felt worried that the soldier in whom he had confided would tell old Sokolović, or someone else, what he had heard. He considered leaving Romanija altogether and forgetting about Jelena entirely. But his guilt sent him back to her. He watched her closely for signs that she might have heard something, but he didn't detect anything unusual about her. She was just as she had been, struggling with her own soul and with the reality of a life she could not accept. Once, he tried to talk to her about emigrating.

"Where would you go?" she asked.

"Canada," answered Milan promptly. And Jelena, who was standing at the stove over the coffee, turned away from him and began to weep. He was confused and sorry, and didn't know what he should say and what he should not. Even so, Milan kept returning to her. And now it seemed to him that he returned to her to try and discern whether she had heard the story he told to the soldier in Sokolac. He watched her closely day after day, observing her behavior, analyzing her words, his heart pausing fearfully at her every look.

And then, one night, unexpectedly, Jelena laughed. Milan could not even remember what she had found funny, because he was so shocked to hear her laughter. It transformed her instantly, and in that moment, while her laughter rang out through the kitchen, Milan thought he felt love for her. He felt that he had finally succeeded in making something right after Luka's death—however small, however long it had taken, however fleeting it was. Jelena's mother turned and looked wordlessly and long at him with grateful eyes. He slept on the couch that night. Her mother laid the bedding, and Milan stretched out to sleep. He slept easily and well for the first time in months. In the thin light before morning, he awakened to find Jelena slipping beside him under the wool blankets that were covered in coarse, clean cotton. She pressed the whole length of her body against him and he wound his hands into her hair. They stared at each other and there seemed to be some recognition between them, some understanding, some mutuality.

So Milan returned to her, back and forth on the steep roads between Sokolac and Pale, Pale and Sokolac, across the high hills of Romanija, past Mokro and the river canyon. Months—years—of war passed, and all those things which seemed so unimaginable before became part of everyday life. Stories floated up from the bottom of the hills, where the besieged city of Sarajevo crouched on the edge of oblivion. These were broadcast up across the radio, and on the television, and the soldiers brought them back into the mountains. Milan had almost grown used to it. After all, they were just stories from the bottom of the hills, and he was on their tops, in Romanija, in Sokolac and in Pale, where war was news and Ratko Mladić sometimes stopped for coffee in a café with a blue awning. Later, in its attempt to locate Ratko Mladić, the NATO Stabilization Force came and blew the door off of the Pale priest's rectory, and with it, they blew his son off the skin of the earth. Milan wondered why they couldn't just knock. But that was only later. At that time, Serbs looked like they were doing alright. And then, after a while, they were not doing alright.

So, with no warning at all, Milan was mobilized again. Everyone was mobilized. All the students were pulled out of university and now there was no way out. He was sent to one of the lines around Višegrad, south of Srebrenica. He wondered vaguely if Stojan Sokolović was still there somewhere. He spent his first night on the front line, his heart faithfully beating in his mouth. There was chaos there, and the discipline was breaking down, so Milan deserted. He knew he would never survive that last mobilization and the only chance he had was to get to Serbia so he could apply for refugee status at the UN mission there. So he ran. He crossed the border into Serbia at Kotroman. Had he been further north, he would have been prevented by the Drina River, but here there were only checkpoints to prevent him crossing, and high, unforgiving hills. He dropped his rifle, stripped off his camouflage jacket and skirted around the checkpoint on the Republika Srpska side. Amazingly, he made it around them without being seen.

But on the Serbian side, he was seen and stopped, and he told them that he had just received word of his mother's death in Belgrade. Milan had never been to Belgrade. He made up a street name. He kicked up a fuss. "What unit did you run away from, little kitten?" they asked him mockingly. He began to cry with exhaustion and fear. The Serbs on the Serbian side were unmoved. He emptied his pockets. He had three hundred German marks that Jelena gave him before the second mobilization, so that he might buy his life back if the circumstances should warrant it. He didn't know that the money had been given to her by Luka's father, or if it would have saved Luka's life had he been carrying it the night he was killed. The circumstances of life and death had now arrived, and he offered it to the Serbian Serbs. He wanted to scream at them: "How can you let us die like this?! How can you turn your backs on us?! We are dying and dying for you and your fucking Serbia!" But he swallowed hard around his betraying heart and managed to keep quiet.

They looked at him long, hard, contemptuous. "Fuck this guy," murmured the most senior officer and he wandered away, shaking his head in disgust. Milan was suddenly aware of the fact that he would be shot. He felt lifted right out of his skin. He felt a strange sensation of lightness, as though the bulk of his cold, sweating body had already disappeared. For a moment, he stopped breathing. The heart in his mouth stopped beating. His wet eyes dried up. He had an almost uncontrollable urge to run, but a quiet, warning voice in his own head spoke to him firmly as if from somewhere else. And, like Luka, he had no choice but to trust. "Stand still," he told himself. "They'll shoot you if you move. Don't move!" Milan Milanović, Bosnian Serb, stood hopeless, helpless, and speechless before these Serbian Serbs, quite sure that they would kill him—quite sure that this war had been for nothing at all, the evidence of which lay precisely in the fact that they would shoot him in the back if he turned away to run. But why? Why? He didn't understand why. Would they shoot him for deserting an army that was not really theirs? For betraying their vision of what all Serbs should have wanted and felt and done? Or would they shoot him simply because they—like the Ivan—just felt like shooting anyone for whom a justification could be found? Or maybe they would shoot him because they did not want Bosnian Serb refugees in Serbia anymore. The internal police were always rounding them up and sending them back to kill and die. The Serbs in Belgrade were tired of hearing stupid Bosnian accents and dealing with stupid Bosnian peasants in their sophisticated city. That was why, Milan realized. The world sees us as one people, but the Serbian Serbs hate us.

Milan stood there before them, and he had run out of ideas. He prayed silently that they could be bribed. His mind was racing. He knew it would go one of three ways: they would take the money and shoot him, they would refuse the money and shoot him for trying to bribe them (after which they would take the money anyway, because what has a dead man to do with a bit of hard currency?), or they would accept the bribe and let him go into Serbia. And just at that final moment, when lies, tears, and begging had all fallen flat, when Milan felt that he had already begun to leave his own body, the German marks worked their neoliberal magic. The senior command officer doubled back, and snatched the packet of cash out of Milan's hand. "Go on. Fuck off." The officer stuffed the crumpled, greasy notes into the breast pocket of his coat and waved Milan away with disgust. "Fucking briber," he spat.

Milan fucked off into Serbia. He hitchhiked to Belgrade in his T-shirt. It was night, and dark, and he had no money. His identity card and his accent would betray him as a Bosnian, and if the Serbian police from the ministry of the interior happened upon him, he would be sent back over the border to a front line above a town he had never been to, but only read about. Every set of headlights that swam out of the blackness of the night to illuminate him walking down the side of the road made him feel like running, because he had no way of determining who might help him and who might destroy him. He walked through the night, cold without his jacket, scared without his rifle, terrified of each approaching car. The night was without moonlight, and Milan could barely see his own hand in front of his face. He thought that there was probably no other darkness in the world like the one in this country at night. The white reflective line that delineated the side of the road from the fields around it was badly faded, hard to see, and Milan concentrated on the few visible meters in front of him. How many meters to Belgrade? He walked and walked, and after a while he sank down on the pavement and wept his guts out. He would give anything to get back to Jelena, and then he thought he understood how Luka felt on the night he died. He understood why Luka had been running. His heart would not leave his mouth. It beat in such a way that it made him sick, and now he saw there was no way to get away from it, no way to fix it, no way to undo all of this.

As his crying wore him out, Milan became aware of a sound in the pitch blackness. It was a slow, steady sound—like breathing. He realized that he was being watched and all of the hair on the back of his neck stood up in an enormous current of fear. He listened, straining his ears because his eyes were useless in the dark. He couldn't tell where it was coming from. It seemed to be coming up from behind him in one moment, and ahead of him in the next. He was immobilized, listening. It was definitely breathing, he realized, and his heart staggered wildly. His whole body started to shiver.

"God, please!" he cried out. "Why are you following me? What have I done?"

The breathing paused for a moment, and then picked up again. Milan cried silently.

The darkness was suddenly broken behind him by a set of glittering headlights in the distance, and the fear rose up in him again. He staggered to his feet. "Please, please, please, please," he begged out loud as he stood and turned to face the approaching car. It seemed to pass him in slow motion. Then the brake lights flashed, and the car slowed rapidly. The tags were from Belgrade. "Christ, have mercy on me," he whispered into the darkness as he walked toward the car. He looked around fearfully in the illuminated arc produced by the headlights, both wanting and dreading to know the source of that breathing in the dark. And suddenly he saw it—a hedgehog trundling along the side of the road with two of its babies in tow. He couldn't hear it breathing now over the idling engine of the car. A hedgehog, he realized absurdly. He turned and slowly approached the window of the car to find a young, pale woman behind the wheel and a man beside her with a shaved head and a pleasant face. In his relief over the hedgehog, he had a sudden urge to tell them everything there on the side of the road, to babble out all of what he had seen and experienced, to beg them to help him. Please help me get out of this, for the love of Christ. Please. But instead he was silent.

"Where to?" asked the man with the pleasant face.

"Belgrade," answered Milan in a shockingly calm voice.

"Come on," he offered.

Milan stuffed himself into the back of the tiny car with a murmur of thanks, and his camouflage-clad knees were nearly up to his chin.

"I'm Marko," the passenger announced. "And this is Vesna." She nodded as he motioned to her. "Milan," said Milan. The little red Yugo was pumping out heat like there was no tomorrow. And Milan felt that heat on his skin and he wanted to sleep. He was so exhausted and this felt now as though it was the first time in his life that he had ever been warm. His eyes were closing, despite the terminal presence of his fear and his heart in his mouth. He was so tired now that his betraying heart beat on nearly unnoticed. He stayed awake in the back of the car long enough to see the city limits of Užice and couldn't believe how far he had walked from the crossing at Kotroman. The heat was so nice. God help me, he thought automatically, disinterestedly. When he awoke, it was daylight, and his legs were cramping in the tiny space. He watched the landscape slide by—the flat expanse of Serbia stretching out into an unseen distance. It was so different from the high hills of Bosnia.

Milan shifted his weight, uncomfortable in the small space, and the man with the pleasant face—Marko—realized that Milan had awakened. He passed him a cigarette.

"Thanks." Milan did not usually smoke. But he felt like doing so. And he would have taken anything then that anyone was willing to give him.

"Where are you from?" asked the passenger Marko.

Milan wanted to say Toronto, Canada, though he had never been there. So he laughed strangely and answered, "I want to be from Toronto, Canada."

"Who doesn't?" asked Vesna with a short burst of laughter.

"No, seriously," Marko pushed. And Marko was not laughing.

Milan sighed. "Sokolac."

Marko turned his head violently to face Milan and looked at him closely. His eyes were very dark. "Have you been demobilized?" he asked, trying to sound casual and not succeeding.

Milan looked at him steadily and did not answer. He drew gingerly on his cigarette.

Marko changed tack. "Where did you come from last night?"

"Kotroman," answered Milan truthfully, exhaling the smoke from the cigarette sharply.

"From the Bosnian side?" asked the passenger.

"Yes."

"There's no war in Sokolac, is there?" asked Marko interestedly.

"No."

"Did you come from Sokolac, then?" he asked.

"Yes."

And because Marko was annoyed with these one-word answers, he asked Milan, "You're not a Muslim, are you?"

"No."

Marko nodded, obviously relieved. "We should take all of Bosnia. Forget partitioning it. These are historical Serbian lands, and have been lived in by Serbs forever. All those fools who think they're Muslims are just converted Serbs." Vesna shook her head quietly in opposition, but said nothing.

"We?" Milan wanted to ask. But instead he said, "I guess."

"Are we going to win this war?" asked Marko. "I mean, do you think NATO will bomb us?"

"Us?" Milan wanted to ask. But instead he shrugged and said, "I don't know."

"What are you doing in Serbia?" Marko pressed.

Milan remembered the lie he had manufactured at the border, and it was a lie which might force this Marko to forgive him his silence. "My mother died."

"Oh, no!" Vesna exclaimed.

"I'm sorry," Marko added quietly.

Milan pulled the smoke from his cigarette down past his troublesome heart and into his lungs. He shrugged. He imagined that he looked bad enough by now that they would believe him.

"How long did they give you to be in Serbia?" Vesna asked.

"Three days," Milan lied.

Marko nodded. "You know, for a second, I thought you were a refugee. You know, maybe deserted the army over there."

Milan looked out the window, and hoped that they were almost at the limits of Belgrade. "God, get me out of this," he prayed silently.

Marko went on. "There are so many refugees from Bosnia in Belgrade it's ridiculous now. And most of them are completely uneducated. And there are also deserters everywhere. I don't understand why Bosnian Serbs say they want support from us, and then they desert their army and run across here into Serbia to hide." He trailed off and shook his head in disgust.

"Stupid Bosnians," Milan offered derisively.

But Marko did not answer that, because he could not tell whether Milan had really meant it or whether it was sarcasm.

After a while, Marko said, "It's good that you're not a deserter."

Milan smoked in silence.

"I'm sorry about your mother, though. I really am." It came across as an afterthought.

They drove through the industrial outskirts of Belgrade, which would be bombed mercilessly by NATO a few years later. Milan would remember that passenger, that Serbian Serb, that Marko, when the bombs started falling, and he would not have a drop of sympathy for him. He would not have a drop of sympathy for Serbia at all. He would only wish that NATO would level the place. He would hope that Marko was trapped somewhere in Kosovo, being shot at by Albanians armed with American guns, being bombed into fucking oblivion. He would hope that Marko was shitting himself somewhere in a little fold in the earth while the Kosovo Liberation Army led by the thug and murderer Hashim Thaqi advanced against his trapped unit. For Milan, later, this would be a lovely little fantasy—a bite of pleasant bitterness. Vesna pulled into a petrol station in the suburbs of Belgrade and asked Marko to buy a package of cigarettes. Marko obligingly got out of the car, and then turned back to ask Milan if he needed anything.

"No, thanks." Milan Milanović was without a single dinar. But he was thirsty. He stared out the window, watching two young men smoking as they perched on top of one of the petrol pumps.

Vesna was scribbling something on a piece of paper. And as she wrote, she asked him clearly and without any trace of emotion in her voice at all: "Where did you escape from?"

Milan looked at her closely. She turned to him with unwavering eyes. She had twisted around in her seat, and was staring at him. Her eyes were very bright. And he realized that she was sympathetic. He also realized that he was out of options. "Višegrad," he answered quietly after a considering moment. He did not avert his eyes. He did not feel ashamed. He just felt he had come to the end of his rope.

"How bad is it there?" she asked in a staccato voice, firing questions, seeking answers.

"Bad," Milan answered without hesitation and without looking away.

She nodded. "And your mother?"

"In Sokolac," Milan answered. And then he did feel ashamed—he could feel shame blooming across his face—and he looked away.

"Dead?" she asked.

"No."

Marko was coming back toward the car now. Vesna quickly reached back between the seats and pressed a small bundle of paper into Milan's hand. He slipped it into one of the utility pockets of his trousers without looking at it.

"Where are you going?" Marko asked Milan as he climbed back into the car.

"Republic Square is fine," he answered. It was the only place in Belgrade that he was sure existed, except for the old fortress at Kalemegdan that he had seen in schoolbooks growing up.

"No problem," said Vesna quickly, and they drove on in silence for the rest of the journey. Belgrade seemed huge and unknowable as Milan watched it slide by—a massive, unintelligible, seething gray grid.

"Pleasure to meet you, Milan," offered Marko as he climbed out of the car on the edge of Republic Square.

"Thanks," answered Milan.

Vesna looked at him with dark, sympathetic eyes. "Good luck," she said.

"Yes," Marko chimed in. "Good luck."

"You, too."

"Remember the ancient saying, brother," Marko said through the open window. "Only unity will save the Serbs."

"Yeah," Milan answered noncommittally.

They drove off in a sputter of smoke, and Milan walked across the square on legs that were tingling from being cramped for so long. He looked around at the dirty stone buildings and the ornate window frames and at all the beginnings (or were they ends?) of streets that branched out into unknown places from a knot of traffic around the city center. There were a handful of women dressed in black gathered at one end of the square, and they seemed to be gathering some attention. One held a placard which read simply "ENOUGH". There was a small crowd, and angry voices floated across the square on the breeze.

"Why don't you traitorous bitches go home and take care of your own business?" called a young man from the safety of his group of friends. There was a murmur of assent from another small clutch of friends. An old man in a lambskin hat nodded approvingly.

No one from the group of women answered him. They just stood there silently. It reminded Milan of Luka's funeral. Their silence was strange and palpable.

After a moment, two policemen sauntered up to investigate the commotion. So Milan moved slowly in the opposite direction. He walked over to have a look at the statue in the middle of the square. Knez Mihajlo perched proudly on his horse. Milan found an empty bench and reached into the pocket of his trousers. Rolled up into a flattish cylinder were fifty German marks and a square of plain paper. He unrolled it and read: "Come any time and I will give you a place to sleep," followed by her name—Vesna—and her address on March the 23rd Street.

Milan dropped his face for a moment and stared unseeing at the cobbles beneath his feet. Then he went shopping for clothes. The first thing he bought was a pair of jeans. He was desperate to get out of the camouflage. He paused to look at a cheerful bright blue shirt. He meant to buy it, but then he reconsidered, wondering if the bright color would draw attention to him. He hesitated for a few moments while the women in the shop looked at him curiously. Then he settled for a drab moss green shirt instead. He wandered up and down Knez Mihajlova, getting to know Belgrade. As the afternoon wore on, the wind began to carry a chill on its edge. He walked up to the fortress at Kalemegdan, built on the fortuitous juncture of two rivers, an unlikely tourist in a city full of refugees whom the government was trying to relocate into Kosovo to bolster the Serbian population there. He stopped an old woman and showed her the address Vesna had written on the slip of paper. He tried to speak with a Belgrade accent. He did not want anyone to know he was Bosnian. The woman looked at him strangely for a moment, then she nodded, and directed him. "It's only about half a kilometer."

Milan stopped and ate a slice of cheese-filled *burek* with yogurt. It was steaming hot, crispy, flaky outside, soft and tart inside. Then he started for Vesna's. It didn't take long to get there. There was a narrow doorway cut into the concrete between two shop-front windows. The corridor that disappeared beyond was shadowy and dim and smelled vaguely of old cooking oil. For a moment, Milan hesitated on the pavement while men and women passed back and forth along the street beside him, and then he ducked through the doorway. A wall-mounted light flickered for a moment and was illuminated with a loud buzz. Milan jumped, and felt a brief pulse of adrenaline rush across his skin. It lingered even after he realized with relief that the light was simply wired to a motion detector. He moved deeper into the corridor with soundless, tentative steps, and came to a flight of stairs. At the top of the stairs, on either side of the landing, nondescript apartment doors unfolded along the corridor. Milan turned left, and did not find the door with the name correlating with the one Vesna had written on the slip of paper. He doubled back, retracing his steps to the stairs, and walked down the corridor in the other direction. At the end of the hall, he found it. But still, he stood quietly outside the door, unsure and indecisive, trying to gather enough guts to knock. His body felt weak—that physical tingling weakness which comes when one realizes that one is completely at the mercy of another; the weakness that comes when men of little faith have no choice but to trust. Milan made a fist with his sweat-slicked hand, and tapped gingerly on the door. Fear had heightened his senses. He thought he heard the pad of stocking feet on a parquet floor. The deadbolts were thrown back. The door opened.

Vesna smiled a gentle, welcoming smile and ushered him inside. Beyond the foyer, Milan could see a section of the living room. Its primary theme was red velvet and brocade. The fringed corner of a Turkish rug was visible. Milan bent over to take off his shoes, but Vesna touched his arm and told him it was not necessary—the difference between Bosnia and Belgrade, Milan realized. He followed her into the living room. In every patch of afternoon sun, there was a potted African violet. They were purple and pale pink, white with red edges and pale, pale blue—like the color of Luka Sokolović's uncomprehending eyes as he stood in his sneakers in the woods above the hollow where Milan and the others lay in wait for him.

Vesna's television had been turned around so that the screen faced the wall. Milan stared at it for a moment, puzzling over its backwardness.

She looked at him looking, and said, "I don't want to watch the war anymore. So I took measures to avoid the temptation of the television."

Milan nodded. He stood, uncomfortable with the soles of his street shoes on Vesna's carpet. He lifted one foot. Then another. And he saw that he could not lift them both at once.

"Bitter or sweet coffee?" she asked him.

He cleared his throat. "Sweet, please," he answered.

Her dark eyes were kind. She was smiling at him, and something about it seemed not-quite-right. It had been so long since he had seen anyone smile this easily. She turned toward the kitchen, and then she turned back.

"Milan, my home is yours. Be comfortable, and stay as long as you need to. My brother doesn't come often." Her voice was kind, her eyes sympathetic, but not pitying.

He looked at her in confusion.

"My brother," she repeated, seeing his perplexity. "Marko."

"Oh," he nodded.

She tucked her dark hair behind her ear, and regarded him for a second, as though she wanted to say something else. Then she went to make the coffee.

He followed her into the kitchen. Her lunch dishes were piled neatly on a tea towel on the counter. Nietzsche's *Beyond Good and Evil* was tented open on the table.

"Marko is quite supportive of the war effort," Vesna offered as she waited for the water to heat in the plain stainless steel džezva. "I am a member of an organization that opposes the war," she went on.

Milan said nothing. It seemed safer just to listen. He thought about the lines in the hills, the absurd rumors of executions, the men who should have been studying but instead were killing and dying. He thought about the thin attempt at control and command, which was useless in the face of the paramilitaries and militias that were roving all over the villages of the east, burning everything they found and leaving their names spray-painted on the exterior walls of the houses they had robbed after tossing the bodies of the occupants into the spring-swollen rivers. Finally, he said dispassionately, "It's a bad situation."

"We are going to lose this war," said Vesna evenly. "What do you think?" she asked.

"You're right," Milan answered readily. "For nothing."

"And it will take us twenty years to recover from it, if we ever do," she shook her head sadly.

Milan didn't respond. He had never thought of it that way.

"Where will you go when it ends?" she asked.

"Canada," he answered evenly.

Vesna thought for a moment. "You know, Milan, you shouldn't be out on the street in Belgrade right now. Since this last big push, I've seen the interior police stopping men for their identity cards very frequently. They arrest the Bosnians and send them back to Republika Srpska."

Milan nodded. "I know this."

"So you should stay here."

He nodded again. He wanted to ask her why she had helped him. But he felt he was afraid to know, so he did not.

Milan tried to sleep that night, and though he was exhausted, he could not find the anchor line that would draw him down below the surface of consciousness. He got up and walked out to the living room, where Vesna was stretched out on the couch, reading Camus' *L'Étranger* in French. A cup of sweet mint tea was cooling beside her on the table. He knelt down on the floor in front of her and looked into her dark eyes. Her gaze was unwavering. He thought about Jelena. And then he ceased to think about Jelena. Vesna was pliant in his hands, and there was no other motive for Milan but to wring a bit of pleasure out of his weary body. For this reason, and because at that time, in that place, there was little for which one could plan or hope, Milan and Vesna drank each other down like water. In the mornings, Vesna left her apartment for her job as a French tutor. In the evenings, she joined the black-clad women in the square and endured the abuse of the passersby. At night, she curled up in Milan's arms. There was no one to see them. Vesna's head fit perfectly in the hollow of his shoulder, and Milan thought that he now slept better than he had in his whole life. His guilt evaporated, his memory was mercifully blank, and his failures were forgotten. He almost forgot about Luka Sokolović. And while his heart was still beating in his mouth, it was less discernible. Or maybe he had just grown used to it. Milan and

Vesna clung to each other like moisture on trees and, after a while, Milan mistook his feeling of peace for love.

And then the war was ending. Srebrenica was gone in two days. Thousands of prisoners were set loose in the woods around Potočari, hunted down, and executed. Years later, Milan would watch the thirty-two-year-old commander of the Zvornik Brigade admit his guilt in a live feed on CNN in this way:

"I have thought for a long time, and I'm always followed by this same thought—guilt. I find it very hard to say this truth. I am to blame for everything I did at that time. I am trying to erase all this and to be what I was not at that time. I am also to blame for what I did not do, for not trying to protect those prisoners … I ask myself again and again, what could I have done that I didn't do? … I am responsible for this. The guilt for this I feel remorse and for which I apologize to the victims and to their shadows." The commander of the brigade was imprisoned for twenty years.

The Serbs had finally gone too far, so NATO bombed their positions while Milan and Vesna were lying in the bathtub together. And then, with American air support, the Croats emptied their Krajina of all its Serbs, who came flooding down the absurdly named Highway of Brotherhood and Unity, and they were all stopped on the Serbian side to pay the toll tax at the border. While the ink was drying on the Dayton Accord, Milan applied to the UN mission in Belgrade for refugee status. He checked the box beside "Canada" on the form that asked where he wanted to be resettled. "Canada is a good state," the voice of old Sokolović echoed in his head. Milan believed this. He had visions of Canada, hopes for Canada, and for himself. He felt no fear. He had only one dilemma. On the form where it asked for information about a person's dependants, Milan Milanović checked the box indicating that he was married. But he hesitated with his pen poised over the line that asked for the name of the applicant's spouse. He was not sure whose name to write there. He realized that he wanted to write Vesna (Vasić) Milanović. He considered this. Lowered his pen. Raised it again. His heart began to pulse harder in his mouth, his guilt slipped in between his ribs and crouched like an insatiable animal in his chest. So he lowered his pen again, and he carefully filled the blank line with the name Jelena (Dragojević) Milanović. He knew he could not return to Vesna's after that, so he left his few possessions behind, and he returned to Sokolac.

IX

"I will bribe the registrar," Milan told Jelena as she sat still and silent over her untouched coffee in her mother's house above Pale.

"It doesn't matter," she shrugged.

"Why? Why don't you want to get out of here? We can go to Canada. We will get the clearance." Milan was insistent.

"I don't want to go to Canada," Jelena answered.

Milan was dumbfounded. "But we talked about this. We agreed." Had they? He could not remember.

"What will I do in Canada?" she asked simply.

"What will you do here?" he shot back. "Everything is fucking destroyed."

Before she could answer, he cut in again, and heard the bitter edge creep into his voice. "I told them you were my wife. I promised you we would go to Canada. That's what you wanted." He thought of Vesna, with whom he had spent nearly three months and whom he had wordlessly abandoned by the simple act of not returning to her apartment on March the 23rd Street.

Jelena contemplated Milan's persistence. She was not sure why he had come back for her.

"Jelena, there is nothing left here, can't you see that?" Milan pressed quietly.

She could see it. All of the roads were overrun by NATO military vehicles. Foreign soldiers were wandering around everywhere. The humanitarian aid organizations would not help Serbs. No one with a Serb name could get a passport from the "multicultural" government in Sarajevo. She knew there was something left in Bosnia, but that whatever it was, it was not for Serbs. For Serbs, there would be only The Hague and the humiliation of disaster and defeat and indictments for war crimes.

Finally, she said, "I can't have a child."

Milan was confused. "What do you mean?" he asked carefully.

"I can't have a child here. The hills are full of landmines." Her voice was flat, almost emotionless.

"Not up here," Milan answered. "Not in Pale." But then he saw that his reassurance was helping her make the decision to stay in Pale, and that was not what he wanted. So he corrected himself. "But you're right. The whole fucking place is overrun with mines and foreigners. Why don't we just get out?"

While Milan was in Belgrade with Vesna, Jelena was tending Luka's grave. She brought packages of cigarettes and bottles of plum brandy. She brought fistfuls of wildflowers. In her sleep, Luka's long shadow hunted her down without mercy. She could not escape it. The breeze blew in through the open windows at night, and no matter the direction it came from, that breeze always brought the smell of the Sokolović graveyard. The scent of those mountains became the scent of Luka's death. She knew that. And she knew that she could not have a livable life in Pale. She looked up at Milan. She thought of the day he came crashing through the kitchen door of her mother's house with the frozen mud on his boots. She thought of the way his legs had trembled as she curled up on the floor between his knees. He had prevented her death, and she was not grateful. But she had never again found the courage or the strength to make a second attempt at suicide, and it made her ponder his role in her life. She could not stay. But she was afraid to leave, and afraid to leave with him.

"Let me think overnight," she said.

Milan was exasperated. "What is there to think about?" he demanded.

"I have to think," she persisted quietly.

Milan was angry at her hesitation.

"I can just go back to Belgrade," he warned. And he pulled the last option he could think of—the final option. "Do you not love me?" he asked sadly.

She didn't answer right away, and Milan sat in disbelief for long moments with his heart thundering in his mouth. She did not ask him in return if he loved her. It did not occur to her to ask that. He had come every day from Sokolac. He had stayed with her all that time while she sat at the kitchen table with her life destroyed and her eyes leaking out the contents of her soul. She didn't wonder if she loved him. She wondered what she owed him.

"I do love you," she said hesitantly. "Let me think about it. Just overnight. Please."

"Alright." Milan scraped his chair back and walked out of the house, closing the door firmly behind him. If she hadn't existed, none of this shit would ever have happened, he realized as he walked to his car. If she hadn't existed, Luka would not have been running through the night when his leave was granted. He would have waited for morning like a normal person. Even the Ivan would not have had the balls to shoot him in broad daylight with the possibility of someone seeing him. And the Ivan would not have been drunk. None of them would have been drunk. And now she was resisting the move she had agreed to make. "So she can cling to a fucking grave," he said to himself angrily.

After Milan left, Jelena slowly climbed the hill to old Sokolović's little cluster of buildings. The evening sun was sinking slowly, and long, glowing filaments of light sieved through the pines.

Old Sokolović opened the door and ushered her in. While the water was heating on the stove, the old man asked her to wait a moment, while he went out to his shed to get something.

"Of course," she said.

She watched the water in the džezva for a moment and then realized that she had never been in that house alone in all her life. Someone had always been there: its sons, its uncles and aunts and neighbors and friends. She walked softly from the kitchen and out into the living room. The sun cast its long light on the white walls. There was no sound but the soft ticking of a clock on the wall. Out past the living room, a shadowy corridor led out toward the bedrooms. She tiptoed through the silence, feeling the loss wash over her as she moved into the hallway and out of the sun. At the end of the hall was Luka's small room. The door was open. Slowly, as though she were moving on someone else's feet, Jelena crept softly to the doorway. She peered into the room, and let out a muffled cry when she saw Luka sitting on the edge of his bed with his back to her. It was him. It was! He hadn't died! It had been a mistake! A wave of vertigo spilled across her skin.

Luka turned around and looked at her with his pale eyes. And then she saw that it wasn't Luka. It was Stojan.

Her heart felt as though it had leapt out of her chest. "Stojan," she whispered from the doorway. "Stojan!" She stepped across the threshold and went toward him to embrace him, because he was alive.

He looked at her expressionlessly. His skin was pale.

"Stojan," she whispered as she stood over him. "You came back."

He just looked at her. He said nothing. It was as though he didn't recognize her. "How can that be?" she thought. She reached out and rested her hand on his shoulder. For the first time in her life, she was afraid of him.

"It's me. Jelena," she whispered helplessly.

Stojan reached up and covered her hand on his shoulder with his own. But he still said nothing.

"Stojan?" she whispered again. "Are you alright?"

He did not respond. He slowly turned his face away from her and looked out the window. His eyes were terribly bright.

"What happened?" she asked. But she knew already that he would not answer. She saw that he couldn't.

"Jelena!" she heard old Sokolović call from the kitchen.

"I'm having coffee with your father," she said to Stojan. "Come on, please," she begged. "Please."

He continued to stare out the window.

So Jelena retreated, and went back to the kitchen on numb legs.

"Father, Stojan is here," she said to the old man.

He nodded as he poured the coffee.

"I invited him to join us," she said. "But he can't." She didn't know what had caused her to say "can't." It sounded strange to her own ears. She stood helplessly in the kitchen. She didn't know how else to put it.

"No, he can't," his father agreed.

Jelena felt like screaming. She wanted to scream until all the windows were blown out of the house, and all the glass bottles and cabinet doors were shattered. She wanted to run out of there as fast as she could go. But instead, she sat down at the table. And she knew then that she would go to Canada with Milan.

"I will go to Canada with Milan Milanović," she said quietly.

"I know," old Sokolović nodded. He reached into the pocket of the same sweater that had once held Stojan's invitation to report for active duty, and withdrew an envelope. He handed it to her across the table, and she saw that it was stuffed with German marks.

"Please don't, father," she said to him, embarrassed. "I'll be alright."

"No, no," he insisted, and his voice was hoarse and weak. "Canada is a good state, but you need money."

"Please, father," she begged. "Give it to Stojan."

"There is enough for Stojan," he said firmly. "This is what is left, and it is for you and Milan." He pressed the envelope upon her, and she reluctantly accepted it.

"Now drink your coffee," the old man implored her.

She did, and they sat together in those difficult, painful circumstances, looking at each other and knowing that, if the war had not come, things would be dramatically different. Sokolović sighed, and gave voice to her own thoughts when he said helplessly, "I don't know what this war was for."

Jelena was silent. She had never understood what the war was for. All it produced were the dead and disappeared. All of this terrible loss, tides of refugees, hillsides covered with landmines. All of these rumors about concentration camps and rapes.

"We lost, we Serbs, didn't we?" he asked.

Jelena nodded.

"I lost my son for nothing," the old man whispered. "We couldn't hold our own lines."

"How could they be held against NATO?" she asked in return. "The mood of the world turned against us." She thought about the things she had heard about what Serbs had done. She thought of Stojan, sitting blankly in the next room.

They looked at one another across the table, and the coffee steamed pleasantly between them.

"Daughter," Sokolović began, and then hesitated.

She waited for him to go on. She thought that he had always loved Luka the best. It was strange for a man to love his middle son the best, but Sokolović did. He loved Luka's gentleness, and his good faith. They shared it in common.

"Daughter, don't come back here after you leave. These hills will be full of old men and ghosts, and you won't recognize them anymore."

Jelena understood him. But she said, "I'll come back to see you."

Sokolović smiled at her with affection. "You and I will always belong to one another, even though we will not see each other again. It doesn't matter that you will be Milanović. In my heart, you are still Sokolović. You always will be. If you need something, come to me. If I am dead, go to Stojan. He will not deny you."

"Don't say that!" Jelena implored him, but he dismissed her with a wave of his hand.

"Don't forget what I've said," he ordered. Then he kissed her three times, embraced her with surprising strength, and walked her to the door.

The next day, Milan bribed the registrar in Pale to produce a marriage certificate. More German marks, and the lover of Luka Sokolović became the wife of Milan Milanović.

Old Sokolović called down from the hillside on the morning that Jelena and Milan left for Belgrade on their way to Canada. He was calling to invite them for coffee before they left. Milan did not want to see old Sokolović. So he went for a walk despite Jelena's request that he accompany her up the hillside for coffee.

"Milan," she pressed him, "he is supportive of us."

Milan did not want to stay but he could not say it, so instead he kissed her on the top of her head with dry, passionless lips and told her, "You should spend time with him alone. It's you he wants to see, and not me. It's you he loves. I don't feel offended, so please don't worry." And with that, Milan twisted everything around, for the sole reason that he could not say the truth.

Jelena believed him, so she reluctantly agreed. She walked up the hillside for the last time, alone.

X

Stojan sat on the edge of his dead brother's bed in a haze of incomprehension. He was trying to make some sense of how it had come to pass that Luka, who had sought refuge in Belgrade, had been killed and he, who had been sent up to a front line almost immediately, had stayed alive. He tried to think about a possible answer to this question, but there was none. His brain just seemed to stutter over the ground of every attempt to make sense of anything, and he could see no possible explanation.

The fear in his belly that afternoon when his father came out with the letter requesting Stojan's presence at the front line above Višegrad had grown until it blotted out almost everything else he might have wanted to think about or feel. In the personnel carrier that carried him the hour-and-a-half run to Višegrad, Stojan stared at the eleven other men in the truck and felt a novel fear staining what had up until then been disbelief. He could feel it overtaking him. His hands were sweating and he wiped them in what he hoped was a nonchalant motion across his camouflaged thighs. He sighed deeply, and looked out the canvas flap of the personnel carrier at the little squares of Bosnia that were rolling by—a republic that was now a country.

There were many long tunnels on the road to Višegrad; endless, seamless tubes of empty black, airless space blown deep through the Bosnian bedrock. They were so long and so full of that blackness that even the headlights on the personnel carriers were incapable of adequately illuminating the surrounding tunnel. They produced little puddles of light directly on the asphalt in front of them, but the tunnel walls were not discernible, and the light seemed to end abruptly against the unnerving density of that dark. Stojan grew more and more claustrophobic as the blackness of each tunnel enveloped them, and before they had passed through the third tunnel, he felt a wash of cold sweat break out across the flesh of his chest.

"What's with all the fucking tunnels?" he finally blurted out to no one in particular.

Some of the men laughed. "What? Are you worried about having an accident?" one asked.

"No," Stojan answered. "It's just fucked up."

"What you really have to worry about is whether or not some fucking Turkish sniper might be waiting for us at the other end of one of these tunnels," said another.

"Shut the fuck up!" someone said sharply.

Stojan gritted his teeth against the tunnels and wrapped his hands tightly around his rifle.

When they arrived behind the lines, the man sitting beside Stojan said to him, "Get ready, cousin."

Stojan looked at him quizzically.

The seatmate, who looked to be just a little older than Stojan, studied his face and nodded. "You'll get used to it soon. If you stay alive, that is." He smiled, but there was nothing amused in either his voice or his face.

Stojan was processed in a barn that was serving as a field command, and accompanied up to a second-line trench, which he learned was situated a hundred or so meters from the frontline trenches. These trenches were not much more than little hollows dug at uneven intervals and in haste as the Serb army moved forward against the under-equipped Bosnian government forces.

"Pas," one of the young soldiers in the trench offered his hand to Stojan.

"Pas?" Stojan echoed in confusion. The word meant "dog."

"That's my name!" he clarified in an agitated voice. Stojan looked closely at him. He looked disheveled and unwell. His eyes were bloodshot.

"Oh," Stojan offered uselessly.

The second man down the line was lying on his back with his rifle resting across his chest. He didn't acknowledge Stojan's arrival at all.

He was humming to himself as he looked up at the vast expanse of blue sky above them.

"How long have you been here … Pas?" Stojan asked.

Pas looked at him with a sage expression on his face. "My whole life, brother," he answered dolefully.

The soldier lying down in the trench broke out into song. "I can see a thick fog descending over Kosovo!" he sang.

"Ignore him," Pas advised easily. "He's high."

Stojan did not say anything. He peered over Pas' shoulder at the singer. "Nothing is alive anymore. We can see nothing except for one tall tree!" he sang.

"Shut up, Branko!" Pas offered in a mild voice.

Branko did. And then, seemingly unable to help himself, he continued his song in a whisper.

"How does this work, Pas?" Stojan asked. A mortar round suddenly exploded nearby with a loud cough. The hair on the back of Stojan's neck stood up and he shuddered involuntarily.

Pas did not seem to be affected by the shelling. "It works like this," he offered. "We are here to defend the territory behind us if the Chetniks in front of us get overrun by the Turks." Stojan listened to Pas refer to the Serbs as Chetniks—royalists from the Second World War—and to the Muslims as Turks. He nodded at Pas. "And if we get overrun, we die," he finished simply.

Stojan nodded again, as though that outcome would be perfectly alright with him. His lips felt numb.

"And from time to time," Pas added, "they will exchange some of us for some of the ones up front, so they can have a rest. The remainder of the time, we chill out."

A second mortar shell landed in the space between the first and second trenches. The earth trembled beneath Stojan's haunches, and small handfuls of dirt crumbled down from the hastily dug walls of the trench.

"Fuck!" whispered Pas. Apparently, even he hadn't expected the shell to land that close. "Get up you crazy fuck!" He kicked Branko in the ribs with the toe of his boot. "Get up!"

But Branko was still lying supine in the trench, his arms wrapped around his rifle. He was singing with tears streaming out of his eyes. "There is a thick fog falling over Kosovo." He whispered his song.

"Come on!" Pas cajoled him. "Come on, cousin!"

Branko didn't respond.

"I'll watch what's going on. You go and try to get that lunatic on his feet," Pas said to Stojan.

"OK," Stojan responded. "His name's Branko, right?"

Pas nodded.

Stojan crouched down beside Branko and tried to make eye contact with him.

"What song is that?" Stojan asked him.

"I don't fucking know!" Branko answered clearly.

"It's a threshing song, right?" Stojan asked.

Branko ignored him.

"Do you know all the words?" Stojan inquired.

"No," Branko shook his head.

Stojan nodded at him. "That's because the second and third verses are written in some weird dialect that is only spoken in certain pockets of Kosovo."

Branko looked at him as though Stojan were the insane one.

"Seriously," Stojan offered. "I know that song, too, but I don't know the final verses, because it's not standard Serbo-Croatian."

"Serbian!" Pas shouted.

Stojan looked up at him. Pas was staring down the barrel of his rifle, which was pointed out at the first trench. He didn't turn to look at Stojan, but seemed to feel Stojan looking at him.

"The language is Serbian!" Pas clarified. "Not Serbo-fucking-Croatian!"

"I don't want to be here anymore!" Branko whispered, ignoring Pas. "Can you write me a pass so I can go home?"

Stojan shook his head sympathetically. "Listen, Branko, why don't you get up? It's safer that way, you know?"

Branko laughed. "Safer? There is no 'safer' here. It's 'safer' in Banja Luka!" he said bitterly, referring to his hometown.

"Yeah, Pale, too," Stojan responded. "But here we are, so come on."

"You're from Pale?" Branko suddenly perked up.

"Yes."

"Do you know Radovan Karadžić?" he asked.

"Not personally," Stojan answered.

"Do you know General Mladić?" he asked.

"Not personally."

"Have you ever seen them?"

"Not personally."

Branko seemed disappointed.

"I'm sorry," Stojan offered with a shrug.

A second shell landed in the expanse between the trenches.

Branko scrambled to his feet.

"Jesus Christ," Pas breathed.

"What the fuck are you two doing?" An angry voice came floating across from behind them. Stojan looked around and saw one of the officers glaring at Branko and him. Branko lifted his rifle and rested it on the ground above the trench. He stared down the barrel, imitating Pas, but, unlike Pas, Branko's hands were trembling.

Stojan turned and raised his own rifle, too. He watched the scrub-covered ground sloping away in front of him. There was a cluster of little white houses off to the left. He wondered if anyone was still in them. The damp earth under his knees was starting to feel uncomfortably cold. He looked out of the corner of his eye at Branko. Branko looked dangerously pale. Stojan wondered what he was high on. He wouldn't have been able to guess. Stojan watched Branko's lips moving as he silently sang his song about the thick fog that had fallen over Kosovo.

"You should change the words," Stojan advised him at one point. "Fuck Kosovo. The thick fog is falling over Bosnia."

But Branko ignored him, and whispered the whole night away, staring down the barrel of his rifle as though in some kind of trance, even after the mortars had stopped falling. Around midnight, the Bosnian army prisoners were taken back behind the Serbian lines. Stojan watched them marching past, wondering where they would take them. He asked Pas.

Pas shrugged disinterestedly in the dark. "Who knows?" he answered. He struck a match and brought it to the cigarette that was waiting between his lips. The light from the flame illuminated the dust in the lines of his face.

"You really don't know?" asked Stojan.

"Nope," answered Pas definitively. "And I don't care."

"I know," whispered Branko in the dark.

"Bullshit," answered Pas. "You don't know anything."

Branko was silent for a moment, considering. Then he insisted, "No, I think I do know."

"Where?" asked Stojan.

"We release them behind our own lines, and they go around our positions to rejoin their army on the other side. Then, tomorrow, we have to capture them again. And it goes on and on like that. I keep shooting at the same men, over and over again." Branko's voice was dull and flat, and he spoke with conviction.

Pas laughed.

Branko went on. "They are shooting at us with our own ammunition. We traded it yesterday for a truckload of cigarettes."

Stojan did not believe him.

Pas laughed again.

"Let's get high," Branko sighed. "Come on," he cajoled the others. "It's not like there's something else to do."

"Sure," Pas agreed easily.

Branko's smiling voice came through the dark. "Pass me your matches, Pas."

Pas did, and Branko lit his joint. The fragrant smoke blew across the trench.

He passed it to Stojan, who politely declined.

Branko laughed kindly at him. "Go on, brother," he joked. "You'll feel calmer."

Stojan drew gingerly on the joint and passed it on quickly to Pas, who lingered over it for a long time.

"Do you think they'll send us up front tomorrow?" asked Branko.

"Who knows?" answered Pas in a tired voice. "Here," he nudged Stojan to pass the joint back to Branko.

"Pas! You smoked the whole thing!" Branko declared.

"Man, you have hundreds more of them stuffed in your pockets!" Pas retorted.

Branko laughed. "That's true," he conceded. "Here," he said to Stojan, "have a few for your own pockets." He felt around for Stojan's hand and pressed three joints into his palm.

"I don't really smoke," protested Stojan. "But I'll save them for you." He carefully placed them in a padded utility pocket in his coat.

Pas sighed. "Fuck, it's cold up here at night."

A burst of automatic gunfire broke the silence.

"What the fuck?" Pas scrambled up onto his knees and peered over the trench.

There were a few seconds of complete silence, and then a barrage of confused shouting from the frontline trench followed by a volley of automatic weapons fire.

Stojan crouched with his back pressed up against the wall of the earthen trench, his tongue too thick in his dry mouth. Branko began quietly singing to himself.

"Does somebody have a radio transmission?" Pas yelled down the trench at no one in particular. "What the fuck is going on?"

"No transmission and no answer!" a voice called back through the darkness.

"We're being overrun!" Pas announced in a voice tinged with disbelief. "I don't fucking believe it. Fucking Turks! They told us these fuckers were under-equipped!"

"We traded our fucking ammunition to them!" Branko shouted. "I saw it happen!"

"We're fucking being overrun!" Pas repeated incredulously.

"I guess they aren't impressed by our prisoner of war tactics," opined Branko sarcastically.

Stojan looked at him. The starlight just illuminated him enough to show the crazy shining in his eyes.

"A great fog has descended over Kosovo!" Branko sang out.

"Shut the fuck up!" Pas whirled on him. "I can't take anymore of this with you!"

"Fuck you, Pas," Branko answered calmly.

Stojan did not know what to do. He stayed with his back against the rough wall of the trench and felt the cold of the earth leaking through his skin. Pas fired a few rounds in the direction of the front trench, but it was random, because he couldn't see anything. After a moment, he, too, sank down into the trench.

"Why are they doing this at night?" he asked helplessly.

"Maybe because that's when we're all stoned," offered Branko between verses of his song.

Pas didn't answer him. They sat in their trench, helplessly listening to the gunfire from the front. After a while, the shooting stopped, and there was silence.

"Do we pull back now?" asked Stojan in a whisper.

Branko laughed quietly and put his arm around Stojan's shoulder.

"No, Stojan," he answered gently, as though to an old friend. "We don't pull back. We become the new front line."

Stojan couldn't feel his fingers. He felt like he was freezing to death.

They sank into silence. The trenches on their side were full of men, but no one made a sound.

Suddenly, through the darkness a high, falsetto voice came shouting from the direction of the front trench.

"Chetniks! We greet you in the name of the government of Bosnia!"

Branko let out an involuntary groan and a collective sigh seemed to pass through the Serbs gathered there.

"Don't worry!" the voice went on. "We have only come to kill you! It won't hurt, we promise!"

"Fuck you, Turk!" an outraged voice came floating down from what had now become the Serbian front line.

"How many are you?" the voice from the overrun trench shouted. "I hope for your sake there are enough of you to hold your second line, since you've failed so miserably at holding the first!"

"Fuck you! Try it!" taunted someone from the Serbian side.

"Come on, kittens!"

Stojan's heart was pounding in what seemed like a single, endless beat behind his ribs. He sat in the ensuing silence, which seemed to go on forever.

There was a scream in the darkness. "Look!" shouted a Bosnian soldier. "We left one alive!" A single pistol shot rang out.

Branko stood up in the trench, his head and shoulders exposed above the ground-line. "There's a thick fog falling over Kosovo!" he sang at the top of his voice.

Pas reached up to try and drag him down again, but Branko kicked him and he fell back. Stojan stayed glued to the wall of the trench.

"You'll lose Kosovo, too!" the Bosnian called back.

"Nothing is alive anymore!" Branko sang. "We can't see anything but one huge tree!"

Stojan was immobilized. He stared at Branko silhouetted against the sky.

"There are tailors under the tree, making a new suit for me!" Branko sang.

Stojan wanted to drag him back down into the trench but he didn't move.

"There are as many patterns on it as there are stars in the sky!"

Stojan heard a rifle shot and Branko collapsed into the trench.

Pas scrambled over on his hands and knees and rolled Branko over from his stomach onto his back. Stojan saw an empty space where the back of Branko's head should be, and it took him long seconds to register that Branko was dead. He felt all the blood drain out of his face as the shock of disbelief washed over him.

Pas crouched over Branko, regarding his dead friend in an almost perplexed silence, as though what had happened was not registering with him, either. Then he began to rummage through Branko's pockets. He found Branko's stash, and handed the joints to Stojan, who did not take them at first.

"Take them!" hissed Pas.

Stojan looked at him blankly in the starlight.

"His family doesn't have to know he was stoned! The army doesn't have to know it, either!

Stojan accepted the joints, and pocketed them.

The Serbs held their second line that night, and in the morning Branko's body was taken from the trench to be returned to his family. Stojan thought about him for a long time afterward, cursing himself for not hauling Branko back down into the trench. He had been close enough to do it. But he hadn't.

XI

In the lengthening light of late morning, Stojan Sokolović tapped on my office door, and asked me if I would go shoe shopping with him. "I'm from a small, pathetic village," he smiled. "Which means I have no taste for fashion." He looked expectantly at me from the threshold of my office doorway. He wore a deep blue button-down shirt that intensified the pale hue of his eyes.

I looked at the pile of essays on my desk and felt torn.

"I'll grade the essays for you tomorrow," he offered, pre-empting my excuse.

And this made me smile.

"Come on," he smiled. "We'll have lunch."

I shook my head in feigned disdain at his tenacity.

"The sun is shining so nicely outside," he went on.

"Stop! Stop! I'm coming!"

"Excellent," he said with a satisfied smirk.

"Can I shut down my computer first?" I asked.

"No." Emphatically.

I shook my head. "You're tough, you know that?" I asked.

"I do know," he answered seriously.

"Come on," he rushed me.

"I'm coming!" I snatched up my jacket from the back of my chair.

"You don't need that," he said.

I looked at him disbelievingly.

"Trust me," he said. "You've been hiding in here for weeks and in the meantime it became summer."

I laughed at that, dropped my jacket, and we went out.

Stojan and I wandered all over the city in the long, late spring sun. People were lying around everywhere, soaking up the warmth that had finally chased out one of the longest, bitterest winters on record. Every green spot in the city seemed to be occupied by a body—they were reading, eating, drinking coffee, flirting, kissing, laughing, joking, throwing sticks which were chased down and brought back by different colors and textures and sizes of dogs. Babies were out in strollers, carefully shaded from the sun by cotton hats and netted screens. Toddlers trundled around all over the grass in front of the imposing legislature buildings like beetles, and older children kicked balls and swatted table-tennis balls back and forth. We bought sandwiches and found a small clear spot on the grass near a fountain where children were splashing in knee-deep water.

"Do you like this city?" I asked him, looking around.

He nodded. "I do."

"Me, too. I like how it wakes up in summer."

Stojan nodded. "I like how it's full of foreigners," he offered. "I feel less homesick."

This was a point I did not feel, but thought I could understand.

"Are you homesick?" I asked in response to his statement.

"Yes," he answered easily. Then he qualified, "I'm homesick for something that doesn't exist anymore, though. I don't know if I would go back now, but I wish I could go back to the time before the war." He trailed off. "It's strange." He shrugged.

"Do you feel at home here?" I asked.

"I don't really know," he confessed. "Sometimes I do, and other times I feel confused a lot. When I'm translating things sometimes, I forget English words, and then I forget Serbian words. I feel like I'm losing my Serbian, but then I think my English will never improve enough. You know?" he asked. I didn't know.

"It's like being trapped between two worlds," he went on. "But more than that, it's like being trapped in two different times. It's strange."

I thought about this. I could imagine it, I thought, but all I could ever do was imagine. I couldn't know. I couldn't feel that. He leaned back and lay down on his back across the grass, looking up at the sky with thoughtful, searching eyes.

This is a different sky than the sky in Pale," he said after a while. "This sky is paler. The biggest difference between the skies, though, is at night. At night in Pale, the stars stretch across a huge distance—millions of them. You can see the whole galaxy, it seems like."

We were quiet for a while, watching the city wake up to early summer.

"What about you?" he asked.

"What about me?"

"What was your home like?"

I considered this for a moment. I thought of the morning sun on the ocean, too bright to look at; the nor'easters that sometimes broke the boardwalks like matchsticks in winter; the smell of salt in the air on early spring evenings; the lowing of foghorns and the distant rumbling of diesel trains moving through the night on their way north to New York. I thought of the fishing boats in the Shark River; the trawlers on the Manasquan. I thought of my mother's hands, and the smell of her perfume.

"There's not a lot to say," I answered. "It's just a big clump of oil refining and heavy industry." But this was not true. It was not all like that. There were truck farms and gardens and pre-revolutionary postage-stamp towns on the national register of protected historic sites. There were walls of lilacs in spring.

"Really?" Stojan asked. "That's all?"

I shrugged. "Pretty much." But it was a lie.

"It sounds like Pančevo," he said sadly. "Did you have a house or an apartment?"

"We had a small Victorian cottage on the ocean," I answered. "It was green."

"It sounds nice," he offered.

I shrugged again.

"What kind of shoes will you look for?" I asked.

He answered with a wry smile, "I don't actually feel like shopping." He was still staring up at the sky, flat on his back on a soft cushion of well-tended grass. He was looking at something—maybe thinking about something.

"You could have said you just wanted to go for lunch, lunatic," I laughed at him.

He turned his head and looked up at me seriously. "No, I couldn't."

"Why not?"

"Because you wouldn't have come."

I thought about this. Was it true? Would I have declined? Stojan went on, "I have the sense that, for you, everything should have its purpose. And a lazy lunch in a park is not a purpose."

"Maybe." I felt a little bit defensive.

"Not maybe," he said gently. "Definitely."

"So what?" I challenged.

"So I thought you would respond better to the lie than the truth," he said simply. "Some people respond better to something which is not the truth, but which makes sense to them."

I looked at his pale eyes, which were deeper with the sky reflected in them. He looked back at me kindly. I wasn't sure whether he was insulting me or not.

"Am I that transparent?" I asked.

"Actually, no," he answered. "But I read your book, remember."

"Which you didn't agree with," I added with a pained smile.

"That's right," he said pleasantly.

"And can you tell so much about a person by reading a book?" I asked, disbelieving.

"Of course you can," he answered, looking back up at the sky. "There is no unnecessary word in your book, and no ambiguity. You only say exactly what you want to say, and nothing else escapes from you. A book maps an author's soul—the part you're willing to show, anyway." He smiled and closed his eyes. "But you shouldn't worry about me," he went on pleasantly. "It's the reviewers you have to worry about, and I will most definitely not be asked to review it."

"You actually should be the one to review it," I mused.

"Maybe," he answered with a laugh, "but I'm not qualified."

"Actually, you are probably better qualified than most of my colleagues," I said.

"I am not the one you have to answer to," he said, and he was absolutely right. "You have to answer to them."

I said, "I should answer to you anyway, though." I felt a strange tightness in my chest.

He burst out laughing and opened his eyes. "You couldn't do it!"

"Why not?"

"You wouldn't understand the question," he said gently.

"Try me," I offered.

"I would ask it in my own language," he pointed out. "You guys writing on Bosnia don't hear our questions, because you don't speak our language."

I stared at him and, again, I had nothing to say. He was right. My Serbian was shit. That was why I had needed him in the first place.

We spent the afternoon wandering around the city, peering into shops and admiring the flowers that cropped up here and there with their surprising colors. As the sun poured its last long rays against the steel and glass, we found ourselves at the entryway to his apartment building.

"Come on, I'll cook this time," he said with a smile.

"I don't believe you," I answered solemnly.

"I promise," he responded.

Later, on the balcony with our coffee balanced between us on the milk crate, Stojan told jokes about Bosnia from before the war. I didn't get them. But I laughed in some moments anyway, because his laughter was infectious. He laughed, and it was a deep, rich laugh that made him seem happily unaware of himself. He laughed almost as though he didn't mean to—almost as though he had surprised himself. He laughed so hard at one point that the coffee splashed over the side of the cup in his hand. He tried to translate those jokes, but it didn't work. They weren't funny.

"We have the best jokes," he announced, trying to sop up the spilled coffee with half a paper towel.

"It seems to be the case," I offered mildly, smiling myself.

"But they don't translate well," he conceded.

"Apparently not," I agreed.

"But you know, there are two things they say about us—that Bosnians are stupid, and Montenegrins are lazy. I don't know for sure if Bosnians are stupid, but there are tons of jokes on this. They say we have big heads. But in Montenegro once, I experienced the true depth of Montenegrin laziness. My brother and I were there on a summer holiday—in a place called Igalo—and we saw a vendor on the side of the road with grapes for sale. So we pulled over and asked him for half a kilo of them. He was sitting in a little folding chair on the road, you know? And he looked at us and said it would not be worth it for him to get out of his chair unless we bought a full kilo. We thought he was joking, so we started to laugh. But he was serious, and we saw that he would not get up for less than a full kilo. So we had to buy a kilo of grapes."

I started to laugh at this, and Stojan was encouraged.

"Another story, which happened to my parents when they were first married, happened close by in Herceg Novi, where there was a bar and my father said they went inside and asked the bartender for two beers. He pointed over to the refrigerator and asked them to please bring him one, too."

I laughed even more at this story than the first.

"Those sorts of things happen all over Montenegro. I have a friend called Želčević, and he says his family name came from a census that his great-grandfather did not come down from the mountains to register for. The story is that this man had a limp, and did everything slowly. The Turkish officials asked the neighbors who had come to register about this great-grandfather. "I can't remember his name, but they call him 'Želka'—the turtle." "Let him be Želčević, then. So the officials named the family a word that means 'turtle,' and that is how he got his surname." Stojan himself laughed at that one. Then he paused and became more serious. "But there were lots of things like that, too. I had a friend called 'Blagojević,' but in his family cemetery, the first stones are of people called 'Milojević.' 'Blago' and 'Milo' mean the same thing basically— 'mild' or 'kind'—and the story is that these Montenegrin Milojevići killed some Turkish officials during a raid in the nineteenth century, and then fled to Bosnia. In order to avoid capture, they changed their name, but kept the same meaning. All Serbs eventually tell you they are Montenegrin, though," Stojan mused. "In 1912, when the Austrians sent attaches to Cetinje to ask for the Montenegrins to reconsider declaring war on Turkey, the king refused to meet with them, because it was Easter Sunday. So he sent a note that read: 'And even if we wanted to meet with you, the mood of my people is for war.' Crazy Montenegrins!" Stojan laughed, then became more serious. "Every Serb wants to be Montenegrin. Every Serb would prefer this to be his history." He shrugged.

The evening was still warm—the sure sign that summer had essentially arrived.

Stojan looked at the paper towel, which was sopping wet with the coffee he had spilled with his laughter. "Do you want a beer?" He stood up on his long legs.

"Sure," I answered. It was pleasant here on the balcony. It was pleasant to listen to these stories, which asked me to do nothing more than listen.

He disappeared into the kitchen for a moment, and returned with two brown bottles of some beer I had never seen before, called Karlovačko.

"It's some Croatian beer," he apologized when he saw my face. "I don't know what possessed me to buy it," he shrugged.

"It's alright," I said, surprised. "Who would have thought that Croats could make a decent beer?"

"They can't!" Stojan answered, and I laughed, but actually, the beer was quite good. I had laughed more with Stojan on this day than I had probably laughed in the previous year. He made it possible to forget certain things, or to carry on despite them. He made me forget my deadly seriousness, even if he didn't realize it, even as he still accused me of being too serious—too economical. I was now only half as economical as I had been the day before. Here, I had lost the whole afternoon to a whim. I sighed a long, contented sigh and settled back into the rickety chair.

"Let's go make some burek," he said suddenly.

"What?" I asked.

"Burek," he answered.

"Burek?"

"Burek," he repeated with conviction. I am very good at this. I was the youngest, as you know, and my mother was gone, so I cooked a lot when I was growing up. My specialty is burek."

"OK," I answered feebly. "But I doubt I'll be much help."

"Come on," he rose to his feet. "I'll show you."

I followed him reluctantly into the kitchen, and he started piling ingredients on the counter: flour, salt, oil, a package of young farmer's cheese, and a couple of eggs from the door in the refrigerator.

"First we make the dough," he announced briskly.

"You're going to make dough?" I asked in disbelief. "Why don't you just buy it?"

Stojan clucked in contempt but said nothing. He measured flour, water, and salt into a big ceramic bowl that had a chip in its rim. I watched him curiously. Then he went out and dusted the whole dining room table with flour, and turned out the dough in the middle of it. With a thin wooden dowel, he rolled it out thinner and thinner until it was hanging in great long sheets over the side of the table. I didn't understand how it didn't tear off under its own weight and fall on the floor. But it didn't.

When the dough was all lightly bathed with a thin sheen of oil, Stojan mixed eggs and cheese and spread it out all over the paper-thin dough. Then he began to roll the dough over itself until it was transformed into a giant snaking coil. He lifted it in sections and dropped it into a deep, circular baking pan.

"If you can make a respectable burek," Stojan said as he wrenched open the oven door, "you don't need to write books." He looked at me expectantly, pleasantly, and with a slight expression of perplexity. He opened his mouth to speak, but then stopped and looked away.

I felt the contentment of the afternoon fly away then, and my anxiety returned. "Is what I do so useless?" I asked pointedly. "I mean, should there be no books at all?"

He looked more closely at me. His hands were covered with flour, and there was a smear of it on his neck. Then, quietly, he said, "Why does it matter what I think? You asked me to check the translations. I'm not qualified to comment on it."

"But you *are* commenting on it," I retorted. "You're commenting on it all the time." I felt a sharp hostility growing inside me, but strangely, he looked very sympathetic.

"I don't know these theories," he said quietly. "I wish I did know them."

"No, you don't," I interrupted him swiftly. "They fucking ruin your life." I didn't know what made me say that. It was not true.

"Alright," he conceded. "I don't want to know the theories then. But it doesn't matter what I think about it, because I'm not the one who matters. I don't get to decide anything, so I should leave it to people who do get to decide. How can I say whether it's good or not? Right or not? I just don't know." He opened his flour-covered palms in a gesture of helplessness, and my anger softened. It was replaced by a feeling of sadness that washed over me. He couldn't help me. I could see that. But I still wanted him to.

He leaned up against the countertop and regarded me with his pale eyes. "You don't owe me any explanations," he said quietly. "We don't know the same Bosnia. We have different eyes. Different souls. And that's just the way it is." He shrugged. "We want to know different things."

"What do you mean?" I asked.

"Well, I don't really care about why the war happened, or how it happened, or who was responsible," he said. "I don't care who should have done what, or how things could have been done differently."

I felt my anger and frustration returning. I had heard this so many times from so many people in Bosnia. "How can you not care about why you had to leave your own country?" I asked, and there was a sharp, uncomprehending edge in my voice.

"I do care about leaving my country. And I feel homesick. But I can't do anything about it, so what's the sense in being angry about it? What can I do? I can make myself sick over it, but what will it change?" His position was unintelligible to me. I just couldn't understand it.

"Stojan, don't you ever ask yourself why Serbs did what they did?" I asked sadly.

He looked at me long and hard. "I know what Serbs did. And nobody really knows why each person made his choice. You can't tell me with your theories and none of your colleagues can tell me, either. I read many books on that war. Yours wasn't the only one. And when I read them, I felt like I was reading something that took place on Mars. I couldn't recognize the things I was reading, because, for me, it was not as they described it. It was not as they explained it." He paused for a long moment, looking at me. "And another thing," he went on. "I accept that Serbs performed the biggest portion of killing in Bosnia. I'm not stupid. I was there, and to say something else would be a lie. I know what the Zvornik Brigade did. I know why their commander went to prison. It was because he authorized his men to be released to the Drina Corps so they could dig the graves at Srebrenica. I know that's true. But believe me when I tell you that there was no one in Bosnia with a gun in his hand who was innocent."

I looked away.

But he bid me back. "We want to know different things, you and me," he repeated.

"Why can't we do both?" I whispered.

"I don't want to do your job," he said evenly. "All it can do for me is make me crazy. I just want to know what happened to my brother. That's all. If you want to make sense of the whole war for yourself, then you should. But don't ask me to believe what I can't believe." He wasn't angry at all. He was just honest. It seemed that he just wanted me to understand him. But another part of me did not believe him, because he kept mentioning it. I felt uneasy—I felt that there was something else I could not put my finger on. He did want to know, I thought. And yet, he did not. I considered for a moment, trying to think clearly, but finding myself unable.

"How will you find out what happened to Luka?" I asked him quietly. "How will you ever know for sure? Even if you find this Milan, how will you know that he will tell you the truth?"

"How will you ever know for sure what you want to know?" he challenged. "You ask me whether your book is wrong, because you can't ever know if it's right. You have to wait for the reviews, and you still won't know. It will depend on who reviews it—whether he is your enemy or your friend. It will depend on whether he is sympathetic to your position, or not. I can tell you what I really think about it, but it won't matter, because *I* don't matter. If I say it is right, you will still wonder if it's wrong. If I say it's wrong, you will tell yourself that I'm a Serbian peasant who doesn't understand what he's read."

"That's not true," I protested. He paused to give me a chance to say something more. But I slipped into silence again, because I didn't know what to say. So he went on. "Your book is just written in faith, because you don't know, and you'll never know. For some reason, you wanted to write about Bosnia. I don't know why."

I stared at him silently.

He scratched his forehead with his wrist because his fingers were still covered in dried dough. "Maybe you wrote it because your colleagues are interested in this Bosnia—this primitive place where a person can get killed for the price of a package of cigarettes." He paused, considering. "Or for a song," he said with a short burst of cryptic laughter. "Or maybe you wrote it because Bosnia is the big example of evil now, and that makes it exciting. Maybe it's more exciting than writing about what your people have done to the world." He stopped, considering. And then he said, "Or maybe you wrote it so that you will get promoted."

This last statement fell between us like a block of ice. Whether I had written it for that reason or not, promotion would be the outcome. I would go for lunch with the department head. I would casually remind him that the book was in press. He would get the message, and quietly approach the Head of School while I celebrated with a bottle of champagne. It was an intricate game, with its own rules. When it was in print, I would put it on my reading lists for the classes I taught. Students would have to buy it. People would congratulate me at conferences, saying they loved it, even if they didn't—even if they hadn't read it. Its purpose was to make a name for me. Which would make it easier to publish the next book, and which would eventually seal up my career in a nice clean package of emphatic statements—the mark of academic success.

But because I couldn't admit this to him, I said, "I didn't write it to get promoted, Stojan."

He looked at me with a small, painful smile. It was clear that he didn't believe me.

I couldn't think of anything else to say, so I repeated, "I didn't." My voice sounded thin and hollow.

The expression on his face didn't change. I turned abruptly and walked out of the kitchen. My heart was pounding. I stepped out onto the balcony and sank down on the edge of the rickety folding chair to roll a cigarette. I was ashamed enough that I wanted to leave immediately, but I was hopeful enough that I could still make him believe me. And that was when I knew he had been right. He had been right about all the reasons I had chosen to write on Bosnia. He had been right about many things.

The cigarette rolling was slow going. My hands were sweating all over the paper, which caused it to moisten and tear. In frustration, I set everything unrolled on the milk crate. After a minute or so, Stojan came out wiping his freshly washed hands dry on a dish towel. He crouched down and took up a new paper and dumped the tobacco I had tried to roll into it. His hands were perfectly steady, and he handed the cigarette to me wordlessly. I took it with a murmur of thanks, but I couldn't look at him. He stayed sitting on his heels, looking up at me as I lit the cigarette with my trembling, betraying hands.

And then he said, quietly, "I am going to see Milan Milanović."

"When?" I asked, surprised.

"Soon. This week. I will call him." He spoke softly.

Stojan rolled a second cigarette for himself and stayed smoking it, still on his heels. Then he said to me, "You don't have to feel bad about your book. Everyone profited from our war." His eyes were deep in the gathering twilight and he gazed up at me steadily.

"What are you talking about?" I asked in a whisper.

He sighed, and said nothing.

"Do you think I'm profiting from the war in Bosnia?" I asked angrily. I could feel my cheeks burning.

"Well, you've built your whole career on it," Stojan answered easily.

"Jesus, Stojan," I said weakly. "It's not like I'm some kind of criminal or something. It's not like I'm getting rich."

"You have a reputation that is more valuable to you than money," he observed thoughtfully. "But don't worry," he added hastily. "As I've said, many people profited from that war. Even Milan Milanović."

I looked down at him wordlessly.

"Milan married Luka's girlfriend and I don't think she knows that he has a different version of events," Stojan explained. "Sometimes people have a lot to lose by telling stories in certain ways, so they work very hard to hide the things that don't fit with their views of themselves," he went on.

I considered this for a moment, ignoring the possibility that this last statement may well have been directed at me. "Well, the truth is the truth," I offered, but this sounded pathetic to my own ears.

Stojan looked at me, considering. "Do you believe everything you hear?" he asked directly.

"Of course not!" I answered.

"Do you believe everything you say?"

"Yes," I answered, but hesitantly. I had lied to him about theory ruining one's life. I had lied to him about my home. But it wasn't because I didn't want to tell him the truth. It was just because the truth was so tiresome. What was there to say about the yawning chasm of unbroken monotony which animated that life? I was bored senseless, bored stupid, bored beyond redemption. I read to be *On Escape*. I read Kierkegaard. I read Kant. I understood none of it. But I wanted it to illuminate me.

Stojan looked closely at me with his pale eyes, and he was serious, but something else in his look suggested a trace of amusement.

"So if you don't believe everything you hear, but you do believe everything you say, what does that say about you?"

"That I believe my own lies?" I offered sarcastically.

Stojan smiled, obviously pleased with my answer. "Yes," he answered definitively. "Everyone believes their own lies. Milan Milanović has married my brother's lover. In order to live this life, he has to believe his own lies."

"So why did he tell the truth in the first place, then?" I inquired.

Stojan shrugged. "Maybe he couldn't live with it." Then he stood up and went to pull the burek out. I trailed after him quietly and watched him retrieve the pan from the oven. The burek was bubbling, golden, and perfect. When it was cool enough to touch, we went back out on the balcony to eat it. It was the simplest and best meal I had ever eaten. We sat for a time in silence with the lights of the city splayed out before us. One by one, the windows in the apartment building across the street went dark.

"It's late," he announced after a while. "Why don't you stay? I'll sleep on the couch."

I stirred and stretched and considered this. "No, I have to go," I said automatically.

Stojan looked closely, sympathetically, at me. "Stay," he said firmly. "It's too late to leave now. I'll lay the bedding." He stood and yawned and stretched, and then he went in to make up the couch. We argued rather heatedly for five minutes before I finally agreed to stay. The truth was that I was too tired to leave and I was too lonely to go home. When he went to his bedroom, I stripped down to my underclothes and climbed beneath the blankets. I had trouble falling asleep, though. I struggled with the urge to get up and go into his bedroom. I was hungry for something, but I wasn't sure what it was. So I didn't go. Sometime before sunrise, I woke with a strange start, thinking I had heard something. I listened, straining to hear in the dark, but whatever it was, if it was anything at all, I didn't hear it again.

XII

The dead do not stay dead when those who love them are still looking for them, still dreaming about them. The empty space where there was once a brother, once a lover, once a son, still contains the trace of him in the lives of those whose work of mourning never ends. The morning sun poured through the blinds in Jelena Milanović's bedroom. She rolled over and stretched her arms above her head. Milan was already gone, walking along the waterfront. Jelena pressed weakly clenched fists over her eyes for a moment to block out the sun. She couldn't remember what she had dreamed—there remained only fragments: colors, shapes, a sense of urgency captured in shallow breathing that the waking did not dispel. Then she hurled herself out of the bed and padded into the kitchen to make coffee. She stood naked at the window, the diminutive coffee cup clasped between her long fingers. The rising east sun cascaded across her body through the glass, the light bending to wrap around her hips, her knees, her shoulders and chest. She felt a dull, slight weight in her ribs that never went away. Coming to Canada had not lifted it. She felt that she had lost something that could not be regained, that she should be looking for something that did not exist. She felt a desire inside her that she could not quite place. She thought it was the desire for a child. Jelena was thirty-two years old. In another world, without war, she might have already had two. But here, where the grayness of winter buried every needed thing, desire did not bloom. Desire was a small seed buried under a blanket of northern snow, and it never got warm enough to grow and be satisfied. That small seed could not be found. There were no mountains or villages to act as reference points to identify where it was buried. The sun did not shine long enough or strong enough to illuminate the spot where one should dig to find it again. Now it was spring. Spring in a cold country. Spring in a country where the land lay low and flat as far as the eye could see. The city sprawled out beyond the figure of the woman in the window—repetitive, stone, steel, concrete. Monochromatic. The buildings, the walls, the slushy streets in winter, the endless procession of unfamiliar, weather-worn faces along the wide concrete sidewalks and gathered in tight human knots at the street corners, waiting for traffic lights to change so they could safely cross enormous white-painted intersections. No one ever stopped. And no one laughed.

XIII

"Why don't we ever go to your apartment?" asked Stojan unexpectedly one night.

"Because nobody lives there," I replied promptly. I had arrived at his apartment later than I had said I would, and he had been waiting for me. On my way there, knowing I was late, I stopped to buy him a small crown of thorns plant on the street. The crown of thorns is difficult to kill, I reasoned, and it rewards even the laziest owner with a multitude of tiny, lively red flowers virtually all the time.

"I'm sorry I'm late," I said to him. "I have a performance review tomorrow, and I really had to prepare for it."

"What is this?" he asked, pointing to the small plant in my hand.

"It's a present," I answered. "And an apology for being late."

"It's covered in needles," he said doubtfully.

"It also has poisonous sap, so be careful not to prick yourself with the thorns," I pointed out.

He looked at me in amazement. "You brought me a poisonous plant with spikes all over it as a gift?"

"It's a plant, Stojan," I explained carefully. "You have no plants, and you need some, so I bought you one."

"What do I do with it?" he asked doubtfully. "It looks really dangerous."

"You put it in the sun and water it every ten days or so, and it will show its gratitude by flowering," I answered proudly.

"Are the flowers poisonous, too?" he asked.

"Can you just take it and put it somewhere?" I asked sharply.

"Yes, I can," he responded, and gingerly took it from me. He carried it at arm's length over to the window ledge, as though he was afraid it would injure him. He placed it on the windowsill and regarded it for a moment.

"Why does it have these thorns?" he asked me.

I shrugged. "I guess to deter predators?" I answered.

"But if it already has thorns, why does it need poisonous sap, too?" he persisted.

"Stojan, I really don't know. I'm not a botanist," I answered. "How can you have so many questions about a plant?"

"I am interested in knowing everything about it," he said solemnly, and I could not tell if he was teasing or not.

"Well, I'll print something about it off the internet for you, then," I offered.

"Excellent. Thank you," he added.

"If you want to prune it back at any point, the branches that you remove will grow new roots and can be re-potted," I informed him.

He looked at me in obvious confusion. "Perfect," he answered. "Thanks." He backed away from the plant slowly, which made me laugh.

"But watch the poisonous sap if you decide to cut it. They bleed a lot," I couldn't resist adding.

He looked at me with wide, disbelieving eyes. "Excellent," he murmured. "I love it."

I smiled at the fact that he obviously did not love it, and did not know what to do with it.

"I'm cooking. Here is your coffee." He poured the coffee out of the džezva into my tiny blue china cup and I took it out onto the balcony, where the milk crate was set for dinner. I sat down to roll a cigarette.

"So!" Stojan emerged onto the balcony. "Tell me about your performance review."

"There's really not much to tell." I answered. "It's just this thing I have to do, where they review what I've done over the last year, and then tell me whether it's good enough. Then, we set targets for next year." I shrugged, as though it didn't matter.

"What kind of targets?" he inquired.

"Targets for publication," I replied.

"And are you going to be good enough?" he quizzed me.

"I guess I'll find out," I laughed. I felt ashamed to tell him how confident I was.

Stojan set a roasted chicken down on the milk crate.

"Why don't you tell me why you hate engineering?" I invited him.

"It has a logic in it that I dislike," he answered easily.

"Do you prefer translating for the courts?" I asked.

He thought for a moment. "I think I do like it, yes," he affirmed. "I don't have to worry about performance targets," he added. He sat down, and with no further comment, tore a leg off of the chicken and began to eat. He indicated with his other hand that I should do the same.

I leaned forward in my creaking folding chair with its precarious hardware and took a wing from the chicken.

"What would you do if you could do anything you wanted in the whole world?" he asked me with an expansive note in his voice.

I chewed on the chicken thoughtfully for a moment. "I don't really know. Maybe sail away somewhere. You?"

"I would go home," he answered.

"Why don't you?" I asked.

"Why don't *you*?" he replied.

"Well, sailing away is really impossible," I said, "which is why I probably want to do it."

"What I want to do is impossible, too," he pointed out.

"Why?"

But instead of answering, he asked me, "Do you ever wish you could go home?"

"To New Jersey?" I laughed.

"What's wrong with New Jersey?" he asked innocently. "It can't be all refineries."

I saw again the coast in summer; the Inlet at dusk, loaded with boat traffic waiting for the train bridges to open. I could smell the littleneck clams roasting on the grill outside. I could smell the docks at night as they hosed down the decks after the catch had been sold. I had worked on those boats growing up, and they always sent me out onto the pulpit in the storms to watch for the jetties that flanked the inlet into the Shark River.

"I guess nothing is wrong with New Jersey," I answered feebly.

"So why did you leave?" he asked.

"What do you mean?" I asked in return.

"Well, I left because I had to," Stojan pointed out.

And I understood what he was trying to say. Stojan could not understand why a person would voluntarily leave home. And I began to wonder if we had ever understood one another at all.

"I left because I wanted something, and I could not find it in New Jersey," I answered, and it was the honest answer. I had wanted to leave all my life.

"And did you find it?" he asked seriously.

"I don't know," I answered truthfully.

"If you found it, would you go home?" he pressed.

"I don't know," I sighed. "I haven't thought about going home in a very long time. Sometimes the paths that lead back to places get blocked."

Stojan seemed to understand that, and he nodded in sympathy. "We think we're only going to go a little distance, and when we turn around again, everything is gone."

"Yes," I agreed. "That's how it is." I could see the face of my mother, whose Moroccan heritage I discovered only after her death. I thought of the low, fast moving clouds over the ocean on the day that she died. I thought of the terrible hollowness in my heart, the terminal loneliness that accompanied me afterward as I left again.

We ate in silence, watching the night creep into the hollow spaces between the buildings across the street. I felt tired. There was a well of exhaustion in my bones these days that never seemed to lift. Stojan had an expression on his face that suggested he felt the same. He seemed tired, but he also smiled easily, and there was a difference between a genuine smile that came from within the depths of a person and the mechanical stretching of muscles around teeth that I was accustomed to in many of my daily interactions. The difference between these smiles could be detected not in the mouth, I thought, but in the eyes. Stojan Sokolović did not waste energy on polite smiles. He did not waste resources on responding to what was expected of him. When he smiled, he smiled. When he didn't, he didn't. It was not that he spoke truth, but that he *was* truth, in some way. He was only what he was, without needing to be more or less or otherwise than himself.

"When I came to this place," said Stojan, gesturing with his head to the stolid, sweating city that lay out beyond the balcony, "I didn't speak English very well. I could not understand the people around me. This is a hard language—I don't mean that it's difficult, but rather that it sounds hard and unkind to me." He looked over at me, and I looked back. "English has sharp edges," he went on. "I never liked it. That's why I studied Russian. It's softer. Even at the height of the war, when Serbian became the language of death, it was never as sharp as English can be."

I thought for a moment of the sharpness of language. I remembered a poem I read once, or a passage. It told of a foreign word, spoken against the frost on a winter windowpane: *Wstawać. Ustajte. Get up.* I picked up my coffee to find that it had grown tepid. I put it down again without drinking and sighed deeply.

Stojan looked sharply at me out of his pale eyes, a considering expression on his face. And then he asked, "When you were a child, did you ever dream that you could fly?"

I was surprised at this. "Yes."

Stojan nodded. "I used to have that dream all the time; that I was flying, but very low to the ground. I never got above the treetops."

"Me, neither!" I exclaimed. "And I never went very far—only a block or so. It seemed like a struggle to stay aloft," I remembered aloud.

Stojan nodded. "Everyone I know has had that dream in their childhood. It goes away, though," he added. "I never had it as an adult."

"No," I agreed. "Me, neither."

"Do you think there is something to that, then?" he asked.

"What do you mean?"

"I mean, do you think that this means there is some basic connection between us all?" he clarified.

"I don't know," I answered thoughtfully.

"What if our dreams are not our own?" he asked suddenly.

"What do you mean?" I asked again.

"I mean, what if we can dream one another's dreams? Whose dreams are these—these flying dreams—if we all have them? Are they our own dreams, then?" Stojan looked perplexed and thoughtful.

I shrugged. "Maybe."

"Maybe what?" he pressed.

"Well, maybe they belong to all of us in some way, as human beings," I offered, but it seemed a naïve statement to make, and most of the theorists I read would not have agreed. I paused, and thought for a moment. "Some philosophers pose that we have a natural connection to each other—like Rousseau, for example, who says that we have a natural pity for each other."

Stojan raised his eyebrows questioningly. "Go on," he said.

"Well, Rousseau believed that we are essentially good by nature, and that human evil comes from the corruption of our societies. We get destroyed, morally, by our societies."

Stojan leaned back in his chair and looked up at the sky. "Yes," he nodded thoughtfully. "That makes sense."

"And Wittgenstein," I added. "Wittgenstein says that the man who cries out in pain does not choose the mouth which says it."

Stojan puzzled over this for a moment, nodding thoughtfully. "I don't know if I understand that, really, but it sounds nice," he said.

"I don't know if I understand it, either," I confessed. "But I think it means that we can experience one another's suffering. And if we can experience one another's suffering, maybe we won't cause it so frequently." I shrugged. That didn't make sense. It wasn't what I had wanted to say.

"Can we live one another's lives?" he mused.

I thought about this for a moment. Levinas did not think so. He believed our lives were uniquely our own—like our deaths. He believed that we were not substitutable for one another. We could not take one another's places. But Maurice Blanchot had hidden Levinas' wife and child from the Nazis in France in 1941. "The need for escape," wrote Levinas, "leads us into the heart of philosophy." But he wasn't talking about escaping the world. He was talking about escaping oneself. He was talking about the chill of nausea on the flesh, the shame that crawls through our bellies when confronted with who we are.

Wstawać. Ustajte. Get up.

We went silent for a while, until Stojan stretched his arms over his head and yawned. I heard one of his shoulders crack. I rolled another cigarette and the smoke from the first lighting wandered lazily off the balcony into the lengthening evening. For a while longer, we said nothing at all. I wondered why I kept returning to this apartment. I wondered why I kept returning to him—why I kept building this strange relationship, brick by careful brick. Some affinity was growing there between us on the balcony over the course of that summer. If we were friends, it was an awkward friendship, born out of loneliness, perhaps. We were not the same. We did not see things the same. We were a couple of people who had nothing in common, really. We were not contemporaries. We were not compatriots. Our sadness was not the same. Our exile was not the same. Or was it? I watched the profile of his face out of the corner of my eye and wondered what had drawn us to each other. I did not know. Stojan reached out suddenly and upended his coffee cup into the saucer. The china rim clanked against the plate.

"Are you going to read the grounds?" I asked.

Stojan smiled. "I'll try," he answered. "I always try, but it never seems to work," he continued affably and shrugged.

"How is it done?" I asked. "Can you teach me?"

Stojan looked at the upended cup doubtfully. "I don't think so, really," he answered apologetically. "That is one thing I think you have to be from a certain part of the world to know how to do."

"Oh."

After a while, Stojan flipped his cup back over and peered into the bottom where the grounds had set. He looked for a long time, moving the cup around to look at all the possible angles.

I grew impatient. "Well?"

Stojan was quiet for a moment, and then he looked up at me. "It says that we have a long way to go before we can rest," he announced cryptically.

"Both of us?" I asked doubtfully.

"I think so," he answered.

"Wait. Why does *your* cup tell about *my* future?" I challenged him jokingly.

He looked up and smiled broadly at me. "The grounds read only my own future," he said. "But that does not mean that futures are not mutual."

"You're so full of shit," I laughed in protest. "Show me where it says that!"

He leaned over and tipped the cup toward me. I looked in and saw a series of swirls and cracks in the drying paste of the coffee grounds.

"You see those two lines that run parallel to one another, and they go across the whole bottom of the cup?"

"Yes."

"That is the future, and it is the future of two people walking together, but they don't intersect," he explained.

I was silent.

"They can't intersect, but they are parallel."

"OK … " I said absurdly.

"And you see how around those cracks are the swirls in the grounds that have no pattern to them?"

"Yes."

"This is the world that the two walk through. There are some of those swirls between the lines, and this is why they cannot intersect. When they try, they are prevented," he explained.

"Stojan?"

"Yes?" he answered.

"This is ridiculous," I said authoritatively.

He shrugged, and did not seem to care.

"What makes you think that the parallel lines represent people? And even if they do, what makes you think it has anything to do with me?"

He was surprised by that. "Because you are here," he answered simply.

"How about if I leave?" I replied.

"It will not change that you were here," he answered.

I was silent, regarding the grounds.

"Why don't you read mine?" I asked.

Stojan peered into my cup at a glistening mass of indeterminate sludge.

"It says nothing," he announced.

"Why not?" I demanded.

"Because you didn't finish drinking your coffee, so the grounds did not set."

"I can't drink it all," I explained. The grounds get in my mouth and it's disgusting."

"That's why it doesn't work unless you're from my part of the world!" he laughed, and got up to carry the plates back into the kitchen. I didn't offer to help. I smoked while he cleaned, and halfway through the washing of the dishes, he began to sing. I froze, listening to him. I had never in my life heard such singing. His voice was sonorous and perfect, floating out through the open balcony door. He sang in a strange register that rose and fell in even meter and then dropped off lower at the end of each verse. A chill crawled across my skin. I tried to understand the words. I could understand "fog," "falling," "Kosovo," "nothing," "alive," "tree," and "tall." My grammar was too poor to string the words together. It sounded more like a chant than a proper song—it did not stray from the few staggered notes that rose and fell with the tenor of his voice. It was beautiful and haunting and it seemed to reach into my chest and twist my heart in a painful vise. I wanted him to stop. But when he stopped, I was sorry.

He emerged on the balcony with a bottle of Corona that had a wedge of lime stuffed into its neck. "I like Mexican beers," he said apologetically. "They seem to do less liver damage." He looked at me with a puzzled expression.

"Why do you look like that?" he asked with his brow furrowed.

"What is that song you were singing?" I asked. My throat felt unexpectedly tight.

"I think it's a threshing song," he shrugged.

"What do you mean, 'a threshing song'?"

"A threshing song," he repeated. "We sing when we thresh fields."

He thought for a moment. "Or maybe it's a wedding song," he offered. "I'm not sure." He shrugged again.

"Can you teach it to me?" I asked.

He sat down, still holding the two Coronas. "Really?" he seemed surprised.

I looked away. "That's OK," I said, suddenly embarrassed.

"It is a women's song, I think," he said. "I'm not sure where it comes from, actually. Kosovo, I guess." After a moment of silence, Stojan started to sing, slowly. "Gusta mi magla … "

He paused, and I looked at him. He nodded at me.

"Sing," he offered.

"I can't," I answered immediately. I felt that my request had ruined the way I felt at hearing him sing. I saw that I wanted him to go back in the kitchen and sing the song again so I could just listen to it.

"Gusta mi magla padnala … " he sang again.

I looked at him silently.

"OK," said Stojan matter-of-factly. He handed me one of the Coronas. "Drink this," he ordered.

I accepted the bottle with a murmur of thanks and took a few swallows.

"Gusta mi magla … " he sang again. He wasn't going to let it go.

"Stojan, I don't think I can do it," I said doubtfully. "I've never threshed anything in my life," I tried to joke, but it sounded dull and contrived and I was embarrassed.

He laughed at that. Then he turned to gaze out over the balcony railing, the sweat from his Corona pooling on the milk crate and dripping down between the evenly spaced perforations. He started to sing it again, from the beginning, and his voice swelled up with so much emotion I couldn't look at him. For long seconds, I listened with my breath coming tight in my chest, but I couldn't look at him. Again, I only understood those few words.

When he had finished the song, I asked him what the words meant.

He considered for a moment. "I can see a thick fog falling over Kosovo," he translated carefully. "Nothing is alive; we can see nothing but a single tall tree." He paused. "It goes on strangely, about how many stars are in the sky and then something about tailors, and I have to say that I don't understand all the words myself because they are written in a very specific old dialect that is spoken in Kosovo. We would just change the words in Bosnia. We change words to these songs very frequently, but their musical measurements don't change."

I drank my Corona. "Sing it again," I half-asked, half-commanded.

He did and it seemed to fill up my veins with a kind of strange, muted ecstasy.

I went home that night, and climbed into a bed that had not borne my weight for some time. The sheets were crisp and clean and taut and did not smell like anyone's skin—not even my own. My mind wandered around for a long time, caught in the unfamiliarity of my own apartment. It was a lonely, empty place. It had not even witnessed the cooking of a proper meal. It had not received guests, or been laughed in. And in order to stop thinking about this, I thought instead about my book, which would go to the publisher shortly in its final draft form—my whole professional life stretched across its pages in ordered, even, predictable print. I was less confident in it now, though. Somewhere inside me, there was a faint, insistent voice whispering that I should not send it. Where had that voice come from? I had never heard it before. Perhaps it was the impending performance review, lingering over my shoulder with its rationalized scheme for success like some watchful vampire. Have you given enough of your time? Have you given enough of your resources?

Have you given enough of your soul? Have you published in the best journals, with the best presses, presented your research at the most prestigious conferences? I had, on occasion, done some of these things, and I was confident about tomorrow, but I also knew that it was never enough. It would never be enough. Stojan was right. At the end of my life, I would be alone with my books and their words would be no company at all.

I climbed out of my cold, unslept-in bed and padded in bare feet across the apartment to the refrigerator. There were two English bitters in the door, and not much else. I took one and cracked it open, and the tab released a burst of gas that turned the amber beer creamy pale. I poured it into a tall glass and wandered out into the living room. I stayed awake deep into the heart of the night, rolling cigarettes and drinking the beer and thinking alternately about the book I had written and Stojan Sokolović. He had interrupted me in some way. He disrupted me, made me wonder about what I was doing, what I was trying to say and why, to whom, and for what purpose? I didn't want to think about this. It made me feel afraid for a reason I could not discern. Maybe it was that mine was just another book on war for a world already choked with them, and nothing was changed by it. All the shelves in my office were groaning under the weight of books on Bosnia, I thought, and Luka Sokolović was still dead and nothing could be done that would undo that. No clarity of theory, no analytical framework, no perfection of writing or amount of reading and research could bring him back, could undo his death or wipe clean the grief from the hearts of those who loved him. I sat in front of my computer all day, pouring words into paragraphs, into chapters, into articles, into books, and still all of that pain throbbed like a fresh and unsuturable wound, despite all the publications in all the academic journals of the world. Lukas are piled up like firewood for the competitive flames of my profession, I thought. And there was nothing I could think of to make it alright.

I sang out quietly into the dark: "Gusta mi magla padnala ... " And then I shook my head, contemptuous of myself.

Somewhere in the long, semi-real world of my professional life, I became hypnotized by my own talent for abstracting and theorizing. It was like a nagging bit of puzzle that couldn't be solved, but that I kept going back to, determined to solve it. After a while, I forgot why I wanted to solve it in the first place, and the solving itself became its own reason, which was no reason at all. This awareness crept up slowly. It was not easily apparent. But after a while I began to realize that I was looking at the caliber of the press to determine the content of the book, and this was because the performance review was coming, and this life was not at all anymore about spreading knowledge, but about ticking boxes on forms handed down from the university administration. And my skin got thicker every year. But Stojan was persistent. He quietly scraped through this skin with his strange pain, so different from my own. He was fucking everything up, and I already knew it then. I was wasting my time with him. I should be doing my work. I resolved to spend less time with him. Better yet, I resolved, I would just stop seeing him at all.

"You're fucking things up, Stojan Sokolović," I said aloud into the silent darkness of my apartment. "I cannot afford for you to fuck these things up."

But then I started thinking about what it could have been like when the soldier from Pale came to the lines around Višegrad to tell Stojan that his brother was dead. I could not feel it. I tried to feel it, and I could not. I could not feel the pain in the other man's body, Stojan Sokolović. I could not feel it, and yet it damaged me.

"Gusta mi magla padnala more na toj mi ramno Kosovo," I sang quietly. Were those the right words? I closed my eyes and tried to remember them. I tried to remember their sequence, their meaning. I tried to feel them in my own body, rather than just hearing them in my head. The need for escape leads us into the heart of philosophy, I reminded myself. When I opened my eyes again, the sun was blaring through the window, and I was still on the couch. I had a moment of real panic thinking I had missed my performance review, but of course I hadn't. It was the first time ever that I was not the first one in the office, though I had still failed to sleep in my own bed. As I walked out the door, I turned back for a moment and regarded that empty space. And it was true. The reason that we never went to my apartment was because nobody lived there.

XIV

Stojan wandered around his apartment after the professor left, wishing he could get a decent night's sleep. He went to bed, struggled to fall asleep, and then woke up in the still light before morning, bathed in sweat. He went to look at himself in the cracked bathroom mirror. He stared at his own reflection and did not recognize himself. What he saw were the eyes of his brother looking back at him. The similarity to Luka, of which he had been so proud growing up, now haunted him mercilessly. He walked out onto the balcony in his shorts and sat down to roll a cigarette. The lacquered floor was cold—it seeped into the soles of his bare feet as he moved through the living room. But the warm night air dried the sweat on his body as he smoked.

"Gusta mi magla," he sang to himself quietly, "padnala more na toj mi ramno Kosovo. Ništa se živo. Ne vidimo do jedno drvo visoko." He thought of Branko, lying supine in the trench with his arms wrapped around his rifle. Branko had two daughters, Pas told him later. Pas said that he would visit those daughters, who were two and five at the moment of his death, and tell them about how brave and loyal their father was.

"I'll tell them," Pas promised Stojan. "He didn't deserve to be here," he went on. "And the men who didn't deserve to be here are the ones who should be respected the most, because they came against their wills."

Pas was referring to all the stragglers who had come over from Serbia—heroin addicts and released criminals and all manner of people who should not be there, not only because they were useless, but because they didn't understand what was going on and this made them unpredictable and dangerous. Branko understood this through his haze of marijuana. He was destroying his own country, and he couldn't live with it. For those Serbian Serbs, it was easy to destroy another man's country. Pas explained all of this to Stojan patiently. But it was at odds with Pas' earlier vehement opposition to the Serbian language being referred to as Serbo-Croatian. Stojan meant to point this out to Pas, but by that time he had already realized that there was no logic in anything that was going on. He believed Branko when he said that he had witnessed the Serbs trade ammunition for cigarettes. So he didn't contradict Pas. There seemed no point in it.

Stojan and Pas smoked all of Branko's joints over the course of the subsequent weeks as the Serbs regained the territory they had lost on the night of his death. The Bosnian government forces paid a heavy price for overrunning those frontline trenches in the middle of night. The Serbs left none of them alive as they gained ground, so there were very few prisoners.

Pas shrugged at this. "They'll just rejoin their army later if we let them go," he justified. "I don't want to keep shooting at the same Muslims over and over again," he said, echoing Branko's explanation of what happened to the prisoners of war. "I want this fucking thing to be over so I can go home."

Stojan was in agreement. He could feel himself growing less and less interested when he saw what few prisoners there were being taken back behind the Serbian lines. The expressions on their faces alternated between fear, defiance, exhaustion, and resignation, but after a while, Stojan found that he didn't really care what happened to them. He had stopped looking at their faces. Reports were circulating that the Bosnian army was cutting the heads off of Serbian prisoners and stuffing them inside the sliced open bellies of pigs. And now there were mujahedin in the hills as well.

"If you see an Arab," advised one of the battalion commanders one morning, "you shoot him immediately. I don't care if he promises you all the oil in Yemen. Shoot him, because he's a crafty fucker and he has no business being here."

Pas laughed at that.

Stojan snuffed out his cigarette on the concrete floor of the balcony and went back inside. It was not yet morning, but he knew he would not be able to fall back asleep, so he dressed and went out to the Orthodox church. There were two Serbian churches in the city: one for the communists and one for the nationalists. Stojan chose the communists' church, because the nationalists' church was hostile to the refugees who had come from the Bosnian war. The nationalists' church was populated by the old immigration; the communists' church, by the new. Apparently, the old immigrants were incensed that the new immigrants collected refugee welfare and had the opportunity to complete university degrees. This was the main cause of the divide among the immigrant Serbs in this city of their exile, and it plagued all their attempts to do anything collectively. But Stojan did not care. He didn't want to do anything collectively anymore. He wasn't interested in community. He went to the church for different reasons.

He stepped out into the silent street. The light was bruised and purplish with the impending sunrise, and there was a ghostly glow about everything. He walked alone along the sidewalk, finding it strange that there was nothing to be heard in this big city but his own footsteps. As he passed an alley loaded with garbage bins, he heard a high, thin mewling and he paused to look. A tiny black kitten was sitting on the stained sidewalk beside one of the bins. When he stopped, it ambled out onto the street and mewled again. Stojan stood regarding it for a moment. It responded by pausing and sitting purposefully down on the pavement, looking up at him steadily.

Stojan sighed and bent over with his hand outstretched. The kitten stood up and came cautiously closer to him. He reached out and picked it up. It didn't resist, and he placed it carefully in the pocket of his spring jacket. It stayed there quietly, and Stojan went on to the church.

The heavy oak door of the church was always unlocked, and Stojan slipped through the doorway into the comparatively cool nave. It smelled faintly of incense and the heavy, honey scent of melting beeswax candles. The iconostasis was a massive, shadowy screen brooding in the low light. In the back of the nave, near the entrance, there were pyramid piles of candles sorted by thickness. There was a small wooden hinged box with a slot in the top for depositing money. Stojan reached into his pocket for his change, and found the kitten instead. It raised its head and peered anxiously around the church. Stojan felt around underneath it and came up with a few bills. He deposited them in the box and gathered several candles from the thin pile.

As he walked over to the troughs of sand where other candles were still burning, he heard the low creak of the door that led through the iconostasis into the sanctuary. The shadow of a young priest filled the cracked doorway. When he saw Stojan with the candles, he closed the door quietly again and retreated. Stojan stood in front of his candles for a while, feeling a hollow emptiness creep into his bones. He watched the small flames on the candles, mesmerized by them, and felt nothing. He couldn't understand that nothingness that welled up in him. He came to light candles so that he might feel something—so that he might make sense of the fact that he so often felt nothing beyond a vague sense that the things he had seen had actually never happened, so far removed did they seem from this new life. The kitten squirmed in his pocket and cried out thinly. Stojan lifted it up and it settled against his chest in his cradled arm.

The door in the iconostasis creaked open again, and the priest peered out of the shadows.

"God's greetings, brother," he said quietly. The cavernous church amplified his voice.

Stojan turned and nodded at him. "Hello," he replied politely.

The priest tiptoed out into the nave, leaving the door open behind him, and crossed the stone floor to where Stojan was standing.

"What an impressive example of a cat," the priest offered.

"I found it on the way here," Stojan explained, turning to face him.

The young priest smiled. "Would you like a drink?" he asked Stojan.

"No, thank you," Stojan answered politely.

The priest nodded. "I am new to this church," the priest explained. "I don't know many of the parishioners yet."

"I'm not a parishioner," Stojan replied.

The priest nodded. "Do you know Father Ilija?" he asked.

"No," answered Stojan, "I don't."

"He is one of the regular priests here," the young priest explained. "The other is Father Petar. I am only here as an interim, for a month, while Father Petar is away in Bosnia."

Stojan nodded. "I haven't met them," Stojan said to him. "But I only come sometimes at night." He shrugged at his own feeble attempt at explanation.

"Many people come at night," the young priest replied, as though this were a perfectly normal thing to do. "The Serbs of this city are night people," he added thoughtfully.

Stojan nodded and looked around. "I have to go now," he apologized.

The priest nodded. "Come and go as you please," he said quietly. "We leave the doors open always."

"I know." Stojan nodded again and retreated toward the street.

The priest sighed. He was looking forward to the end of his time here. Father Ilija had instructed him to leave the doors open at night, and the young interim priest soon understood why. Serbs wandered in at all hours, depending on the depth of their grief and when it struck them. Father Ilija had also instructed him to invite any late night visitors for a drink of brandy, which he kept in a cupboard in the sacristy. The interim followed the instructions, sitting up in the dim glow of the lamplight while he read the epistles of Paul and waited for his visitors. At first, he thought that Father Ilija must be exaggerating. But then they began to arrive. And the interim would creep out through the door of the sanctuary and invite them to the sacristy for a brandy.

More often than not, the visitor would sit down bewildered for a moment, women and men alike, and then they would gather themselves and tell some story: a son who never came home; a mother who died trying to cross the lines; a brother who was captured crossing the Miljacka River in Sarajevo, and who was forced to drink a bottle of cola mixed with crushed glass before being sent back to his own side to die slowly and in agony. The interim priest had already heard many, many stories. One or two drinks would usually calm them down long enough so that they could take temporary comfort in the word of God. The priest was aware of the irony of this, but he did not know what else to do.

Most of the tales that blew in with the wind at night were tales of loss and grief over dead family members and friends. But some of them were different. Some of the tale-tellers, invariably men, told other stories, and they were stories that made the priest drink of his own brandy after they had left. They talked about what they had witnessed, and some gave veiled impressions that they were responsible for Muslim women and girls locked in a barn on a threshing floor, and all the weeping and begging in the world—all the appeals to decency, honor, family lineage, and Serbian saints—could not save them from soldiers drunk and sober, brutally cruel and unreachable. Sometimes they knew them. Sometimes they were neighbors. Sometimes they would call them by name in the vocative case: a desperate query to which the soldier would never respond, because he had already denied what he had done before he ever decided to do it at all. He had forgotten their faces, which were pale with terror at first, and dark with shame afterward, and blank with disbelief when it didn't end. Prisoners were often shot in their faces, their feet; they were lined up by twos and executed without a second thought. Houses were burned carefully, after the registry had been checked first to identify and separate those who waited for Yeshua as the Messiah, and those who considered him only a prophet of God. Even the lambs that had their throats cut on the day of a feast died for a reason. But those who carried out these executions did not know why they were doing so. One says that he heard a survivor's account of Srebrenica on the radio from Tuzla. Everyone in the trenches on the Serbian side was listening to this broadcast. The commanding officer came and told them to turn the radio off. "We are not listening to enemy radio," he said. A soldier asked the commanding officer about the deaths. He said to the interim priest, "I had said that we knew the people killed were all simple people, and asked for the reason why they had to be killed. I said that even if they were all chickens that were killed, there still had to be a reason." The officer didn't answer him. If the Serbs in the trenches would only turn off the radio, it seemed, the dead would miraculously disappear.

"I'll tell you, priest, why Serbs bulldozed the people they had killed into mass graves," offered one of the night visitors. "They weren't worried about the evidence. Who was thinking about war crimes? The Geneva Conventions? They weren't thinking about any of that shit. No one used the word 'genocide.' It was their job to make things 'clean.' And they did. They already knew that the satellites can pinpoint the graves. Burying the dead wasn't about hiding them from The Hague. It was about getting them out of sight, so that it could be forgotten. If we can just get them buried—get the job done—then we can get drunk, and pretend that it didn't happen, pretend that the bodies are not there. Pretend that they simply never existed. Soil can cover up consciences as well as bodies. We didn't want to see them anymore. And we never talked about what we had done. Can you absolve me, priest? Can you make it go away?"

"I cannot," said the priest, ashamed, and ashamed of his shame.

But even these were not the hardest ones for the young priest. The people who came into his sacristy at night could put their lives and deeds into language—could trace out the contours and the parameters of what they had seen and done. There was a finitude to these stories. They began and they concluded. The hardest ones were those who wandered into the nave from the street with faces that were unreadable, who did not weep, and who could neither remember nor forget, and who thus occupied a strange place from which it seemed they could not articulate anything. These were the ones that truly terrified the priest—that haunted him into a state where even the Sermon on the Mount could not comfort him. They stood facing the iconostasis in such a way that it seemed as though they wanted to flee their own skins. They scanned the icons, searching for something that was never found, because they kept coming back, again and again. They didn't call on the priest. They didn't tap on the sacristy door in the hope of obtaining absolution so they could sleep at night and get on with the somnambulism of their reconstructed lives. They always declined the priest's offer for a drink. These night visitors already knew that forgiveness was impossible. The priest, after weeks of watching them, suspected that these were the ones who knew why they had done what they had—the ones who could not allow themselves to forget the faces of the people who had implored them in vain to make a different choice. These were the ones who were aware of the delicate balance between the killing and the dying. And they were meting out time like knots on a prayer rope, unsure of where to go, what to do, how to get out from under it. They knew the priest couldn't help them. And the priest also knew it. They came to the church on instinct alone, knowing in their hearts that there was simply nothing to be done. They made his blood run cold.

XV

The sun climbed up over the horizon in the eastern sky, staining the scattered low clouds with a delicate blush. Jelena dropped her coffee cup in the sink and stepped out of the apartment. Milan came home from his walk to the sound of the telephone ringing, and he reached over to answer it. For a long time afterward, Milan would wish that he had not. On the other end of the line was Stojan Sokolović, who was asking after his brother, Luka, who died on the front line north of Sarajevo on the 19th of December, on the feast of Saint Nikola in 1992. Milan went slowly numb with shock. In his misplaced heart, he had always known it would happen someday. The phone would ring, or the intercom would buzz to alert him to the presence of the seeker who would be waiting in the lobby of the apartment building. Milan's knuckles burned white as he clutched the phone. His head swam. He had known, but no amount of knowing could prepare him for the day.

Stojan was careful and hesitant. He said that he had heard the story that Milan Milanović told. He heard it after the war, in a café in Pale. He did not attend his brother's funeral, he said. He was on a front line in the ancestral mountains of the east. It was very bad fighting there, and they would not let him leave. But this was beside the point. Stojan said in his careful, hesitant way that he needed to know what happened to his brother, and that he needed Milan to help him.

The blood returned to Milan's face and he sank down onto the couch with the phone line wrapped around his hand. The sun poured through the blinds. He heard Stojan as though from very far away. His ears were ringing, and his heart was pounding in his mouth. He cursed himself for ever having spoken. He cursed himself for his weakness. He cursed himself for not going to Australia. His tongue felt too thick, his mouth too dry. Something felt lodged in his chest—something constrictive that prevented him from catching his breath. Milan met Stojan's request with complete silence. It was not because of his hardness, but because of his shock.

It had not occurred to Stojan that shock would be the visceral, gut reaction of the man on the other end of the phone. He interpreted the silence as intransigence. "Please meet me," Stojan implored in a new, persuasive voice. He said that he couldn't sleep. He said that he couldn't live. He said he had panic attacks. He all but begged. "I live very close to you," Stojan announced into the silence of the telephone wire. "We can meet for coffee. We can talk." He paused, and then breathed into Milan's silence: "You can tell me why you took my brother's girl with you to Canada."

And Milan, whose shock might have given way to mercy had he enough time to process what was happening, became angry at this. He bypassed mercy entirely, and headed for the safety of outrage. "Why I took his girlfriend? She is not a pet, cousin. She comes and goes as she pleases!"

"I'm sorry," Stojan conceded rapidly, backtracking. "But I'm begging you."

Milan was silent for a moment. He was thinking, thinking, and could not think. "Why do you want to ruin my life?" was finally all he could whisper into the phone.

"Because mine is already ruined," Stojan answered softly, without hesitation. "And you are the man who knows why."

Milan panicked silently. He knew he could not say no. If he did not go, Stojan would come to the house. He would come to find Jelena. He would tell her what he had heard, and she would want to know everything. She would recognize him, Milan, for who he was—she would know about his lie—the lie that had brought him to Pale in the first place, which was the lie on which their whole subsequent life had been built. Jelena would offer Stojan Sokolović—who was meant to be her brother-in-law—a place at their table if he came to the door. She would make him coffee. Maybe she would even cook him a meal. Most importantly, they would talk. And she would know. He felt as he had felt at the crossing to Serbia at the last mobilization—trapped. And the German marks were long, long gone.

"Alright," Milan relented.

"When?" Stojan asked.

"Tomorrow," answered Milan. "I'll meet you tomorrow."

Fear and anger are first reactions and, in more or less time, they give way to more useful cerebral phenomena, such as calculation. Milan lay awake all night after hearing Stojan Sokolović's voice on the telephone line, trying to figure out what he should do. Jelena slept beside him with her arm flung up over her head in her characteristic way, oblivious and unsuspecting. His mind raced everywhere, looking for a way out of meeting with the brother of the man who had ill-fatedly decided to go home through the forest so long ago. He tried to remember how much he had told the soldier in the café in Pale, but for Milan that conversation had taken place in another lifetime and, although he could remember every single detail about the death of Luka Sokolović, he could not remember what, exactly, he had told the soldier who had taken his story to all the small villages of Romanija. Hour after endless hour, his mind raced around and his thoughts dashed back and forth through bits of the past that could not be accurately sequenced or clearly remembered.

The dead should be buried in such a way that they stay dead, he thought feverishly. They should not come back to haunt this life, which is hard enough as it is. He could not figure out if he was angrier with himself, Luka, or Stojan. He hated them all, including himself, equally. He rolled over to look at his wife, and felt a flash of hatred for her, too. Why was it his fault that she tried to kill herself? Why was he responsible for that? He felt overcome with hatred for a moment. Then his guilt softened him, even as he tried to absolve himself for telling the story that had now caused Stojan Sokolović to finally seek him out. And he remembered the approach of that long-dead soldier through the woods, moving fast, running in sneakers because his army had run out of proper boots in his size.

Milan lay awake, and he remembered. He was scared, and had worked hard to keep his mouth shut. So why couldn't he continue to keep his mouth shut afterward? Milan simply couldn't believe what had happened in that hollow on the feast of Saint Nikola. It had been so flatly sickening that he often wondered whether he had dreamed it. He had had to tell someone. He couldn't bear the memory of what he had witnessed, and in some way he knew even then that time would not make it go away. It could not go away. It was still fresh in his mind all these years later, present in a visceral way, in the tides of blood that washed around inside his body and in his heart, which had betrayed him so unforgivably at the moment of Luka's death. This meeting is pointless, he thought hopelessly. What is the point of this? I can't do anything about it. Why does he want to meet me? What difference would it make now? It did not occur to Milan that his hatred might more rightfully be leveled at the Ivan. But for Milan, the Ivan was a constant in an equation animated by other variables. Luka Sokolović could have been anyone, and Milan always knew that. He did not die because he was Luka Sokolović. He died because he had the misfortune of encountering the Ivan—he became an unfortunate variable trapped in an equation that was not of his own making. And yet, Luka's death remained his own, despite the Ivan's attempts to deny him that.

And then Milan Milanović, who had a keen desire to protect himself, realized that he could lie. He could tell Stojan Sokolović that he didn't know what he was talking about. That he didn't know anything about what he was asking, that he had never seen anything, but only heard some stories that he later repeated because the whole war was full of stories and everyone was worried for his own skin, and they were all talking about what they had heard in the hope of discerning from someone else's fate what the future might bring for themselves. Wondering at other people's deaths was like reading coffee grounds—you looked for some sense of your own fate in them. The war had made everyone a liar, thought Milan bitterly. The war had made it so that one could not distinguish at all between what was true and what false, between victims and perpetrators, or between perpetrators and perpetrators, or victims and victims. They had all been in some measure perpetrators and victims simultaneously, and this was the measure of that war—one could not insert a cigarette paper in between the skins of the killers and the killed, so close were they, and so inextricable from one another. But Milan felt Luka staring at him from somewhere out in the dark with his big, uncomprehending, paler than pale eyes, and Milan thought that Luka would probably not agree with that assessment.

"I was not guilty," Milan whispered to him the darkness. "Go away!" And Luka retreated a bit. Milan was encouraged. Then he whispered another lie, a larger one, the one that he planned to tell Stojan Sokolović: "I was not there."

Milan watched his wife sleeping in the soft glow of the streetlight, and he felt more trapped than he had ever been. He wished that he had stayed in Belgrade with Vesna.

The next day he entered the café to wait for Stojan, his face drawn with sleeplessness. He ordered a double espresso and dumped three sugar packets into it. He found a quiet corner table and waited, peering through the window into the street in the hope that he would see Stojan before Stojan saw him. He wanted that precious extra time to think over his muddled mental notes and to prepare himself for a conversation that he knew at some level could not be rehearsed beforehand, because a conversation always involves at least two people, which inevitably destroys the well-laid plans of both. Milan did not want to be tricked, persuaded, or threatened into telling any more than what he had already decided to tell, which was nothing.

But Stojan was already there in his blue button-down shirt that exaggerated the strange hue of his eyes. He had been there for an hour, waiting to get ready to wait. He had seen Milan walk through the door and recognized him immediately, though they had never met. Despite his unease, Stojan found it almost amusing that he could almost always recognize another Serb, though he could not explain to himself why this was so. But around the edges of that absurd amusement, seeing Milan made him feel physically ill, and he could not decide whether or not to stand up and walk over to him. He was not sure that his legs would bear his own weight. His stomach turned, as though it had been suddenly filled with some kind of hot oil. His espresso grew cold while he was searching himself and trying to determine if he could get up or not. Milan continued to peer out the window, his cup left untouched in front of him. It was torturous, watching and waiting and being unsure if one's body could carry one's weight across a small coffee shop to hear a tale either confirmed or denied, and not knowing which of the tales would be worse. His heart was slamming steadily against his ribs, and he felt a flush of sweat under his arms. This was the man who saw his brother die, Stojan thought coldly, and he studied the other man's face. He was unshaven, and his brow was furrowed with lines too deep for a young man. He looked out into the street, and his worry was a visible thing. He wore it on his skin. Stojan wondered if it was true that his heart beat in his mouth instead of his chest, and then decided that this was technically impossible—just another unbelievable story from a nation of people that were full of them. But Stojan did not realize until later that his doubt in that moment was its own measure of betrayal against the stories that he himself had told and believed. It was a betrayal of his own sense of the order of things.

Stojan finally tried to stand, not because he felt he was ready to do so, but because Milan was looking more and more nervous and Stojan thought he might leave. His skin was pale underneath the day's growth of beard, and he looked like he might bolt out the door at any moment. Stojan walked across the tiled floor of the café, weaving between the flocks of new mothers who were flanked on all sides by massive baby carriages. He barely noticed them. It took him what felt like the better part of a lifetime to arrive at the pale veneer table where Milan was waiting and wishing that he was not waiting.

"Milan Milanović," Stojan greeted him in a voice that was a whisper.

Milan's heart began to pulse in his mouth, and he said resignedly, quietly, "Stojan Sokolović," in reply.

They stared at each other, one with dark eyes, one with light, each of them struggling over the same thing, but differently. Stojan stood over the table, unsure of what to do. His body felt cumbersome—a burden of weight measured in flesh and bone. The chair in which he wanted to sit was too far away. The sun was too hot, flooding through the double-glazed window that amplified its heat a thousand-fold. His stomach was filled with that oil. A droplet of sweat broke loose and ran in a rapid rivulet down his chest. It felt like an insect moving there on his skin, and Stojan rubbed the palm of his hand over the place where it had passed. The patch of sweat was absorbed by his shirt and it darkened the fabric.

Milan waited for Stojan to say something more. He had resolved that he would be economical. He would not offer any information about which he had not been directly asked. He would keep it short, and then he would leave. He would go back to his life. But Stojan looked lost instead of angry, and Milan had not expected this. He had not expected him to look so like his brother. He had not expected to see beads of sweat on the man's face, which was already too pale, or the bloodshot network of veins in the whites of his eyes that betrayed his own sleeplessness. He did not expect to feel such sympathy for this other man, who was confused and quiet and unsure of where to begin. He did not expect to see Stojan Sokolović wearing his grief on his skin, or that it would still be so raw. Milan was instantly transported to the day that Luka Sokolović was shot, and somewhere inside him he felt something begin to crack.

So despite his plans and his careful logic, he said flatly, "Sit down, Stojan Sokolović. I'll tell you everything I saw."

Stojan sat down across from him and they looked at one another, Milan with eyes so dark that one could not distinguish between the iris and the pupil, Stojan with the strange light eyes that he shared with both of his brothers, and with all the other members of his family up in the high hills of Romanija.

"Tell me," sighed Stojan. But now that he was faced with it, he was not sure that he wanted to know, and he thought that he might heave his body up from the table and run out the door at any moment.

Milan looked at him, his heart pounding in his mouth. He could feel himself coming apart, and he had a fleeting sense that he was nothing but an empty shell held together by the ever-weakening glue of his evasions and lies. Already, he was being hollowed out. Already, he was being taken over, and he remembered with perfect, unbidden clarity the approach of this man's brother in the hills behind the lines. He remembered the Ivan. Holy Christ, he thought suddenly. How do I tell him this? How do I tell him what I saw? Where can I start? It was now clear that there could be no lying to this other man, who did not know what had happened to his brother, and who could not live with that unknowing.

XVI

I stalked confidently down the hall toward the departmental committee room with my briefcase tucked under my arm and my heels clicking authoritatively on the tiled floor. The performance review committee was waiting. The dull fragrance of percolating drip-coffee hung in the air of the stuffy, windowless room.

"Good morning!" I smiled at the three committee members as I took my seat and opened my briefcase.

"Good morning," Bill replied. "Help yourself to coffee." He gestured to the carafe perched on a little side table.

"Thank you," I answered, and rose to pour the thin, watery liquid into a fresh Styrofoam cup. It looked awful. I stared at it for a moment and then turned to take my seat.

There was a brief shuffling of papers as each of us arranged and organized our documents.

Bill was the first one to speak. "As you know," he addressed me, "you are here under the terms of the accelerated performance review. We would like you to briefly summarize what you consider to be the most salient contributions to the profession over the last year. We would like you to speak for fifteen to twenty minutes, and then the members of the committee may have some questions for you. Does that seem agreeable?" he asked politely.

I nodded tersely. "It does, indeed." I looked down at the stack of documents that contained my curriculum vitae, copies of my journal articles, and teaching evaluations. There was a page of talking points that I had drawn up, to remind myself of what I wanted to emphasize. I paused to take a sip of my coffee. It was disgusting. I forced myself to swallow it. I thought of the copper džezva with the desert animals stamped on it. Then I gathered myself together, looked up at the members of the committee and began.

"Thank you all very much for coming this morning. I really appreciate your time and the opportunity to talk to you about my research and teaching." I paused briefly for effect. "My most significant contribution to the profession this year has been the completion of my monograph, which was successfully reviewed in early April and is ready to go to press. I have also authored two journal articles, both of which were accepted with minimal revisions." I named the very respectable journals. I noticed one of the reviewers nodding appreciatively. I went on: "One of those articles was accepted into a special forum on genocide, and it appears alongside articles by academics widely regarded as eminent leaders in their respective fields."

I talked for my fifteen minutes, detailing my contributions, the articles I was currently writing, and the status of progression on my funding proposal. I walked them page by page through my curriculum vitae, pointing out elements that were of particular importance. But really, on the face of it, the only thing that mattered was my book, which was sitting smugly in the very first line of text.

When I had said what I wanted to say, I reached over to pick up my coffee, looked at the liquid that appeared to be dirty water, and then withdrew my hand again. I felt a brief flash of nausea.

Bill was nodding slowly. "I have to say that the production of the monograph is extremely impressive for such an early career scholar."

"Yes," one of the other members murmured.

"Is it actually in press right now?" the third committee member asked.

I hesitated. "It is sealed and ready to go," I answered.

"So it is not actually in press yet," he clarified.

"No, but the contract is in place and the draft is sealed and ready to go. All I need to do is walk it down to the mail room," I answered firmly. "I'll do that this afternoon," I promised. But I didn't.

XVII

"I'll tell you everything," Milan whispered across the table. "But please forgive me. I should have killed the Ivan myself. I didn't know it would happen. I didn't. How could I know? I didn't know. It was cold ... December ... the feast of Saint Nikola ... " Milan Milanović trailed off, and the desolation in both his words and in his voice was obvious. He realized with a wash of shock that it was Serbian coming out of his mouth. Serbian, the language he had tried to forget—to shed like an unwanted skin. The oily feeling rose in Stojan's stomach, threatening to spill out of his throat across the table—a liquid volley of grief built up over all these years of his exile—winter after winter, feast day after feast day.

"What happened to my brother?" he managed to ask.

And Milan told him everything. He told him about how the Ivan had been so excited earlier in the day at the prospect of "shooting something." He told him about how much brandy they were drinking, about how Milan was afraid of the Ivan, so kept close to him, because of his fear, and because he didn't want to be the "something" that the Ivan shot. He told him about their joking in the hollow, their boasting about how many they would kill, and the criteria for targets. "Who would you kill?" asked one, who was called Nebojša, and who came from the rock-strewn, scrub hills of Hercegovina. "I would kill every Muslim on the planet," answered

Milan, though he never knew what made him say this. "I would kill everyone who married a Muslim," declared Dimitrije, a skinny kid with pitted skin from the town of Omarska in the north. The Ivan leaned close to them, and took the bottle of brandy from Nebojša. "I would kill a deserter," he declared after he had swallowed down a mouthful of the clear, plum-fragrant liquid.

Dimitrije from Omarska, whose uncle would be the first to be convicted by the court at The Hague for his role as a commander of the detention camp there, hissed to the others to be quiet, because someone was approaching. They grew silent, listening. They heard the creak of the leather strap on the rifle of the one who was coming—the one who was coming but who had not yet arrived. He was in-coming. They heard his sneaker-clad feet crunching against the frozen ground, snapping twigs. They heard him slip on some patch of icy ground, and then recover. They heard him breathing heavily. Were they frightened? Milan wanted to believe they had been, because that might provide some measure of justification for what followed. He searched his soul, desperate for Luka to bear in some measure the responsibility for his own death. So he wanted to say that they had been frightened. Who was coming? How many were there? But it was obvious that the runner was alone and that he himself was not concerned about the noise he was making as he moved. Why was he running? Where was he going? And Milan knew that they were not afraid. Even he was not afraid, being armed to the teeth and pleasantly warm and slightly drunk from the brandy. The approaching runner became terribly important simply by virtue of the fact that they were bored. They were warm and drunk in a hollow in a forest in the middle of a war, each of them wishing vaguely to be somewhere else. Sometimes, the war was a terrible tedium of boredom. That was true. And in this way, they had also forgotten that they were in the middle of a war. It was easy to forget that one's whole life had been torn open like a bag of grain, because the torn-ness of it all quickly became normal, and it was thus possible to forget what one suddenly found oneself in the middle of. It was no longer an exceptional place to be and after a while it just became a life indistinguishable from any other. It became a life of drunkenness and boredom and boastful stories about how many they would kill, interspersed with the actual killing itself, which, as the neighbor from Pale who brought the news of Luka's death to Stojan outside of Višegrad had observed, was easier than the mourning.

The runner was louder now. Closer. The Ivan readied his rifle, clicking off the safety. The runner must have heard it, because he stopped moving immediately. He looked around, and they could see him now as he stood indecisive, trying to determine where the sound had come from. He seemed as if he was trying to decide if he should call out—if he should stop. Milan knew all these years later that if he hadn't stopped, they would have hunted him. Maybe the runner knew it, too. He stopped at the sound of the hollow click of a rifle at the ready. The runner began to move again, but cautiously, having guessed right as to the direction of the sound, and he slowly approached the hollow. He never even pulled his own rifle from his shoulder. It hung down uselessly at his side, the barrel pointing at the frozen ground. He paused again, again unsure, and the Ivan, who was in charge of the soldiers in the hollow in practice if not in fact, called out to him in a voice that was unusually reassuring. He asked the runner his name. The runner hesitated, maybe wondering for a split second whether he hadn't stumbled across somehow into Federation territory.

"Sokolović, Luka," he replied softly.

"Which is your saint day?" the Ivan asked.

"Today. Nikola," Luka answered, and he slowly approached to find four soldiers of the Serb Republic huddled together with a bottle of brandy.

"Brother!" declared Milan Milanović. "Where are you rushing to? Stay and have a drink!" But for some reason, Milan did not feel drunk anymore. He realized that it was cold, that his fingers were numb, and that he wanted to go home.

"Why are you wearing sneakers?" inquired Nebojša from Hercegovina.

Luka laughed. "They ran out of boots in my size!"

The Ivan, disappointed, lowered his rifle. He had wanted to shoot a Muslim. Even a Croat would do, though there were few of them around these lines. But he couldn't shoot a Serb, and this man wore the colors of Serbia on his uniform. He listened as Luka Sokolović explained where he was going. He had a permit to leave for three days to celebrate the feast of Nikola, he said. He was going to see his girl in Pale.

The Ivan suddenly looked up at Luka with contempt.

"You've abandoned your brothers on the front line!" the Ivan declared. How could this be permitted? The Serbs were more exposed to the enemy now. One of them might be killed as a result of this idiot's desertion. "What the fuck were you thinking?" The Ivan raised his rifle against the lone figure of Luka Sokolović. "Go back to your fucking position," he said softly. "There's a fucking war on."

Luka Sokolović stood above the hollow looking down at them, and he wore a look of simple puzzlement in his pale, pale eyes.

"No, no," he said with easy reassurance. "You misunderstood me." Luka smiled. It was not a fearful smile, but a confident smile. He reached into his pocket and said, "I have three days of leave."

"I don't have three days of fucking leave!" announced Milan. But he did not know why he had said it. He really didn't begrudge Luka his leave. It was his saint day.

"Me, neither!" complained Dimitrije from Omarska.

And then, amazingly, Luka took several steps toward them. He was open-handed, completely exposed. His pale eyes registered his confusion. He trusted them. With a rifle pointed at his chest, he trusted them.

"This is Europe!" Stojan heard his brother saying as Milan spoke.

"It's not fucking Europe!" he now heard Jelena's voice that day beneath the trees when Stojan was mobilized. But it *was* Europe—a Europe that justified its own history of outrage by identifying it now everywhere else.

"Who's your girl?" asked Nebojša, who did not really understand, Milan thought, what was unfolding here.

"Jelena Dragojević, from Gorni Pribanj above Pale. Do you know Pale?" asked Luka.

The Ivan stood up with some effort and faced Luka Sokolović. "I know her," he declared. "I'll go and fuck her for you." His rifle was nestled in the hollow of his shoulder, pointed at Luka. And Luka did not even have time to react. Milan had the strange sensation that, even given the chance, Luka might not have reacted at all. He fell like a sack of grain on the hard ground. It seemed to Milan that Luka fell before he heard the shot. The rifle report echoed through the night. The Ivan stared at the body on the ground impassively. He turned and looked down at his friends, suddenly confused. "Did I shoot myself?" he asked them.

No one answered him. The Ivan strode over and kicked the body on the ground. "Fucking deserter! You're a disgrace to the Serbian nation!"

Stojan put his ashen face in his hands, and Milan stopped talking.

"I'm sorry," he said uselessly, but there was no amount of regret that could take it back. He fell into a momentary silence. Yet Milan could not stay silent now. The words, walled up in him for so long, now poured out of him. He moistened his bloodless lips with his cold espresso, and went on with his confession.

It was Dimitrije who figured out that they would probably all go to prison if they were caught. So he suggested that they try to hide the body.

"I'm not hiding the body!" shouted the Ivan. "This man is a fucking deserter!"

Milan walked on numb feet over to where Luka had fallen. His heart crawled slowly up his throat and into his mouth. Milan reached into one of Luka's pockets and found a folded sheet of paper. It was a leave permit, and it was in order. He stared down at the dead runner with disbelieving eyes and lips pressed tightly against his teeth. The paper fluttered in a sudden gust of wind.

"Ivan, we'll go to prison," begged Dimitrije.

The Ivan finally seemed to realize that this was, in fact, a possibility. So he ordered Milan to help him lift Luka's body, and to drop it along with his rifle in the hollow where he had come upon them. Milan wiped his bloodstained hands on the frozen grass, but it remained under his fingernails. And although he scrubbed his hands until they were spotless and raw, he could feel the traces of it lodged there for months afterward.

"Take off his sneakers!" ordered the Ivan. "I want them as a souvenir."

Milan unlaced Luka's shoes with frozen fingers, and tossed them up to the Ivan, who stuffed them into his rucksack.

The Ivan warned his companions in no uncertain terms. "If you talk, you die."

They looked at him wordlessly. They understood.

What happened after that was rumor, heard secondhand, said Milan. The body of Luka Sokolović was found at first light. The officers knew he had been murdered, and they knew that he had probably been murdered by someone in his own ranks. But there was a war going on, and a full investigation would require resources that they were not prepared to spare. One of the officers offered up the possibility that the Muslims had snuck up behind the Serb lines and picked him off like wolves after a lone sheep. It was not outside of the realm of the believable, and it was easier that way.

"Let's clean it up," he pressed the others.

And the others agreed.

And then Milan stopped.

Long minutes passed, and Stojan struggled to hold onto himself. He struggled with the desire to kill Milan, who was looking at him miserably. And then, in the wake of that rage, Stojan just felt empty and sick. The heavy, oily feeling was now in his throat, announcing a familiar nausea from which vomiting could never fully deliver him. He looked up again, and Milan felt that he could see everything in his eyes. He felt that he could smell the grief on the other man's body. Milan saw all of this, maybe even saw that Stojan wanted to kill him, but he did not know what else he could say.

He whispered uselessly, "I'm sorry."

Stojan looked at him with bloodshot eyes and wiped his hand across his mouth.

"I'm sorry," he said again.

But Stojan couldn't answer. He wanted to, but he couldn't.

Milan had wanted to lie, and found that he couldn't lie. Stojan had wanted to know, and found that he couldn't live with knowing any better than he could live with not knowing. They were each overtaken there by Luka Sokolović, and by others, each silently asking for his life back, a gift which no currency could ever buy.

"My father gave you his blessing," Stojan whispered suddenly.

Milan did not answer. He looked away in shame for a moment. And then he looked back. "What can I do now?" he asked helplessly. "How can I make it right?"

"How could you think it was possible to make it right?" Stojan asked incredulously.

"Stojan, I would give my life to go back so I could tell you a different story. But I can't." Milan looked at him miserably. "I can't," he said again.

"You can tell me his surname," said Stojan suddenly.

"What?" Milan asked.

"This Ivan. What is his surname?"

"Vuković," Milan remembered.

"Where was he from?"

"Rogatica. But I heard that secondhand, so I'm not sure." Milan put his head in his hands.

"What is his family's saint day?" Stojan pressed.

"What?" Milan looked up.

"His saint day."

"I don't know," Milan answered truthfully.

Stojan looked at him closely, and Milan saw that Stojan would look for the Ivan. Knowing a man's saint day is crucial to distinguishing him from another man with whom he might share the same surname. Saint days distinguished families, and were unique. "If I knew, I would tell you. I only know that it was not Nikola," Milan insisted.

"Alright." Stojan got up to leave. He was going to be sick, and there was only a small window of time left before it overtook him.

Milan stayed alone at the table for a few moments longer with his cold espresso before him. He watched the thirtysomething women showing off their expensive baby carriages to one another. He felt disconnected, utterly unable to think himself into the normal space that they obviously occupied. He had tried with all his energy to make this country his own—this good state—but he knew somehow that it would never happen. Despite his best efforts, Milan was permanently trapped in the folds in the hills of Bosnia. One of the women was pulling baby clothes from a massive shopping bag—tiny yellow and white socks, buntings, and the white cotton shirts that snap between babies' frog legs. There was a murmur of conversation around him, and laughter. One of the infants let out a low wail of protest for some unknowable reason. The ceramic mugs clinked on the counter as the server deposited them back for washing. He expected to feel better telling Stojan Sokolović the truth. But grief is not a thing that can be cleansed from the skin like salt.

A young girl approached him with a tray of tiny plastic cups. "Sir, would you like to try our new mocha coconut cappuccino?" she asked brightly.

Milan reached out without meaning to, and accepted the little cup with a murmur of thanks. He looked into the girl's smiling face and felt absurdly alien. He felt that he was going through the motions of another man's life, in another man's body. He watched the coconut cream melt into the cappuccino for a moment, and then he left.

XVIII

"Do you know anything about cats?" asked Stojan anxiously when I arrived at his door.

"Cats?" I asked, surprised.

"Cats," he confirmed.

I peered through the doorway behind him and saw a small black kitten sitting placidly on the parquet floor.

"Where did you get a cat?" I asked, pushing past him into the apartment.

"I found it on the street," he answered.

"Well, have you bought anything for it?" I inquired.

Stojan thought for a moment. "I bought food, and a box, and sand," he ticked off the items on his fingers.

"Then you're in good shape," I answered. I picked it up on my way out to the balcony and it settled in my lap quietly.

"What did you name it?" I asked.

"I didn't name it," Stojan answered. "I don't know what to name it. I just call it *mačka*—cat."

I think it needs a name," I offered tentatively.

He shrugged.

I looked more closely at him. He looked exhausted. Stojan wore sleeplessness on his face. Sometimes, I would awaken on his couch in the middle of the night to see him—a massive shadow—leaning over the kitchen sink in the dark, splashing his face with water, and drinking from the faucet out of his cupped hands. Then he would pad across back to his bedroom. As high summer approached, I often grew to stay too late with him on the rusting balcony, and I couldn't be bothered to find my way home again, or to return to the solitude of the office. So I would sleep on his couch. After that whole year spent plagued by loneliness, I was beginning to find that it was increasingly difficult to find my way back and re-enter the frame of my life. But I had not exchanged a difficult life for an easier one. I could feel my academic expertise dissolving all around me, like flesh melting away from my bones. I could feel myself losing the reference points by which I had grown to define my life, first out of curiosity, and then out of habit, and finally out of a chronic inability to choose differently. At first, it was almost imperceptible. It manifested in my increasing disinterest in the journals that arrived in my departmental mailbox. Everything I read seemed completely pointless. Since I had stopped reading, I was slowly beginning to be unable to write anything. I was beginning to feel a cringing shame at my book on Bosnia, which was maybe why I hadn't sent it to the publisher yet. It sat on the edge of my desk day after day, the address of the editor at the press written boldly across the padded envelope in the thick, smug lines of a black marker. But things were beginning to change. I was less and less sure of myself. I was less and less sure of what I was doing, and why. I wanted to escape from myself. I felt in my bones a nausea, a shame, and a strange sense of growing ineptitude. The padded envelope that cocooned the manuscript within it mocked me from the corner of the desk.

Stojan and I shared no past, we shared no memories and no faith— what we had in common was only what seemed at first to be the innocuous intersection of a manuscript proof that had brought us together in an indiscernible way. And I knew after everything was done that it was true that even the things that people seemed to share—the need to eat, to sleep, to love, to know—were still always executed differently. We are not born the same, we do not die the same, we do not sleep the same, and we do not see the same. I saw but could not see. I was lost, and the self that I later found was unrecognizable to me.

On the night after my performance review, which was the night after Stojan Sokolović had met Milan Milanović, I slept on his couch. I slipped uncharacteristically easily below the surface of sleep, but then I fell into a bad space where dreams begin to be senseless and formless and frightening. In the first of these dreams, I thought I could hear Stojan calling out from somewhere far away. But I couldn't see him anywhere. I looked around the doors of the dream, beneath the floorboards, behind the crumbling plaster walls. I heard him now closer, now louder. And all at once, I snapped awake, unsure of where I was, and tangled up in the blankets. I had the sense that there had been some shouting. Of this, I was completely sure. I got up on shaky legs and padded across the floor toward the open door of the bedroom. Stojan was perched on the edge of the bed with his back to the door, his silhouette illuminated by the moonlight which poured through the panes of the window glass. I could see the vertebrae of his spine beneath the white cotton shirt that was plastered to his skin. I curled my hands around the doorframe and looked at him in silence. He held his head in his hands with his elbows propped on his thighs.

"Stojan?" I whispered, and wrapped my arms around myself. I felt cold. "Are you alright?"

He nodded silently, and did not move.

I moved closer until I was standing at the foot of the bed, looking at him from the side, and hesitated.

"Are you sure?" I whispered tentatively.

He nodded again without taking his head from his hands. His breathing was slowing, but still coming in those irregular fits and starts.

I didn't move. I didn't know what to do. I wanted to sit down beside him, to comfort him, but I was also scared of him in some way, because I was afraid of what he had dreamed. I stood in the shaft of moonlight and watched him slowly recover from whatever it was that had happened to him in his sleep. He rubbed the palm of one of his hands along the top of his head, as he had done that day when he wiped the rain from his hair in my office, and raised his face to me. His eyes were literally sparkling in the pale light of the moon. "I'm sorry," he whispered, and he seemed to be looking past me.

"It's alright," I answered quietly. I walked over and stood over him. The sheets were soaked through with sweat. "Jesus," I exclaimed involuntarily. "What the fuck did you dream?" I asked.

Stojan shook his head and turned away. He was not going to answer.

"Seriously," I pressed.

"I don't remember," he answered in a whisper, but I knew it was a lie.

I leaned over and twisted my head so that I was looking up into his flushed face. He didn't look back at me, but he heaved a heavy, long sigh and pressed the heels of his hands into his closed eyes for a second. "It's alright," he said with more conviction and it was more believable the second time. "I'm sorry I woke you."

I looked at him closely. His body was glowing with sweat. The sheets smelled of it—thick and sharp. "Alright," I replied hesitantly, and Stojan nodded. I retreated slowly back out of the room to the couch. But it took me a long time to fall asleep again. When I finally did, I dreamed badly myself. Are our dreams our own? Stojan had asked this question that day on the balcony. I was not sure. I dreamed of places I had never seen. It was not that I passed through the night, but that the apparition of the night passed through me. My sleep was laced with an undercurrent of dread, but I could not understand why, because in the dream I was only standing in a sun-soaked, yellow field which was long overdue for threshing. I could see several young men in the distance, swinging scythes rhythmically. Behind them was a snaking swath of cleared space where they had already passed. "Call them for lunch," a woman spoke behind me. My heart was filled with dread, as though something terrible were about to happen, but I didn't have any idea what it might be. "Hurry, there's not time," the woman implored me. She smiled kindly at me, but there was an urgency in her voice that I could not understand. She wore a white dress, and she was thin to the point of malnourishment. Some distance behind her there was an uneven line of whitewashed houses with terracotta roof tiles. One of them was burning. Smoke was pouring out of its windows. I looked at her stupidly. "Run!" she shouted, and shoved me.

I ran toward the threshers. I was barefooted, and the uncut hay scratched at my legs. I ran and ran, but for a long time, I didn't seem to get any closer to them. Some terrible fear was gathering into a solid thing between my ribs, and I had the sense that someone was behind me—chasing me. I felt sweat running down my back as the summer sun beat down. And then, finally, I started to get closer to the threshers. They saw me coming all at once, when I was still some distance away. They dropped their scythes and began to shout at me. At first, I couldn't hear them. As I got closer, I could hear them, but I couldn't understand them. They were waving their arms and screaming at me. I ran and ran toward them, and didn't have the guts to look back to see what was behind me. Finally, when I was nearly upon them, I understood them to be shouting at me to stop running. So I stopped short, fearful now of both what was behind me, and what lay ahead. I was panting with exertion. And then I looked down and saw that the field beneath my feet was littered with hand-hammered scythe blades. Their sharpened edges were glittering in the sunlight. They were strewn everywhere, dozens of them, and I was barefooted. This must have been why they were yelling at me to stop running. I knew that whatever was behind me had already caught up. I whirled around with my heart pounding in my throat. But there was nothing there. At the end of the field behind me, I saw that all the houses were now burning. The sun began to fade all at once as the smoke filled the sky. One of the threshers strolled up and stood beside me with his scythe resting across his shoulders. "Nice villages burn nicely, too," he opined. Behind us, one of the other threshers began to cry out as though he had been wounded by something.

I woke up with a start. I knew I was awake then, but the thresher's crying had not stopped. And then I realized that the crying was coming from Stojan, who was dreaming his own dreams—and maybe I was dreaming his dreams, too, I thought crazily, because I did not recognize what I had dreamed. It was completely alien. My legs were all tangled again in the sheets. It took me a moment to extricate myself from them. When I finally managed to do so, I got up and tiptoed back toward the bedroom and stood in the doorway, shivering. The moon had set, and it was darker now. I couldn't make out the corners of the room. Stojan had stopped calling out, and was now panting heavily in his sleep. I walked up to the edge of the bed and looked down at him. He was covered in sweat. "Stojan," I whispered. His breathing slowed for a moment, and then he said clearly in Serbian from the depths of his dream, "Stop running!" I leaned down and put my hand on his shoulder. He recoiled violently and his eyes flew open. For a second, I'm sure he didn't recognize me. He threw his hands out in front of him, still half in the dream. I scrambled back out of his reach. And then he was suddenly all there again, all himself, and there was some expression on his face that I could not read, but which made my skin crawl.

I sat down on the bed beside him as he sank back down into the pillows. Out of the darkness, he said in a thick voice, "I saw Milan Milanović, and I can't live with it."

"Tell me," I whispered.

He did.

In the morning, I awakened to the sun pouring through the window. The kitten was curled up asleep in the block of sunshine at the foot of the bed. My head felt like it was stuffed with cotton from the heat of the sun and the sleepless trace of that traumatic night. I felt like I had been hit by a truck. I rolled over to look at the clock. It was noon. I slipped out from under the blankets, which were now warm and dry, dressed silently, and went back to my office.

I tried to recover my life at that point. I really did. I went back to my office, and I finished my funding proposal, and it actually looked pretty good, even to my own critical eye. It was the last big push, fueled by fear more than anything else. I was afraid of who I was becoming. I stood in front of the mirror in the faculty bathroom, and I felt like I had someone else's eyes in my face. I marked the essays. I organized shelves. The only thing I couldn't do was send my book. I walked along my avenue of books, touching the spines with my bloodless fingertips, ensuring that each was intact, ensuring that they were alphabetized by author. When I came to Levinas, I saw that *On Escape* was missing, and I went hunting all over the office for it. But I couldn't find it, so I tried to convince myself that I had lent it to one of my colleagues, even though I knew I hadn't. I forced myself to believe it anyway, and I watered my succulent plants. Afterward, I took the soft toothbrush that I kept in my desk drawer, and I dusted each leaf to increase their capacity to photosynthesize. I screened for mites and other insects with a tiny Japanese jeweler's glass. I removed the few deadish-looking leaves that always appeared from time to time, and admired the flowers that had sprung up between the woody stems on the crown of thorns. Finally, I turned and looked at the envelope on the edge of my desk.

I was never able to explain to myself why I destroyed my manuscript. Something welled up in me that was larger than my ability to control it. First, I wiped clean the hard drive on my computer. It calculated for a few moments because there were so very many documents to delete. It asked me if I was sure. I responded that I was. It warned me that this could not be undone, and asked again if I was really sure. I responded that I was. In one stroke of the keyboard, all that I had ever written vanished. I looked at the hard copy of the manuscript on my desk. I looked at the filing cabinets, choked with articles, fragments of thoughts, the supporting documentation for my book. I looked at the folders and the notebooks piled on my shelves. I felt nothing. And the person who was not me—could not be me—tore open the envelope that contained the manuscript, and began to shred it page by page. I sat cross-legged on the floor and shredded everything into little confetti ribbons—interview transcripts, hand- and type-written notes I had used to remind myself of various points and arguments, drafts of chapters, notebooks full of citations and bibliographies. There was so much to shred that the portable machine could not handle it all. I had to turn it off from time to time to let it cool down.

While I waited for the shredder to recover, I pulled the ribbon out of cassette tapes that contained hours of interview material with members of international organizations in Bosnia and stretched it taut until I was sure it was unsalvageable. Then I took the scissors to them, snipping them up here and there until everything was unrecognizable. After a while, there was a huge pile of shredding stuffed into my wastebasket, and more piles on the floor. They looked like white paper bales of Bosnian hay, and before long I was surrounded by them. I emptied whole filing cabinets on Bosnia. When the shredding of my own book manuscript was complete, I began to shred all the articles that other people had written on Bosnia. I shredded David Campbell, David Chandler, Florian Bieber, Noel Malcolm, David Rieff, Thomas Weiss, Ronnie Lipschutz, Susan Woodward. I shredded Serbs and Muslims, I shredded Germans and Americans and Britons. I shredded Canadians. I shredded the Bosnian Muslim Serb who had asked to be cut in half at that long ago conference, even though I had liked his article.

As the shredder whined and ate, whined and ate, Stojan appeared at my office doorway and regarded me with a perplexed smile. He looked awful. He was as pale as my piles of shredded paper, and his eyes were rimmed in red. I stopped shredding and turned off the machine. The office was quiet, and dust from the shredding hung in the air.

"Thank God," I heard one of my colleagues across the hall sigh. I guess the shredding was bothering him. "Fuck you," I wanted to call out, but didn't. And I felt shocked at myself.

"What are you doing?" he asked curiously.

"Shredding," I answered calmly.

"Oh." He came in and sat down cross-legged on the floor amid the piles of paper-hay. He pulled an orange from his pocket and began to peel it. Its fragrant citrus scent filled the room. He handed me section after section, wordlessly. I ate them, one after another, and they were sweet and refreshing.

After a while, he said to me, "You write about war."

"Not anymore," I answered flatly around a mouthful of orange.

He swiveled his head to look at all the little mountains of shredding on the floor. I ate his orange. He produced another one from his pocket, and began to peel the skin back.

"This weight," he said, "it sits like a bear on my heart." He shook his head.

I sat silently, thinking about his nightmares.

"How can you and your colleagues sit here and write all day and still not have anything to say?" His tone was pleasant, conversational, even, and I could see by the way he looked at me that he loved me. I realized with some surprise that I could recognize that.

I swallowed down the orange section with my constricted throat. "I've told you everything I can. I've tried to explain myself a million different ways. I care about what happened in Bosnia. I care about what happened to your brother, even though he was not my brother." I sat quietly for a moment, thinking about it. "I don't know what you want from me, Stojan," I said.

"You can say something else."

"What?" I asked helplessly. "I have already destroyed everything I wrote. Tell me what I should have said."

"I don't know," he answered back with a note of frustration in his voice. "I just know it should be something else. I read the books on Bosnia. All these professors, building their careers on what I lost." He looked closely at me, and said, "You're building your whole career on what I lost, and you never came to even ask me what that was like."

"What would you like me to do?" I asked quietly.

"Say something else!" he repeated emphatically.

"What should I say?" I asked defiantly, but I felt that I might cry soon.

"I don't know. Say anything but what you're saying now. Come and live inside my skin."

"I can't, Stojan," I answered. "I can't get out of my own skin."

"You said that we could feel each other's pain," he said in a quiet, sad voice.

"I was wrong. I'm sorry."

"You said that the one who cries out in pain does not choose the mouth which says it," he went on.

"I was wrong."

Stojan ignored this. "You talk about ethics," he went on. "You act like it can be calculated. 'The ethical moment of decision,' you call it. But sometimes we just have to choose—like Petar Petrović chose when he unloaded his rifle. We don't, or can't, see all the consequences, and we just choose. And the thing we think is the right thing turns out to be the worst choice imaginable. And the thing we think is the wrong thing—well, sometimes it stays the wrong thing, and sometimes it's even worse than that. And then we have to live with it."

I looked at him. "I agree with you," I answered. "Decisions can't be calculated."

"No, that's not what I'm saying," he insisted.

"What are you saying, then?" I asked. I was coming to the end of myself now. I was at the point where no theory I knew of could help me proceed.

"I'm saying that we do calculate, but that you can't recognize it as a calculation because you would never be able to bring yourself to believe that someone would knowingly choose the worst option," he said. "When you come upon a problem like that, you have nothing to fall back on but evil."

"What about Ivan?" I asked. "Isn't he evil? Isn't what he did evil?"

He looked at me, as though trying to decide something. He was struggling with himself over something. Finally, he said, "I had to decide what to do, and the range of options was very narrow. I tried to leave, but I couldn't. My brother tried to leave, and they shot him. I couldn't even go to his fucking funeral. I asked to go. I begged my commanding officer to let me go. "Let me go to my own brother's funeral—the son of my dead mother—for the love of Christ," I begged him. And you know what he said to me? You want to know? He said, "If you can kill thirty Muslims before sunset, you can go to your brother's funeral." I went away wondering whether it would be possible to kill thirty Muslims by sunset. It was already afternoon. There were only maybe three hours of daylight left." His voice was flat and tired, remembering.

"Stojan, you can't say this here," I whispered, horrified.

"Why not?" He was emphatic, and he raised his voice. "One of you experts on war, tell me! What should I have done? My father was alone, burying his favorite son."

"Stojane!" I called him in the vocative case.

He wouldn't look at me, but he grew quiet. He swallowed audibly.

"Please don't do this," I said quietly. But even then, it was really too late. It could not be taken back. My skin was humming with dread.

He sighed and the breath caught in his throat. "Alright."

He handed me the last orange section, which he had been cradling, forgotten, in his hand. It was warm from being held for so long. It was warmer than I was. I had gone cold. I couldn't eat it.

"Alright," said Stojan again absently. "I'm going to the church. Why don't you come with me?"

I was startled at this. I didn't want to go. I didn't want to see anymore. I didn't want to know anymore. I wanted to go home. I wanted to get out of this. I could feel myself unraveling. I stared at him, unsure of how to answer, unsure of what I wanted. He nodded, and smiled gently as though he wanted to comfort me. In all of this, he wanted to comfort me. I thought it absurd.

"Why, Stojan?" I asked in response to his invitation.

He answered easily, "Because you have lost your context."

"What?"

He motioned to the piles of shredding on the floor. "All the things you thought were real are gone."

"They are," I confirmed.

"But that does not mean there is nothing that matters," he went on quietly. "It's just that you have to find it, and to find a way to say it."

I didn't answer him. I couldn't see where he was going. The unfamiliarity of what he was saying weighed on me. And I saw that I didn't know him at all. Maybe I didn't know myself.

"Find a way to say it. To write it." His eyes were shining, unwavering.

"I can't anymore, Stojan," I protested.

"You can."

"I can't."

"My friend, you can."

"Please, Stojan," I answered. But my intentions were no longer my own. I was his hostage. I was a hostage of his dreaming, a hostage of his pale, searching eyes. It was not love, although there was also love in me for him.

"Why did you answer my note looking for the translator?" I asked. I realized then that I had always known he wanted something. And I had always known that, when the time came for him to tell me what it was, I would not be able to deny him. That was the nature of our proximity to one another. That was the nature of the inescapability of it.

He thought for a moment. "Because I wanted to find someone who would write this differently. In English. It had to have happened for a reason." And this was why he had come. He was not looking to simply translate a few lines of text. He was looking for the reason his brother died, knowing all along that there was not one—knowing that no reason would ever make it alright. Petar Petrović was right. Countries are stone and wood. And they're not worth it. Stojan Sokolović was not looking to have his world explained for him. He was not looking for closure. He was looking for something else, something otherwise: a difficult freedom.

"Why did you think it could be me?" I asked, shaking my head.

"At first, I didn't know," he answered. "But now I do."

"Stojan, what do you want me to say?" I asked helplessly. "You want me to say why all this happened to you?"

He smiled sadly and shook his head at me. "You don't understand me, even now," he said. "Your book already told the reasons. You made reasons where there are none. And then your solutions are flawed from the beginning. You do not see me."

Stojan held out his hands to me, palms up, and I looked at all the creases there; the lines that mapped out the course that his life had taken and would take, the fingers that deftly peeled the oranges. I looked at their length and their uniqueness.

I looked at the confetti piles on the floor of my office, and felt a hum of terrible confusion growing in me. We went to the Orthodox church, and we lit candles. The priest passed through the iconostasis, a watchful raven in a black cassock. He looked at us for a moment, and then went on as though he had not seen us.

XIX

After the meeting with Stojan, Milan hoped that his life would go on as though it had not been interrupted. But things didn't work that way, and his hope was not enough to make it so. All that is hidden is eventually revealed, Milan thought, and this was particularly so when there were others around everywhere, scratching, scratching into the deep soil of the past. How it happened was that Jelena, who had lost the slip of paper on which she had written a friend's new telephone number, went scrolling through the caller identification that was attached to the phone. It was thus that she saw the name "S. Sokolović" swim up across the digital screen.

Jelena regarded the name curiously. She felt a crash of memory land in the pit of her stomach with an internal, audible thud. She stared at the screen with a measure of confusion that contained within it a grain of recognition, a suspicion, and then a denial of suspicion, a desire to forget, knowing also that one could not forget the name burning across the pixels of the screen—the name chiseled into the gravestone. And so then she looked for an explanation to make sense of it in an easier way, to believe what she wanted to believe was believable. Jelena had become this type of pragmatist, because she had lived these years with Milan. There were dozens of people with the name Sokolović, she told herself. But she stared at the number until it was memorized, and then spent the next three days repeating it to herself, a number recited quietly in time to the steady ebb and flow of her everyday tasks.

Jelena lay awake for a long time that night beside her husband, thinking of the name on the call display. She did not ask Milan about the telephone call. Something in her heart told her that he would lie. If she asked, he would quietly and expertly accuse her of worrying too much about nonsense. He would say it was a business call, or a cousin of a friend, or a friend of a cousin. He would dismiss her. If she pressed him, or wept, he would say she was too emotional and retreat into another room. Worse, he would feel badly that she still thought of Luka. Somewhere inside her, she felt that she was the one responsible for his withdrawal. She had waited years for Luka to fade away so she could get on with the task of living. But he didn't. And she didn't know how to make him go away. He had become now not a loss, but a comfort which she used to navigate the dissatisfaction with the way this life was turning out. So, while she wanted to forget him, she could not, because Luka was now doing other work for her.

So she kept quiet, curled up beside Milan in their comfortable bed in the middle of the night in that sheltering, alien city. Milan slept soundly, his breathing deep and even across the comforter that covered them. Jelena stared out into the darkness, luring herself into the spaces of memory that were still hidden in the tall grasses of summer in the village where Luka Sokolović had been born and buried. As the moon rose higher in the night sky, Jelena began to drift away along the currents of these memories. Gradually, slow currents gave way to swifter ones, which carried her down into a sleep that was without familiarity or pain.

At work on the third day, she thumbed through the phonebook, and found only one S. Sokolović. And she discovered that S. Sokolović (who was most certainly not Stojan Sokolović, she told herself reasonably) lived six metro stops away from her office. She allotted herself three more days to see if she really wanted to pay a visit to this address. And then, after the three days had passed, which made six in total, she packed up her briefcase and took the metro in the opposite direction than she would have done had she been going home. She alighted at the station, and walked up onto the street. It was not hard to find the building; it was close to the university where she had studied engineering, and she knew the area well. The street was lined with sprawling tenements between which the city had planted pathetic sapling trees with dull, dust-covered leaves. They would not build parks, or install playground equipment, so they planted slender little trees instead. Nothing would have helped but a demolition team, Jelena thought sadly. The endless blocks of gray concrete-dominated buildings rose up into thirty-story monstrosities that stretched on and on for city block after city block. She knew these buildings well. She and Milan had lived in one of them for a long time before they finally scraped up enough money to rent a glass condominium closer to the waterfront. The only difference between the glass condominiums and the concrete apartments, though, was the square footage and the description that accompanied the prison. They were all still prisons, she thought—some with large windows, some with small, some with balconies, some with solariums, some with hardwood floors and some with tiles and some with linoleum or carpet. The floor plans were all the same. Sometimes the views were slightly different, and this seemed to be one of the primary determinants of cost. Jelena noticed as she walked down the street past the identical concrete buildings that there was a notable absence of flowers. Each of them had a circular driveway with "Do Not Park" signs plastered everywhere.

"I told you he was a bastard!" A young woman on a bench insisted to her limp-haired friend or sister as Jelena passed. "Fuck him! I told you that he would get somebody pregnant before long. That's just the way he is." There was a note of triumph in the girl's voice, as though being right was more important to her than the pain of the other girl. The other girl seemed not to notice this aspect of the conversation. Or maybe she did, but lacked the power to say anything about it. She hung her head and her lower lip trembled as she dragged on a menthol cigarette.

Jelena wrapped her thin sweater around herself as she moved on. She passed two old men feeding the pigeons on another bench. They were speaking with Sarajevo accents. So many of us are here, she thought. Why? What was the reason? These apartment blocks were full of immigrants and refugees from Serbia, Bosnia, Sudan, Somalia, Ethiopia, Eritrea, Cambodia, Sri Lanka, Bangladesh, and Afghanistan. There was hardly a native English speaker to be found anywhere in this city, Jelena thought. We are all here, taken over this place, the refuse of the world strewn between apartment blocks and plodding along day after day, wishing that things had been different and powerless to do anything about it. But was there a vibrancy here, as well, that she had failed to recognize? Was there not some semblance of acceptance among the new residents, who knew something that the old residents had forgotten? And then Jelena wondered if old Sokolović had understood something that she did not when he had said that Canada was a good state. Maybe it could help you forget, if you would only let it try. She did not know.

At the entryway to the building, Jelena ducked into the lobby and scrolled through the list of residents. She wondered briefly if she had been mistaken—if the name on the call display had simply been a mirage. But it was there. S. Sokolović. She punched in the code on the keypad. It rang three times, and was answered. "Hello." It was not a question.

"Stojan Sokolović?" she asked through numb lips.

"Yes," came the answer through the crackling connection.

She steadied herself against the wall beside the door. She looked at her manicured fingertips, which spoke a togetherness about her that was not true. "Can I come up and speak to you?" she asked.

There was a considering pause. "Apartment 1024," he said, and the heavy glass door clicked open. Jelena pushed against it and crossed the threshold to the bank of elevators.

XX

"Someone is here," Stojan announced to me as he came back out on the balcony after the phone rang.

"You don't know who?" I asked.

"No idea," he said with a shrug.

"Didn't you ask?" I inquired.

"No. I should make coffee, though." He disappeared into the kitchen, and the cat trailed after him.

"It's probably some Evangelical Christians," I called after him as he walked away.

"Don't be cruel!" he replied with a half smile. "I feel bad for them. They always have nice suits on. But I do tell them that they should go to university. Anyway, it is not Evangelical Christians. It is a Serb."

"How do you know?" I asked.

"She said my name perfectly."

The tap came on the door, and Stojan crossed the room to open it. I got up and went inside out of sheer curiosity.

He opened the door, and before him stood a lovely, long woman with dark hair and dark eyes and a strange expression on her face. She looked almost comically surprised. He didn't greet her, nor did she greet him. They just stood standing and staring at each other across the threshold.

I noticed her hand wrapped tightly around the handle of a stylish brief-case. She had a wedding band on that hand—the right hand—the one that Serbs use.

"Stojan Sokolović," she announced in a disbelieving whisper. The briefcase hit the floor with a dull thud and fell over on its side. She reached out to steady herself against the doorframe, as though she couldn't stay on her own feet.

"Stojan Sokolović," she said again. Stojan stepped forward in one smooth motion and silently embraced her. They stayed like that for a long time on the threshold, blocking the exit I thought it was time for me to make. I retreated to the balcony.

I shredded my manuscript, I thought stupidly. This made all that I had said at my performance review a lie. There was no way to prove now that it had ever been the truth. I thought about my missing book, *On Escape*. "Where is your manuscript?" the Head of School would want to know. "The one that you mentioned on line one of the publications section?" "My friend, the manuscript is *On Escape*," I would answer. I could hear the woman inside now whispering a bit. The door to the apartment slammed shut, and I peeked through the doorway. She was lowering herself onto the couch, and Stojan kneeled down on the floor in front of her, looking up at her wordlessly.

I couldn't understand much of what they were saying, those Bosnian-accented speakers. Each word merged into the next one. After a few minutes of listening to them, I began to be able to make out individual words. I heard her say, "Luka," and suddenly the identity of the woman cracked over me like a rogue wave. This is the woman that Luka Sokolović died on his way home to see. I watched them for a moment, and then felt ashamed of myself, watching them like a voyeur—like one watches pornography—in the illusion that one can shame without shaming. That one can see without being seen. I wanted to go back to the office where all my shredding lay patiently in wait for me to see if I would regret what I had done. Instead, I sat down and wished the blue cushion on the back of the creaky chair would just swallow me. After some time went by, Stojan rose and passed by the balcony door on his way to the kitchen, then he doubled back and came outside. His face was badly drawn and his eyes seemed flat. "Would you make coffee?" he asked apologetically.

"Shouldn't I leave?" I asked hesitantly.

"If you want to, you should. But if you would make coffee first, I would be grateful." He seemed smaller than usual.

"I don't think I should be here, Stojan," I whispered.

He looked at me and a shadow crossed his face. "Please make the coffee," he said evenly.

"Alright," I conceded.

He nodded. "Thank you."

I slipped into the kitchen as unobtrusively as possible and made coffee in the copper džezva bought so long ago in a Sarajevo that could not have anticipated its later fate. It glowed warmly, burnished and worn. At the moment when the foam threatened to overspill the vessel, I snatched it off the flame, and the foam subsided. Each cup had its saucer. Each saucer had a spoon. Each spoon got a lump of yellow sugar from the paper bag in the corner of the counter. I carried it out to them. Jelena accepted the little blue china cup with a murmur of thanks.

I introduced myself briefly to Jelena, who nodded at me, and then I left. "You don't have to," said Stojan.

I looked at him closely and his face changed. "You know where to find me."

"There is no reason for you to go back there right now," he said quietly.

"I have to go back, Stojan," I said.

"How long can you wait?" he asked me suddenly as he walked me to the door. I heard Jelena stirring the sugar into her coffee, and the muted clink of the little spoon against the porcelain.

"As long as you need me to," I answered simply. But I didn't know what I was promising, or to whom.

He nodded. "Alright," he said. "Alright."

XXI

Stojan did not know what Jelena knew about her own husband, so he tried to be very, very careful. But he was unsure of how to proceed, because he did not know how she had made the connection to him, unless she had made it through Milan. He did not imagine that Milan would tell Jelena that they had spoken, but he also knew that people often say and do what would not otherwise be expected of them. So he was quiet for a while with her. He simply looked at her, having not imagined that he would ever see her again, and he was pleased in some painful way that she was here. She was, in her features, as he remembered her. But not in her countenance. And not in the set of her mouth. Grief and age had changed her. Her body was sharp and angular in a way that would cause anyone who loved her to worry.

"How long has it been since we saw each other last?" asked Jelena.

Stojan shook his head. "A long time," he answered.

"I saw you last at your father's house, on the day I left for Canada," she said in a flat, hollow voice, remembering. "But you didn't speak to me."

"I tried," answered Stojan quietly, casting his eyes down into his lap. He was silent for a moment, helpless for an explanation. "I just couldn't," he said uselessly.

She nodded, as though she understood what he was trying to say.

"How long have you been here?" she asked. "I didn't know you were here."

"I came a few years after you," Stojan answered. "Lots of us did, it would seem," he laughed sadly and shook his head.

Jelena smiled at that and nodded.

"I'm glad you came," Stojan said to her suddenly. "What made you come?"

"Why did you talk to Milan?" she answered with her own question, and her eyes reminded him of the day under the trees in Pale when she told him that he and Luka should leave Bosnia.

Stojan did not know how to answer this, so he did not answer at all.

"You have to tell me," she said, and her eyes grew harder, determined. "How do you know him?"

Again, Stojan did not answer.

"Stojane!" she implored him in the vocative. Her voice was sharp and penetrating. He felt it vibrate across his bones.

But he did not know how to answer. And so he said, honestly, "I don't know what to say."

"Say why you talked to Milan," she insisted.

"Jelena, this is not easy for me," Stojan began. It was clear that she suspected something was being kept from her, and she wanted to know what it was.

"Were you looking for Milan?" she asked. "Or for me?"

Stojan felt a surge of relief as he saw his way out of her questioning. "I wanted to know what had happened to you, so I asked around and called you. I spoke to Milan, and all I wanted to know was that you were safe and well. That's it."

"Why didn't you come to see me, then, if you knew I was here for all these years?" she asked. She seemed crushed by the idea that he had not wanted to see her.

"Jelena, I didn't want to disturb your life," he said truthfully. "You made a new life, and you should be proud of that, and happy. Believe me. Believe me, because I'm not doing so good at it myself." He rubbed his hand across his unshaven cheek and laughed a little. "I didn't want to contact you and dig up all this past now. I didn't want to hurt you, or remind you." Stojan looked at her with his colorless eyes and she could see by the level of light behind them that he was speaking the truth. He had Luka's eyes; exact replicas of Luka's eyes in a different man's face. She always knew when Luka was not telling the truth, or leaving something out. His eyes would lose a degree of their brightness. It didn't cross her mind that Stojan might be a better liar than his brother had been. It didn't cross her mind that there might be more at stake than she knew. She had believed Stojan's lie, which had been told in a moment of mercy. Stojan simply did not have the heart to tell Jelena the truth. Even though she deserved to know, and to decide for herself what the consequences would or would not be, he couldn't do it. He just didn't have the strength to be responsible for it. It was up to Milan to tell her or not tell her, he thought. He looked at her, and he told his lie, and the lie became the truth in the instant it was received.

"Why didn't you come to Luka's funeral?" she asked gently.

"I couldn't get away from Višegrad," Stojan answered.

"Milan was there," she said.

And Stojan could not help himself. He wanted to know what lie Milan had told her. "How did they know each other?" he asked.

"They were in the same task force," she said.

"Where?" asked Stojan. And he felt something overtaking him. Some anger that was hard to find the edges of.

"I don't know," she said. "Somewhere around Vogošća."

"How did he know that Luka had been killed?" Stojan asked. Stop! A warning voice in his head commanded. And Jelena looked at him with such perplexity that Stojan knew immediately he had crossed the line.

"They were in the same task force," she repeated slowly, as though Stojan had not heard her the first time.

"Were they close?" Stojan asked. "Were they friends?"

Jelena nodded. "Yes."

Stojan was quiet at this, considering.

"Are you happy?" he asked.

"Yes," she answered slowly, unsure. "But it's hard here."

Stojan nodded. "I know."

"Are you happy?" she asked him.

"I'm alright," Stojan answered. And because Stojan was a better liar than Luka, and because the signs of the untruth that always betrayed his brother had failed to appear in his own eyes, Jelena believed him.

She reached out to take his hand. He looked closely at her face and realized that she was the same in so many ways. He saw her in his mind's eye, wrapped in Luka's sweater against the spring chill with her back pressed up against the outside wall of the little house. He saw her perched at the table under the trees in his father's courtyard. He saw her begging him to speak to her when he came back from the war. Why hadn't he spoken to her? Stojan held her hand, and they looked at one another in the afternoon light.

"I thought you blamed me for Luka's death," Jelena ventured quietly.

Stojan was shocked. "What?" he replied. "Why?"

"Because you didn't speak to me when I left, and I know that Luka came back from Serbia because of me. It was my fault he died." Her voice was hard and matter of fact. She told this in a way that suggested that she had believed it for many years.

"No," Stojan breathed. "No." He struggled against the urge to cry.

She looked at him wordlessly.

"It was not your fault. Believe me," he insisted in a low voice. "Believe me." He squeezed her hand, hoping that this would convey what his words could not.

She didn't answer.

"Jelena, I didn't talk to anyone for a long time. I just couldn't. It was insane, what happened to us. I don't know." He trailed off, shaking his head. His eyes were filling.

She nodded. "I know," she said. "I don't talk, either."

Stojan nodded.

"I have no one to talk to," she went on.

"Why?" he ventured.

"Who would I talk to?" she asked, surprised.

"Milan," Stojan offered.

She shook her head. "We don't talk," she admitted quietly, looking away.

Stojan felt ashamed that he knew more about why that was so than she herself did. He looked away, unsure of how to respond.

"It's alright," she said quickly. "It's just the way it is."

They finished the coffee, and Jelena rose to leave. "I'll come back and visit you," she said.

"Alright," Stojan whispered.

She picked up her briefcase and kissed him on the cheek with her dry, warm lips at the threshold.

"Please come back," he heard himself nearly beg her.

"I will," she promised.

XXII

Stojan tapped on my office window on the evening of Jelena's visit. I walked out of the offices and we went to eat at the Gurkha Grill. I was reminded of that first night we had eaten together. I remembered the silence between us, which was very different than the silence between us now. Exams were over and there were far fewer students around the campus. They were all away on their annual migration. Stojan had dark circles under his eyes. By the time we had eaten everything, we were too exhausted to talk at all. But I had grown comfortable in the silences between us. I didn't want to ask him about Jelena then. I thought he would tell me if he wanted to, but he didn't. When the bill was paid, we went back to his apartment to drink the Corona that was stacked up in the refrigerator.

I drank the pale beer through the lime and looked at the strange patterns the rust made along the girding on the balcony. After a while, I roused myself and said that I should leave.

"Please don't," Stojan said without looking at me.

I looked over at him. But he stayed staring with a strange expression out at the lights in the windows of the building across the street. "What's up?" I asked.

Stojan shook his head.

"Are you alright?" I asked.

He shook his head again. No. His eyes were still glued to the building across the street. They were shining in the darkness.

"Is it Jelena?" I asked.

He shook his head. No.

I stared at him, unsure of how to proceed. A tiny, reflective tear slid down his cheek, leaving a trace where it had passed. He leaned forward suddenly with his head in his hands and began to cry. He cried and cried in the dark against his hands. I didn't know what to do. I had never seen a man weep like this. I tried to embrace him but it seemed a pathetic gesture—a failure from the beginning. His body was completely racked with the force of that crying. It seemed like it had not come from inside him at all, but had somehow overtaken him from outside. I kneeled down on the concrete floor of the balcony beside him, as he had done earlier with Jelena on the couch, resting my hand on his back. He went on like that for long minutes, and it didn't subside. I waited for it to pass. It had to pass eventually, I reasoned with myself. It had to. And finally it did, but it seemed to take forever. After a while, his body started to relax, but he didn't lift his face out of his hands. My knees were killing me. It occurred to me that bodies were terrible betrayers sometimes, and often in the most important moments. I couldn't take it anymore. "Come on," I said quietly, insistently. "Come inside."

He didn't move. I stood up, my knees screaming with pain. It took a few seconds for me to straighten my legs as the blood rushed back into them. When I was finally on my feet, I tugged at his arm insistently. "Come on," I said again. "Let's go in." There was a sudden chill in the night air, I thought.

"Stojane," I pressed in the vocative case.

And he moved at that. "Evo me," he answered thickly. Here I am. I'm coming. He shuffled into the house, which was warmer, and stood in the middle of the living room, looking around, blinking against the light, trying to wipe the tears off his face. "Go on." I gave him a gentle shove in the small of his back. "Sit down on the couch. I'll make coffee."

"I don't want coffee." He was emphatic.

I was taken aback. I didn't know what to do then, if he didn't want coffee. He fell into the couch, where he looked around blankly.

"Why don't you want me to make you some coffee?" I asked quietly.

He looked back at me with a cold expression. "Fuck the coffee."

I walked over gingerly and sat down beside him. "Stojane," I said again, and I could hear the helplessness creeping into my voice.

"I'm going to tell you something," said Stojan quietly, in a different voice. "About the offer the officer made me."

"Don't!" I warned him. My voice was sharp. I could hear it. It seemed to echo back at me from the wall with the print of the sailboat hanging on it.

He shook his head. "I took up his challenge."

"Stop!" I ordered him.

But he didn't. And as he spoke, his tears evaporated; it was as though they had never been there, and a hard, dead edge crept into his voice. "I killed as many as I could." He was staring at some point up behind me, blinking rapidly.

"Please, Stojan," I said in a voice I didn't recognize. "Please stop."

"At first, it went slowly. I am a good marksman, but it was slow and difficult, because the winds were high."

"Stop it!"

He ignored me. I was no longer there. "The winds were high, and I had to compensate for that in the trajectory of the shot."

"Please," I whispered. "Please, please."

"There weren't enough people in the streets. They knew we were up in the hills and they ran everywhere they went."

"Please stop," I begged him.

But he was talking as though to someone else. I was no longer there. "So I went back, and told the officer that I needed someone to be a witness, because how would he believe that I had killed thirty?"

"And the officer was surprised. He had made the offer as a joke—he had no expectation that I would do it. He even asked me if I was joking. But I said I wasn't. And because there were several witnesses to the terms of his offer, he couldn't take it back. He wanted to be known as a man of his word, and he was trapped between this and between the stupidity that came out of his mouth. I knew this about him. So I said to him: "I have three hours before sunset. I have to kill thirty. If I achieve this, you let me go to my brother's funeral." Maybe he saw something in me, he saw that I was serious, so he just shrugged and walked away mumbling something about how disgusting this war was."

"I went back to my position with the witness—my friend, called Pas. The officer trusted him. I wanted to kill them. As many as I could. I felt nothing for them down there in that horrible little town. My brother had been murdered by Muslims, and I felt that I could kill all of them in return."

I stared at him, numb with shock.

Stojan laughed. He laughed a cruel, deep laugh. "I wanted to kill them because they killed my brother. But now I know that my brother was murdered by Serbs."

He looked up at me for the first time. "Bring me a cigarette," he half-asked, half-demanded. I walked out onto the balcony and gathered up the tobacco and papers from the milk crate, when what I really wanted to do was run out of that apartment as fast as I could. When I returned, Stojan continued.

"The first one was a child," he said. "Sometimes they sent their children on errands through the side streets, because they trusted us to have some decency. They still trusted at that time that we would not shoot their children. She was wearing a blue winter coat that was too big for her. It was probably her mother's," Stojan mused. "She had a plastic bag full of something in her hand. Bread? Flour? I don't know. I followed her through the gun sight as she ran, and she was in the crosshairs for a long time before I finally got up the nerve to take the shot."

My voice came swimming up from some depth and with some volume that I had not been aware existed. "Stop telling me this!" I heard myself scream at him, and my ears rang from the force of it.

Stojan looked over at me impassively. "But you wanted to write about Bosnia," he said flatly. "You wanted to tell us about what we had done and why we did it. Why don't you listen, then, to what happened?"

"I don't want to hear what you've done," I whispered. "Please."

Stojan was surprised. "Why?"

"Because it's breaking my heart," I answered thickly.

"What do you think it's doing to mine?" he asked, his voice expressionless.

I fell silent.

"Do you want to know what I felt?" he asked brightly, and then he immediately answered his own question. "Nothing. I felt nothing. I shot as many as I could. But it was still not enough. I couldn't get to thirty. I would have killed everyone in that whole fucking town if I could have. But I had only a sniper's rifle, and I could only kill one at a time."

Why I didn't leave, I didn't know. I just couldn't. I couldn't walk out of the apartment. I tried to go. I stood up and started for the door. Then I stopped and turned back and walked to the balcony. Then I went to the kitchen. I came back toward the couch. I stood before him while he talked, and his voice grew deeper and deeper, deader and deader, heavier and heavier with the weight of what he had done. I turned away again, walked to the wall. And back to the door to leave. And then I stopped. I came back to him again, but I couldn't sit down beside him. My heart was racing along, and I felt a sickly shock. I looked at his hands with their long, straight fingers and their symmetrical nail beds, and I couldn't believe what they had done.

Stojan continued. "I watched that child for a long time, and my hands were trembling so badly that I thought at first I would not be able to mark her—she was jumping all around in the scope." He smiled a rueful, dead smile and said, "At first I understood this to mean that I should not shoot her. But I thought of my brother, and then my hands steadied. So I raised the crosshairs to compensate for the wind and pulled the trigger."

"My friend Pas was watching through the binoculars. And he whispered to me: 'God have mercy on your soul, Stojan Sokolović.'" Stojan lit his cigarette. "But I ignored him, and waited for the next shot. I was ready to be infinitely patient. Something just broke inside me. I can't explain it. I couldn't feel anything at all. Just a little cold, maybe, but it was December. When the girl fell, a woman came from around the corner of a house where there was a line of laundry hanging. She saw the child on the sidewalk, and began to run toward her. I followed her through the scope. She was running toward the child—maybe didn't know why she had fallen, maybe did—and then a man appeared suddenly." Stojan narrowed his eyes, remembering. "He must have chased her down very fast because he tackled her down onto the street. He was trying to drag her behind a car, I think," Stojan offered. "He knew. He knew what was happening. He knew us better than we knew ourselves up in those hills."

I had fallen into a stupefied silence.

"I watched all this," he went on, "and I still felt nothing. The woman struggled with him. She was trying to get to her child, who was already dead. I wonder if she knew her girl was dead, or if she really thought she could do something to save her. So I watched these two in the scope of my rifle, and I was trying to calculate, you know?"

I didn't know. I would never know.

Stojan didn't seem to notice. "If I shot the woman first, I thought I might lose the man, because he would definitely run, and would probably make it to cover. But if I shot the man first, I thought I could count on the woman to continue on to the child. So I trained my rifle on the man, I adjusted again for the wind, and I pulled the trigger. Again, my friend Pas begged God to have mercy on me. I thought it was strange for him to do that, and I asked him to shut up. Anyway, I hit the man, and he collapsed on top of the woman. She then had to struggle to get out from underneath him. She was clawing at the sidewalk with one hand, and trying to shove the man off of her with the other. She must have known then," Stojan said reasonably.

"Her face was in complete shock. Her cheek was bleeding, or maybe it was the blood of the dead man on top of her. I don't know. I couldn't tell which it was. But my calculation was right. She managed to get on her feet, and instead of taking cover, she continued running toward her child. I lost her a few times behind cars and trees, but the child was out in the open, so I just trained my crosshairs on the child, waiting for the mother to arrive. And the mother did arrive. But the child was already dead. She picked her up in her arms, and the child's head was bent back unnaturally. The mother didn't know what to do. She headed toward a shaded alley that ran between the two houses that were closest to her. She tried to run, but the child was probably heavy, and the woman was having trouble carrying her. I think at that point she realized that she would not get to the alley in time. So she just turned to face the hill where she knew that we were gathered in force. She stood with her dead child in her arms and she lifted her head so that her face filled the whole scope. I did feel my blood go cold. I even thought for a second that my heart had stopped beating. I watched her, and I just couldn't fire."

Stojan's eyes seemed to be frosted over. He was completely still, his cigarette smoldering between the first two fingers of his right hand. "But when she turned away again, I compensated for the wind, and fired the third shot."

"'That's three,' said Pas," Stojan recounted. "But I knew I could never make thirty. It was a cold winter afternoon, overcast, and nearly evening. We were in the middle of a war, and everyone in that town knew it, so the streets were mostly empty. So I thought I should stop. I wanted to stop. But then a woman came out onto her balcony to pull in a set of white sheets. She was very young, with dark hair. I adjusted again for the wind, and then I saw that her clothespins were red, blue, and white, in deliberate sequence—she was Serbian, and this was her way of announcing it to us. Pas saw this, too, and said to me that she was Serb. 'The deal was Muslims,' he reminded me."

Stojan roused himself and looked at me unpityingly.

"And I realized then that they could all have been Serbs and that, either way, it didn't matter, so I took the shot. It shattered the glass door behind her after it killed her. I waited to see if someone would come out onto the balcony to see what had happened. But no one did. Her husband was probably up in the hills with the army somewhere."

Stojan talked slowly and deliberately while I stood before him with my stomach rising into my throat. I wanted to scream at him, to slap him, to make him shut up. But I was too weak to do it. I was frozen with horror. As he talked, I felt that I could sense those four souls in the apartment around us. They came one after the other, summoned by the narrative of their killer—the child, the man, and two women, none of whom had ever wronged Stojan Sokolović. But he said he went on killing them anyway while the report from each deliberate shot echoed through the hills above their besieged town until the officer came rushing up, outraged, and tore the rifle from his hands.

XXIII

When the officer heard the careful shots ringing out one after the other across the hilltop, he came running to Stojan's position in the tree line. He snatched the rifle out of his hands and struck him in the side of the head with the stock. Stojan fell immediately onto his knees and then forward onto his hands, and his head felt as though it had exploded. He trembled there for a few seconds, and then collapsed on the frozen ground. A finger of blood ran down from the wound behind his left ear. He stared unseeing toward the village into which he had fired. Everything was dimming around the crushing pain in his skull. He drew his knees under him in an effort to get up, and it took him time to figure out how to do it. He scratched at the frozen soil with his fingers, trying to locate his hands through feel because he did not know where they were. And then he managed to get his legs under himself and he tried to get up. He swayed on his hands and knees. "I'm going to die here," he thought disconnectedly. And with an enormous effort, he staggered to his feet. He turned in a drunken spin and began to limp away from his position. He had no idea in which direction he was headed. He didn't care.

"Get back here!" the officer screamed at him.

"Fuck you," Stojan answered without turning around. He staggered for a few yards and then paused to steady himself against the slender trunk of a young birch tree. The white bark peeled away in his hand. He could barely hear anything around the ringing in his head, and he didn't hear the officer coming up behind him. There was another explosion of pain somewhere in his back as the officer smacked him in the ribs with the rifle stock. Stojan clung to the tree.

"Are you out of your fucking mind?" the officer screamed.

"It was your idea," Stojan tried to whisper around the edges of the pain.

"What the fuck is wrong with you?" He shoved Stojan, who managed to stay on his feet by clinging to the tree.

"I want to go to my brother's funeral," Stojan answered thickly, clinging desperately to the birch. "And I'm going. So write me a pass."

The officer raised Stojan's own rifle against him. "I'll fucking shoot you if you move."

Stojan shuffled slowly away from the tree, away from the officer.

"Sokolović!" the officer screamed at him. But Stojan kept going, slowly, slowly, disoriented and staggering with pain.

"Shoot me. Please shoot me," Stojan tried to respond, but he didn't have any air left in his lungs.

"Wait! Wait!" Stojan heard Pas call out. "Let me talk to him," he offered.

"Get the fuck out of my way," the officer responded in a low, warning voice.

"Please," said Pas quietly. "Let me talk to him. His brother has been killed in the service of this army, for Christ's sake. Just give me one minute."

"You have thirty seconds," the officer conceded, but it was not enough time to constitute a concession. And he did not lower the rifle. Stojan heard the crunch of Pas' boots moving swiftly across the frost-covered ground.

"Stojane!" he implored, and Stojan could not make out from where the voice had come. It seemed to be simultaneously behind and in front of him. And then Pas was somehow in front of him, blocking Stojan's way, and his eyes were bright with fear. "He'll shoot you, Stojan," said Pas seriously, fearfully. "Get a hold of yourself."

Stojan shook his head. "Shoot me," he whispered, and tried to skirt around Pas. But Pas reached out and wrapped his arms around Stojan. "No," he whispered. "Turn around and go back."

"Let me go," Stojan looked at him and saw Pas' face torn with sympathy. "I have to go."

They stared at one another for precious seconds. Pas was not convinced that Stojan even saw him. His pale eyes had gone very dark, and he was swaying on his feet. And then the thirty seconds was finished. The officer was still standing behind them with the rifle at the ready.

"I'm going home. Leave me alone now," Stojan said clearly, but his eyes were wet with shock. Whether it was from the concussion or from seeing what he had just done with different eyes, Pas did not know.

He stepped away from his friend, and looked back at the officer, who stood with the barrel of the rifle pointed at Stojan's back. "Make some clearance," the officer ordered, and Pas turned, his heart sinking, and walked away. Stojan began to walk forward again, slowly, painfully. He waited for the shot. But instead, the officer said to him in a remarkably calm voice, "Stojan Sokolović, if you take another step, your father will be burying two of his sons instead of one." He trained his eye down the barrel, and waited. And this made Stojan stop. He went down on his knees again, and pressed his face against the frozen ground. "Please shoot me," he begged. "Please."

The officer shouldered the rifle and turned to the loose group of watchers who had gathered in the commotion. He said to no one in particular, "Somebody lock his ass up somewhere. The provisional charge is attempted desertion. We'll wait for the paperwork."

No one moved. "Do it!" the officer screamed. And two of them came forward as one to lift Stojan back onto his feet. They kept him for three days on the threshing floor of a barn behind the lines. He was frozen right through to the bone by the morning of the first full day, and the plastic bucket of still water in the corner had a skin of ice on its surface. One of the officers who had heard what happened had the bright idea of throwing Stojan in with several dozen of their Bosnian Army prisoners. "They'll tear him apart," he smirked. But the officer who had made the wager with Stojan looked at him in contempt. "Just go and scare him, you sick fuck," he ordered.

So the low-ranking officer headed to the barn where Stojan lay freezing to death on the threshing floor, and he forced him to take off his boots and his winter-issue coat, and he threw the bucket of freezing water over his head, hurling insults that Stojan neither registered nor cared about. Then he hit him over the head with the empty bucket, which was not terribly heavy, but felt like a ton of bricks after the crack from the rifle stock. The wound on the skin of his skull split again, and Stojan was too cold and dazed to ask for mercy. From time to time, he cried out for his brother and, sometimes, for his mother. The officer decided that Stojan should at least be threatened with execution, so he took to pressing the barrel of his pistol against Stojan's head and the back of his neck and under his chin. No matter how cold Stojan felt, the barrel of the officer's pistol always made coldness a relative measurement—the pistol was colder than cold. He did this at least four times for each day that Stojan was imprisoned in the barn. Sometimes he came in drunk at night, and Stojan felt unsure on those occasions of whether he would manage to hold onto the thin threads that connected him to what remained of his life. He searched his heart, looking for his fear, but what he found was that he didn't care. After three days had passed, they dragged him out and sent him back further behind the lines to recover and to get warm again, but they would not give him a pass to leave, because the officer who had made the wager knew by looking at Stojan's blank face that, were he given leave, he would not return. So he got warm again, and he waited for the paperwork that should send him to prison. But it never came. After another week, Stojan Sokolović was proclaimed fit for service, and sent up to the front line. It was Orthodox Christmas Day, 1993.

XXIV

The next day dawned with a sky threatening rain that never delivered. The light seemed dirty and gray as I walked to my office. I unlocked the door and shoved it open. But I couldn't cross the threshold at first. The piles of shredding were all over the floor in great mounds and I stood staring at what looked to be a complete destruction, unsure in that disconnected moment of how it had even happened. I stepped slowly across the threshold as though I had never been there before, and I looked around at the open filing cabinets which were yawning with emptiness in the stunned aftermath of the shredding. I navigated between the strips of my manuscript and all the articles that had supported its architecture, and sat down at my desk. I did not know what to do. There was nothing there to look at; no articles in progress, no manuscript, no book chapters.

It was a strange day. I felt completely detached. I didn't know what to do with myself. I sat in what felt like someone else's skin and stared out the window as the sun crept across the sky. Sometime in the late afternoon, Bill came by to ask me whether I would supervise a master's thesis on the intervention in Kosovo.

"Of course, the student will have to contextualize this in light of the war in Bosnia," he conceded. "I've already told her that."

For a moment, I couldn't figure out what he was doing in my office. Why was he asking me to supervise this? What did it have to do with me? I must have looked completely blank, because he went on, "I think you would be the best person to supervise, based on your regional expertise." And this was the reason he had come to see me, to ask me about my supervision load—to see if I had a space free for one more thesis on Bosnia. Because I was the one people came to when they wanted supervision on Bosnia.

I stared at Bill. A wave of nausea washed over me. I didn't think I could take any more. I didn't think I could live with it.

"I'm not qualified to supervise the student," I said finally.

He had not expected this. It was clear. "Are you already at your supervisory quota?" he asked.

"No. I have two spots left. But I am not qualified to do this one."

"What do you mean?" he pressed suspiciously.

I pointed to the piles on the floor. "Those are my qualifications," I said to him. He looked down at the piles of shredding, which he had been pretending weren't there so he could avoid asking me what I had done. And I would have said, "I am destroying knowledge, Bill. I am shredding all these years of useless text. I am shredding all of these fucking Bosnias. It's not that I don't have empty supervision spots, it's that I can't stand it anymore. I can't stand it." But I couldn't say those things, so I just stared at him.

And Bill, to my surprise, looked at the piles on the floor and said mildly, "You have shredded your whole office."

"Yes," I confirmed, and looked at him steadily.

He nodded warily, then simply turned and left my office, taking care not to disrupt the mountains on the floor. The door closed softly behind him. I saw that a few strips of the manuscript had attached themselves to his shoes when he left. They accompanied him back to his office, and I suppressed a crazy urge to laugh. Instead, I wept, and I gathered the shredding in big fistfuls, stuffing those accusing mountains back in the filing cabinets. I wept, and I scraped up the straggling strips from the carpet. I wept and wept until there seemed to be nothing left inside me but a cold sort of hardness. Then, I went to my computer and looked through all the outstanding warrants on the website of the International Criminal Tribunal for the Former Yugoslavia; I scrolled through the Interpol warrants; and then the Europol warrants. And no one was looking for Stojan Sokolović. What did four lives matter—or one life, for that matter—when there were several thousand dead all at once at Srebrenica? They didn't even know whom to look for most of the time. But I also knew that someone somewhere was looking for him, just as Stojan himself had looked for Milan, as he would maybe look for the Ivan. Someone was looking for him, someone who did not yet know his name, someone who did not yet know where to find him—someone who would maybe never find him, but would never cease looking nonetheless because someone had had to bury the people that he caught in the crosshairs of his rifle.

The department grew quiet and the sun began to set outside my window. I was ill by then. I could feel a fever beginning to burn behind my eyes, and there was a chill that had settled into the marrow in my bones. My teeth were set hard against one another to keep from chattering. My jaw was aching from it. I knew that Stojan would not come that night. I knew he might never come again. I should go home to my apartment, where nobody lived. I should sleep. I should find a sedative and forget this for some time. I should find a new research agenda. Better yet, I should quit this job, pack up my office, get out of this, go home to the coast of New Jersey, watch the boats waiting for the train bridge to open, hose down the docks at the end of the day. But I knew it was impossible, even as I was thinking it. The way back was gone; it had been gone from the moment I left. I stood up to take *On Escape* off my shelf, intending to read it over the next few days while the fever lingered, but then I remembered that it had disappeared. I snapped off the light, and I went out. I thought a hot curry might work to break the fever, so I diverted from the path to my apartment and doubled back through the garden.

But I couldn't eat. I left everything untouched before me, and the servers were concerned that something was wrong with the food. "It's fine," I said absently, staring at my own watery reflection in the window. I didn't recognize myself. I paid and crossed over the threshold that separated the ugly restaurant from the sultry heat of the summer night. Just as I couldn't eat, I couldn't go home. I couldn't stand the thought of that empty apartment now with its scentless, unslept-in bed.

I walked and walked through the long late summer evening, block after block, mile after mile, measuring the depth of the shadows at dusk. I had no destination in mind. My back was wet with sweat in the summer heat. After several hours, I found myself standing in front of the Serbian communist church—that oxymoron of oxymorons—and the heavy oak door was open. I climbed the stone steps and slipped into the nave. It was cool and dim. Candles flickered here and there in long troughs of sand— the upper troughs for the living, the lower troughs for the dead. The number of candles burning for the living and the dead was relatively equal. The nave was an empty, cavernous space surrounded by frescoes and icons. I walked slowly up toward the iconostasis that separated the nave from the sanctuary. My shoes clicked against the stone floor as I crossed it. The smell of incense hung in the still air and I felt the chill of fever in my bones. I stared at the icons—classic Serbian icons—the three-handed Mother of God, the white archangel, Saint Ilija, who disappeared into a ball of fire, Saint Nikola, whose feast it was when Luka Sokolović was shot in a hollow on his way back to Pale on his three-day pass to celebrate his saint day and see his lover.

I stared at those cold images and felt a wash of despair fill my chest. "How could you allow this?" I asked Nikola out loud. "How?" I regarded his image with contempt, the patron saint of half the Serbs. He was the patron saint of so very many Serbs that to let them all off the lines to celebrate their feast would probably decimate half the Serb army. Nikola was the reason that Luka died, I thought bizarrely. Nikola was why he had gotten his three-day pass. If Luka hadn't died in that hollow, his brother, hearing about his death, would not have killed those four. I shook my head in disgust. Above Nikola was Sava—the patron saint of Serbia itself—the youngest son of Stefan Nemanja, who had given up everything to await the new Jerusalem on Mount Athos. "Fuck you, Sava," I whispered, and my voice carried across the church. He stared down at me impassively with his blue eyes and his gold-leaf halo. The icon had blue eyes. Whoever heard of such a thing? I thought derisively.

The carved latticework door that led through the middle of the icon screen creaked open, and a young, cassocked priest emerged. I felt a surge of guilt, because he heard me swear against Sava. We stared at each other for a moment. I fully expected him to ask me to leave. But to my amazement, the priest smiled at me gently. "Is it Sava's fault?" he asked.

I looked back at him with well-trained contempt gathering in my eyes. "It might be," I answered clearly.

"Would you like a drink?" the priest inquired.

"Coffee?" I asked sarcastically.

"Brandy," he responded.

I hesitated and he looked long and curiously at me. "You are not a Serb," he announced.

"No. I'm not," I answered.

"Then I can practice my English with you," he smiled serenely. He held out his hand to me in a welcoming gesture, and with the other, he pushed the doorway between the icons open wider. I followed him wordlessly through the screen, and we passed into the sanctuary, where I was most assuredly not supposed to be. Back behind the altar, which was, ironically, much simpler than the iconostasis, there was a small door which led into an even smaller sacristy. The walls were mellow cherry wood, and there were shelves of books, some boasting Serbian Cyrillic titles, some Old Slavonic, and some in English. There was one that I thought I recognized from its spine, and I walked up to examine it. It was *On Escape*. I couldn't believe it.

The young priest gestured to one of the two empty chairs that were drawn up to the heavy wood table. "Please," he offered. I sat down and he turned to rummage behind the books. He had a prayer rope wound around his left hand. When he turned back to me, he held a half-empty bottle of brandy in his hand, and he placed it on the table with a muffled clinking sound. He turned back and retrieved two tiny, beveled, crystal glasses. Then he sat down across from me and unscrewed the top from the bottle, which bore no label. He poured the glasses full and the tiny sacristy was infused with the scent of plums.

"I take it we should not toast Sava," he smiled as he lifted his glass.

"I'm sorry about that," I said. He was so friendly that I began to feel sorry for cursing those saints in his nave.

"Maybe we should toast to no Serbian saint," he offered.

I shrugged. "It's your church," I answered.

"Let's drink to whatever Serb caused you to come to my church in the middle of the night," he suggested.

"No," I said flatly. "Let's drink to the people he killed."

The priest looked at me sadly. But he was not surprised. "Alright," he said. "To those he killed, then," he offered.

I raised my glass. We touched glasses, looked in each other's eyes in the compulsory Serbian fashion, and drank. The brandy was homemade, and burned my throat going down. He immediately refilled my glass with the clear, oily liquid. "Cheers," I said in a sarcastic voice, and drank the second glass in one swallow. He filled it yet again. And then he settled back in his chair and looked closely, sympathetically at me.

"Why did you come here?" he asked after a while.

"I don't know," I said honestly, and I could hear the edge of anger in my voice. "I really don't know."

He nodded. "Many people who come here don't know why they came, or what they're looking for."

I nodded back. I guessed it must be true.

"But you came because you learned something about someone, and it was not bearable for you," he started.

I looked at him, wishing I hadn't said anything. But I was full with grief, and it had to leak out somewhere. The seams of my own skin were already splitting. "My friend is a murderer," I said coldly.

The priest nodded. "How many did he kill?"

What kind of question is that? I wondered. And then I realized that it was probably just an ordinary question for a Serbian priest, who sat in this sacristy with many other Serbs—with Serbs who had killed their neighbors.

"He said four," I answered. "One was a child." I felt my eyes filling with tears.

"Why do you think he told you?" the priest asked gently.

"How should I know?" I said bitterly. "I wish he hadn't told me anything at all!"

The priest nodded. "Serbs killed many people," he said in a sorrowful voice.

"I don't know what to do," I said honestly.

"You can't do anything," he said reasonably.

"I can't live with that," I said.

"You have to live with it," answered the priest, and he absently counted the knots on his prayer rope.

I shook my head. "No. I can't," I said again. I looked up at *On Escape* sitting quietly on the priest's shelf. I gestured to the book with my head. "I lost my copy," I informed him.

"I'm sorry," he said genuinely.

"Have you read it?" I asked.

He looked up in the direction of my gaze, and nodded.

"Which part do you like the best?" I asked.

The priest considered this for a moment. "The necessity of fleeing oneself is put in check by the impossibility of ever doing so," he quoted. It was the passage I had found underlined in my own copy that day when it fell from the shelf in my office. He looked at me. He was very young; no older than I was. No older than Stojan.

"Escape is impossible," he said, explaining the meaning of the passage he had quoted. "If it was possible to escape yourself, you wouldn't have come here, and I wouldn't have to keep a bottle of brandy hidden behind my consecrated wine," he said kindly.

I was silent again. He poured me a fourth brandy. He was on his second.

"What should I do?" I asked openly.

"What do you think your options are?" he asked by way of answer.

"I don't know," I said honestly. "There isn't any justice in this world," I said.

"No," the priest agreed, and emptied his glass.

"He could be prosecuted for killing that child and the women and the man," I said. And I realized that I didn't even know their names. None of us did.

"Possibly," the priest answered.

We were quiet for a while. I glanced up along his bookshelves. He counted the knots in his prayer rope and ran his index finger thoughtfully around the rim of his empty brandy glass.

"I can't live with this," I said again.

The priest looked up at me and gave his diagnosis: "Your problem is not just that your friend did this, but that you love him. You can't accept the possibility that you love a man who could do what he did."

I looked at him, and realized that if such a thing as perfect truth were possible, the priest had just spoken it. I hadn't shed a single tear while I wrote my shredded manuscript on Bosnia, despite the fact that I had written about deaths like these. I didn't cry, because I hadn't loved them. On this, Stojan had been right.

"I don't know what to do," I repeated.

The priest nodded. "Me, neither."

He went on. "But the fact is that we all laugh and mourn and love and hate with the same breath of air in our lungs. We are guilty and innocent. There is only the difference of a hair between these."

I listened to him speak, and I didn't want to believe him. "Are you saying that he is not a war criminal?" I asked.

"No," said the priest, "I'm not saying that. He is possibly a war criminal, as you say, but he is also something more and something other than that."

I considered this for a moment. "He peeled me oranges with the same hands that pulled that trigger," I whispered.

The young priest looked at me with a quiet, painful sympathy in his dark eyes.

"You want to believe that there is a perfect distinction between guilt and innocence," the priest offered.

I nodded at him.

"But that distinction is impossible, except in very specific moments," he went on.

I felt a tear track down my cheek and I wiped it away angrily. "And it's not Sava's fault," the priest smiled, trying to make it a bit easier with his quiet humor.

The tears kept coming despite his attempt to lighten the atmosphere. I kept wiping at them, but it was futile. For every one that I wiped away, another followed immediately in its wake. "What is the measure of his responsibility?" I asked.

The priest considered this. "Your friend is infinitely responsible. He cannot absolve himself. I cannot absolve him. That is very difficult to accept."

"So, only God can absolve him," I suggested coldly.

And to my surprise, the priest shook his head. "No," he said slowly. "I don't think so. The only people who can unbind him are unable to return from their graves to do so."

"So there is no possibility of forgiveness," I said, following this strange priest's non-canonical logic.

The priest shook his head slowly. "I don't think it's that there is no chance of forgiveness. He can perhaps even forgive himself. But forgiveness and responsibility are not the same thing. No one can absolve him of his responsibility. He will remain responsible for the rest of his life. And he knows it, or he would not have told you what he has done."

"Should he present himself to the families of those he killed?" I asked. "Someone is surely looking for him."

The priest nodded. "This is a very hard question to answer," he admitted. "I have seen it happen once that a Serb who had killed a woman returned to her family to confess what he had done. And the husband of that woman, when he saw his wife's murderer, killed himself that evening. He had managed to survive what had happened—he had married again, had children—and the return of the Serb had opened the wound, and he couldn't go on. It was not made right. It was made worse. But this takes into account only the living. It does not address the question of justice for the woman who was killed."

He went on, "Other times, it is the right choice. In another circumstance, the Serb who had done the killing was arrested on an international warrant and convicted at the tribunal. The families of the people he had killed were pleased. They felt that some justice had been served. Bosnian Muslims mostly support the war crimes tribunal. So it is probably safe to say that they find there to be justice in it. And if they find there to be justice in it, then there is justice in it."

The priest paused for a moment. "In yet another circumstance, the Serb went to the police to confess, and they couldn't bring him to trial because there was not enough evidence; his confession had not been enough to return an indictment because he had gotten some of the details wrong. When they came back and told him he would not be indicted, he shot himself." The priest poured himself a finger of brandy.

"Croats recently reported that over fourteen thousand demobilized soldiers have killed themselves since the war ended," the priest said. "Serbia and Bosnia do not keep statistics on that, but that makes me think the numbers are actually higher there."

"Do you think they were guilty?" I asked.

The priest smiled sadly. "Of course they were."

I nodded.

"We are all guilty in that respect," the priest mused.

"In what respect?" I asked.

"In the respect that there is no place of innocence from which to judge," answered the priest. "No one can be the judge of another until he recognizes that he himself is as guilty for the crime as the one who committed it—and maybe more so. That's Dostoevsky's belief, anyway."

"How can you say that?" I asked. "I didn't kill anyone."

"Did you succeed in preventing the killing?" he asked.

"No, of course not," I said. "But I wasn't there. I didn't know anything about it."

"Do you think this makes a difference?" he inquired with raised eyebrows.

"Yes, I do," I said firmly. But I was not sure.

"I was not there," the priest repeated my statement in a contemplative tone.

I was quiet, waiting for him to say something more.

He drank his brandy thoughtfully. "Denial is a normal response to evil. It's an understandable response. Many people have this denial in them."

I sipped my brandy and looked closely at him. He had warm eyes with deep creases around their corners, as though he had spent a lot of time in the sun.

"But,"—he raised his glass—"it does not actually work. You cannot say that these things were not also your responsibility. If we deny our measure of responsibility, then all we have left are prayers and curses to the icons. And they almost never reply."

"That strikes me as rather non-canonical," I offered.

"Well," the priest smiled, "maybe it is because of my own guilt." He paused and thought for a moment. "Because I *was* there. I thought I could prevent the killing by refusing to kill. But it was not a successful strategy. I failed to load my rifle, and a boy died because I couldn't protect him."

I stared at Petar Petrović in the mute surprise of recognition as long seconds ticked by.

And then I asked him, "If you could go back, what would you have done?"

Petar shifted his weight in the chair and smiled at me sadly. "I cannot go back," he answered simply.

"What if you could?" I insisted. "What would you have done differently?"

"I cannot go back and choose again," he replied. "So I don't ask myself what I could have done. I ask myself how I can live with it today."

"How do you live with it?" I asked plainly.

Petar circled the rim of his glass with the pad of his thumb. "I examine my life," he said quietly. "I live as well as I can in every moment, with love and gratitude, and I try to live in a way that would make the boy whose death I was responsible for proud of me. I remember him, and I think, in this moment, would he be pleased with who I am?"

"Do you ever forget about him?" I asked.

"No," answered the priest directly.

"What should I do?" I asked the priest again uselessly.

The priest shrugged his cassocked shoulders. "You have any number of options," he answered. "But remember that whichever one you choose will not make it alright. There are degrees of justice. Sometimes they happen through law, and sometimes they don't. No one would have prosecuted me for my crime. Yet, I convicted myself. You have to find a way to approach justice, knowing that you'll never achieve it—knowing that nothing will ever make right what your friend did. He will die with it in his throat."

I finished my brandy and stood up. It seemed not to have affected me at all. "Thank you," I said.

"One more thing," the priest said quietly, and I turned back to face him. "When you come near to something that can't be made right, you have to approach it with love, and not vengeance. Vengeance is how we got into this in the first place."

"Are you saying that I should love a murderer?" I asked coldly.

"That you should?" he asked, surprised. "It's not that you should, but that you do, or you would not have come here. You would have been able to live with his evil if you did not also love him."

I stared back at him for a long moment. He was right. It was easy to write when you didn't love. It was easy to convict when you didn't love. I looked up at *On Escape*. "Can I borrow your book?" I asked.

"Of course," he answered, and rose to get it for me. I placed it in my briefcase, thanked him, and left.

On my way through the nave, I stopped at the pile of fragrant beeswax candles. I took five of them. The first four, I lit from the bottom trough, and pressed them one by one into the sand. I lit the fifth from one of the original four and stood it up in the upper trough, a bit away from the others that were already there. I started to walk away. Then I went back, and I lit one more for Luka Sokolović. Petar Petrović was standing in the doorway in the middle of the iconostasis when I went over to the candles, but by the time I was done lighting them, he had retreated again into the sacristy.

XXV

Jelena walked out onto the sun-soaked patio of an Italian café in midtown, thinking that there were some things she would have to learn to live with, even though they made life unliveable. Stojan was waiting for her. She sat down in the chair beside him and took his hand.

"I can't live with things the way they are," she began with no preamble. Stojan nodded. "I know," he said.

"But I don't know what to do," Jelena added.

"I know," he said again. "It's alright."

A waiter came with a bottle of sparkling water in a green glass bottle and two glasses of ice, and took their lunch order.

"Jelena, you don't have to decide anything," Stojan said to her. "Honestly."

"No," she answered, "you're wrong about that. I'm living in limbo. I can't do it anymore, but I don't know how to change it." She struggled to express herself, shaking her head at the inadequacy of her words—at their inability to articulate what she felt she really wanted to say.

Stojan nodded his head and sat perfectly still, waiting for her to go on. She sighed. "I need help, Stojan."

He nodded.

She smiled at him in her old familiar way, remembering. "You know, your father told me that if I needed anything, I should come to you. He said you would not deny me anything I asked of you."

Stojan considered this. "He was right," he answered simply.

"But the problem is that I don't know what I want to ask," she continued. She sat very still in her chair.

"I'm not Luka," Stojan replied evenly.

Jelena looked surprised. "Don't you think I know that?" she asked.

Stojan shrugged. "I don't know," he said. "I'm not as optimistic as Luka was, you know? I'm not as ... " he struggled to find the word. "Certain about things."

"What things?" Jelena inquired.

"I don't know," Stojan shrugged. "The way the world is, I guess. The wrongness of so many things—even things that I have done myself."

Jelena nodded. "I understand that," she said. "I remember when I saw you as I left Pale. You wouldn't speak to me. It was because of something that happened to you."

Stojan nodded.

"I will not ask you what it was, and I do not want you to tell me," she said.

He was quiet for a moment, considering this.

"Will you go back to Bosnia?" he finally asked her.

"I don't know," she replied swiftly, as though she had been asking herself the same question for a long time. "Will you?" she asked.

"I don't know."

She nodded, and Stojan reached over to pour the water. Jelena watched it cascade over the cubes of ice in the glasses.

"Stojan?" she began.

"Yes?" he answered.

"I also missed you during these years," she said quietly, looking away. "I missed all of you. I don't want to lose any more."

"I know," he confirmed, nodding.

Her eyes welled up with tears but this time they didn't spill over and after a few short moments, they had gone again. She pressed her lips together and nodded.

"Jelena, do you remember when we were kids in school, and they told us that the future of Yugoslavia would be—how did they put it?—a model for the world to follow, or something like that."

She laughed. "Yes!"

"It didn't work that way, did it?" he asked with a bemused expression on his face.

"No, it didn't," she confirmed carefully.

"But here we are, in a good state, even though it's lonely and cold," Stojan offered.

She smiled softly at him and her eyes shone in the sunlight. "Your father said that so many times," she remembered.

Stojan smiled at her. "We'll be alright," he said.

XXVI

I saw Stojan Sokolović only once more in that city, on a street close to the university. He stopped, and greeted me by name.

"Evo me," I responded; here I am.

He smiled at that, and his colorless eyes seemed to be backlit from somewhere inside him. I studied him for a moment—the lines at the corners of his eyes, the height of his cheekbones, the curve of his neck. He was holding his leather case—the one that had once carried my manuscript—and his hands were still tanned with summer.

"I miss you," he offered openly. "Your plant is doing well, and that cat, but I miss you."

I smiled at this. I looked at his hands. I looked at them for a long moment. I wanted to tell him that I loved him. But it seemed a waste of words. He already knew that, I thought.

When we parted, I walked slowly to my office. I sat down at my computer. I stared at the blank screen for a moment, considering. Then I wrote: "I am building my career on the loss of a man named Stojan Sokolović, and on the loss of many millions of others, who may or may not resemble him. And one night, he told me … "